Reading the Romance
Women, Patriarchy, and Popular Literature

J A N I C E   A .   R A D W A Y

With a New Introduction by the Author

The University of North Carolina Press

Chapel Hill and London

06 05 04 03 02   8 7 6 5 4

Library of Congress Cataloging-in-Publication Data

Radway, Janice A., 1949–
Reading the romance : women, patriarchy, and popular literature /
Janice A. Radway ; with a new introduction by the author.
p. cm.
Includes bibliographical references and index.
ISBN 0-8078-4349-0 (pbk. : alk. paper)
1. Women—Books and reading.   2. Love stories—Appreciation.
3. Popular literature—Appreciation.   4. Feminism and literature.
5. Sex role in literature.   6. Women in literature.   7. Patriarchy.
I. Title.
Z1039.W65R32   1991
028'.9082—dc20
91-50284
CIP

Portions of Chapter 6 appeared in somewhat different form in
*The Structure of the Literary Process: Studies Dedicated to the
Memory of Felix Vodička*, edited by P. Steiner, M. Cervenka, and
R. Vroon, Linguistic and Literary Studies in Eastern Europe,
vol. 8. © 1982 by John Benjamins B. V. Reprinted by permission
of the publisher.

L
29.5.07

Reading the Romance

For Scott

Contents

Acknowledgments

Upon completion of a project such as this, it is customary for the author to thank all those who have offered assistance and encouragement during the course of the endeavor. It would not be appropriate for me to depart from convention here, for, like everyone else, I have incurred many debts in the process of writing this book. I am especially grateful to two groups of people without whose help this study literally would not have been possible. My most obvious debt is to Dorothy Evans and the Smithton readers. Although this book is certainly about romantic fiction, it is also, first and foremost, about these extraordinary women. I only hope that I have been able to do justice to the complexities that characterize their lives and their engagement with the books they so love. In addition, I never would have met these women had it not been for my colleagues in the American Civilization Department at the University of Pennsylvania. By introducing me to the field of ethnography, Drew Faust and Murray Murphey, in particular, were instrumental in helping me to see that if literature is to be treated as a document in the study of a culture, it is first necessary to know something about who reads, why they do so, and how they go about it. I am happy to acknowledge my intellectual debt to them and to their work.

Two of my friends have shared so much of the process of conception, writing, and revision that I sometimes feel that the final product has been collectively derived. This is as it should be for it attests to the reality and worth of the academic community. In the course of discussing every possible aspect of this study with me, Sharon O'Brien introduced me to Nancy Chodorow's work, nurtured my growing understanding of its implications for the romance, and provided important encouragement when I had difficulty believing that these books really could conceal a search for the lost mother. Later, Peter Rabinowitz read an early draft of the manuscript with such care and precision and then argued theoretical points with an equally astonishing intellectual rigor that he challenged me to clarify and refine my ideas about reading and reception. *Reading the Romance* has benefited enormously, then, from the thoughtful responses of these, my first two readers.

Many others have also helped at various moments along the way. Russel Nye first inspired my interest in the study of popular literature. Peter

Steiner provided early assurances that the study was worth undertaking and Sally Arteseros first brought Dot and the Smithton women to my attention. José Limon helped me to clarify my conclusions and to think through their political implications. Nina Baym, Cathy Davidson, Elizabeth Long, Horace Newcomb, and Jane Tompkins all read the manuscript, criticized it carefully, and offered important suggestions. Elizabeth Zeitz ran the original SPSS program and Selma Pastor typed the first draft. Judy Levin checked the notes and the bibliography and also helped me to eliminate contradictions and logical inconsistencies. Nicole Cawley-Perkins read the galleys with enormous care. In addition to thanking these colleagues and friends, I would also like to express my gratitude to my graduate students in the Literature and Culture seminar who listened to an early summary of my research and, through thoughtful questioning, identified portions of the argument that needed further work. I am also grateful to my editors, Sandra Eisdorfer and Iris Tillman Hill, for their sensitive and careful attention to the manuscript.

My final debt is perhaps the most difficult one to acknowledge because of its very intangibility. My husband, Scott, has helped in so many ways, at once practical and emotional, that it would be foolish to try and list them all here. I hope it is enough to say that I could not have finished this had it not been for his understanding, encouragement, and, above all else, his interest. This book is dedicated to him with love.

Reading the Romance

Writing Reading the Romance

It seems especially fitting that a book about the active and particular nature of reading as a social activity pursued within a specific context should require a new introduction so soon after its initial offering to its own intended audience in 1984.[1] Although less than ten years have passed since the book's first, polemical introduction was completed, so much has changed on the academic scene and in the intellectual environment more generally that that introduction now seems dated, if not entirely beside the point. Indeed, in reading *Reading the Romance* for the first time since the manuscript was completed, I have been struck by how much the book's argument is a product of a very particular historical moment. That moment was colored not only by my own previous academic trajectory and by the past development of the specific community I intended to address but also by a larger intellectual environment that impinged on my work invisibly and from a distance, but no less forcefully for that.

Given the recent explosion of interest in cultural studies, few readers can approach the book now with the set of beliefs about literature, reading, and criticism that I assumed to characterize my audience in 1984 and worked hard to contradict. Therefore, rather than simply repeat the theoretical and methodological claims argued throughout *Reading the Romance* by offering it to new readers without commentary or criticism, I want to situate the book's claims to be doing something new and offer both an explanation and critique of its limitations. In particular, I would like to juxtapose and compare *Reading the Romance* to the highly influential, largely ethnographic work of scholars now loosely identified as "the Birmingham school" of cultural studies. I was wholly unaware of this body of work when I was writing, but it now dominates the context within which *Reading the Romance* is read. Although only constructed retrospectively, the relationship between the work coming out of Birmingham in the late 1970s and early 1980s and this particular volume therefore deserves more than passing comment.

New readers of *Reading the Romance* will note immediately that the book's theoretical argument is directed generally to American studies scholars working in the United States (although this latter qualification is not stated specifically) and more particularly to those who take literature as their primary object of concern. The resulting preoccupation with the question of what a literary text can be taken as evidence for may seem a peculiar and oblique focus for a book that has largely been read as a contribution to feminist scholarship or as an addition to discussions within communications theory about the status of the audience and the nature of mass cultural consumption.[2] This latter fact simply demonstrates, however, that whatever her intentions, no writer can foresee or prescribe the way her book will develop, be taken up, or read. Neither can she predict how it will transform her, a subject to which I will return. Still, I think it will be helpful to know something about the immediate personal and intellectual situation that served as the polemical ground and orienting context for the writing of *Reading the Romance*. That information goes a long way toward explaining why the book was eventually hijacked by its own theory and subject and, en route to its intended destination, gradually found itself directed to another.

As much as the theoretical argument of Chapter 1 is the product of an intellectual quarrel, so too is it the product of an institutional and political one as well. It was born of the fact that I had been hired in 1977 by the American Civilization Department at the University of Pennsylvania, known within the American studies community in the United States for its particular challenge to an earlier American studies orthodoxy. That orthodoxy, formed in the late 1940s and early 1950s, developed as part of the reaction to the hegemony of New Criticism in American English departments. Disturbed by the extreme preoccupation with formalist criticism in a Cold War context that seemed to cry out for a consideration once again of what constituted "the American," certain students of the national literature began to reassert the validity of an enterprise that would reunite the classic American literary texts with the historical context within which they were conceived. Resulting largely in an alliance between literary scholars and intellectual historians, the impulse led to the creation of American studies programs and departments that, whatever their differences from more traditional English departments, at least still assumed that the most reliable and complex record of the American past could be found in the country's "greatest" works of art.[3]

In opposition to such claims, however, the American Civilization Department at Pennsylvania began to elaborate a critique of the assumption that works selected on the basis of their aesthetic achievement would necessarily be representative of the large sections of the population that had never read such books. Writing within the framework prescribed by the social sciences and preoccupied therefore with questions of evidentiary validity and statistical representivity, my future colleagues (who were not, for the most part, literary critics) argued that while "elite" literature might be taken as evidence for the beliefs of a particular section of the American population, assertions based upon it could not easily be extrapolated to wholly different classes or ethnic groups. They argued that if accurate statements were to be made about more "ordinary" Americans, the popular literature produced for and consumed by large numbers ought to become the primary focus of culturally oriented scholarship.[4]

I was hired, then, because much of my graduate work had been preoccupied with popular literature of one sort or another. That work had been directed by Russel Nye, one of the first serious scholars of American popular culture in the United States.[5] Although Nye was himself trained as a historian, he worked within the English Department at Michigan State University. Therefore, under his tutelage, its American studies program articulated the need for the study of popular culture even though it remained theoretically more traditional than that at Pennsylvania. The methods of analysis it taught were still primarily formal analysis and textual exegesis. Thus I went to Pennsylvania as a student of popular culture but also as a literary critic. *Reading the Romance* clearly demonstrates that provenance in the conversations it chooses to join.

By the time I arrived in the department, my colleagues had turned away somewhat from statistical models for the study of society and behavior and had elaborated instead a complex rationale for the use of ethnographic methods in the effort to make sense of American culture. Drawing on anthropology rather than sociology, they argued that cultural investigation must always take account of spatial and temporal specificity. Thus they moved from what Raymond Williams, Stuart Hall, and others have called the "literary-moral" definition of culture to an anthropological one, defining it as the whole way of life of a historically and temporally situated people.[6] The department's required graduate seminars were structured as ethnographies of particular communities which were studied synchronically and in depth. Interestingly enough, these were initiated at almost the same time that investigators at the Birmingham Centre for

Contemporary Cultural Studies, prompted by arguments made by Richard Hoggart, Williams, E. P. Thompson, Hall, and others, were turning to ethnographic methods in their effort to study the necessary "struggle, tension, and conflict" between subcultures or different ways of life.[7] Because this latter move originated within the well-developed Marxist tradition in Britain, even the earliest work at the Birmingham Centre made an effort to consider the nature of the relationship between ethnographic investigation of behavior and cultural meaning and ideological analysis of the structures of determination.[8] Although the turn to ethnography in American studies was prompted by a concern with the relationship (if not the struggle) between subgroups within a complex society and by an interest in the relationship between behavior and "belief systems," the relative weakness of the Marxist tradition in the States meant that most of the early work did not explicitly engage debates over ideology or the place of specifically cultural production in securing the domination of one group over another.

In any case, the ethnographic turn began to have relevance for me when I began to engage simultaneously with the theoretical work on the reader developing within the literary critical community and semiotic conceptions of the literary text. I grappled with this work as a result of discussions carried on within the Penn Semiotics Seminar, which was heavily influenced by Dell Hymes, Erving Goffman, and Barbara Herrnstein Smith, among others. Thus, even as I was attempting to respond to my departmental colleagues' questions about what a literary text could be taken as evidence for, I was gradually being convinced by the theoretical arguments about the social and hence variable nature of semiotic processes. If one could talk of the necessity for ethnographies of speaking, as Hymes himself did, I saw no reason why one shouldn't also assume that as speech varied across space and over time, so, too, must reading. If this was true and one could discover how actual communities actually read particular texts, I thought I saw a way to answer my colleagues' questions about the evidentiary status of literature. If reading varied spatially and temporally, and one did wish to use literature in an effort to reconstruct culture, it would be necessary to connect particular texts with the communities that produced and consumed them and to make some effort to specify how the individuals involved actually constructed those texts as meaningful semiotic structures. Hence my conclusion that American studies needed ethnographies of reading.

Reading the Romance was therefore conceived in response to a set of theoretical questions about literary texts. As a consequence, it was designed initially to see whether it was possible to investigate reading empirically so as to make "accurate" statements about the historical and cultural meaning of literary production and consumption. The decision to move beyond the various concepts of the inscribed, ideal, or model reader and to work with actual subjects in history was thus a product of the difficult questions that had been put to me by colleagues trained in the social science tradition and in culture theory. The resulting empiricism of *Reading the Romance* was embodied most obviously in the book's claim that empirically based ethnographies of reading should replace *all* intuitively conducted interpretation in cultural study because such empiricism would guarantee a more *accurate* description of what a book meant to a given audience. This claim was a function, then, of my situation within the American studies intellectual community as it carried on the familiar debate about the relative merits of "scientific" as opposed to "literary" methods in cultural study.[9]

The book that resulted did not ultimately sustain its initial project, however, because the activity of actually "doing ethnography" produced many surprises, not the least of which was the realization that even ethnographic description of the "native's" point of view must be an interpretation or, in words adapted from Clifford Geertz, my own construction of my informants' construction of what they were up to in reading romances. This, of course, will not be news to anyone familiar with anthropological method or with the ethnographic work of the CCCS, but it was something I only really discovered in the course of attempting to write the ethnography. I tried to acknowledge this point in the first introduction, which, like so many others, was substantially revised after all the other chapters were completed. I attempted to openly proclaim my feminism and acknowledge that it had affected the way I evaluated or reacted to my subject's self-understanding. However, I now think that my initial preoccupation with the empiricist claims of social science prevented me from recognizing fully that even what I took to be simple descriptions of my interviewees' self-understandings were mediated if not produced by my own conceptual constructs and ways of seeing the world.[10]

I would therefore now want to emphasize more insistently Angela McRobbie's assertion that "representations are interpretations."[11] They can never be pure mirror images of some objective reality, she goes on to say, but exist always as the result of "a whole set of selective devices, such as highlighting, editing, cutting, transcribing and inflecting." Were I writing *Reading the Romance* today, I would differentiate much more clearly between the remarks actually made by my respondents and my own observations about them. Perhaps even more significantly, I would attend more closely to the nature of the relationship that evolved between the Smithton women and me by describing the interviews themselves in greater detail and by including representative transcripts from them. In this vein, I also no longer would want to argue theoretically that ethnographies of reading should *replace* textual interpretation because of their greater adequacy to the task of revealing an objective cultural reality. Rather, I would claim that they can be fruitfully employed as an essential component of a multifocused approach that attempts to do justice to the ways historical subjects understand and partially control their own behavior in a social and cultural context that has powerful determining effects on individual social action. However, I would also now stress that any scholar's account of a social formation as a determining context is additionally an interpretation, itself produced from within an ideological position and a particular historical context. For me, the interpretive assumption that cultural activity is in some measure determined was a function both of my developing feminism and of an interest in the then-burgeoning field of neo-Marxist theory.

Although *Reading the Romance* is not very good about foregrounding its account of the social context of the Smithton women as precisely an interpretation (and therefore determined itself), it does at least attempt to theorize context as socially determining, a move that had been prompted more specifically by conversations with Jerry Palmer, the author of *Thrillers*, about Terry Eagleton's efforts to rethink the nature of literary production in *Criticism and Ideology*.[12] These discussions initiated the pursuit of a trail of bibliographic references through the Marxist literature on ideology, an intellectual move that was reinforced by my ongoing reading in feminist literature as I began to grapple with the social situation of the women who were sharing their perceptions with me. The question of determination was thus posed for me by my attention to the material and social context within which romance reading generally occurs.

I had first taken up the subject of romances in graduate school as part of my dissertation on the differences between "popular" and "elite" literature.[13] Searching for a way to trace the variable use of generic conventions across these evaluative categories, I chose the gothic romance. My participation in a feminist consciousness-raising group had made me curious about feminist scholarly writing, and I saw the study of the romance as a way to engage with this literature. I had not previously read any popular romances, although I had recently developed an interest in detective novels. Still, I hoped to bring together my feminist "personal" life with my supposedly nongendered academic work, which, until that point, had not focused on women. This decision set in motion a slow, imperfect, often painful process of transformation that only really gathered steam in the actual writing of *Reading the Romance* some six or seven years later, when the difficulties of accounting for the complexities of actual romance reading produced a more intense and personal engagement with feminist theory and its analysis of women's situations. That engagement was fostered by the romance readers' eloquence about their own lives. Even as I began to see myself in the Smithton women's accounts of themselves and thus tentatively began to admit my identification with them, feminist writers helped me analyze women's situations and begin to trace their various determinants. Thus, another of the major surprises produced by doing ethnographic work was my own growing politicization. This politicization had not proceeded very far, however, by the time I began writing. That fact, along with my preoccupation with the methodological questions about how to conduct the cultural study of literature, caused me to misread earlier feminist work on the romance, resulting in a blindness to the continuity between my own arguments and those of scholars such as Tania Modleski and Ann Barr Snitow.[14]

As a consequence, the way the study was formulated and carried out was largely a function of my first theoretical concerns, concerns that I formulated at the outset within the terms of literary critical debates. Since I was assuming from the start with reader theorist Stanley Fish that textual interpretations are constructed by interpretive communities using specific interpretive strategies, I sought to contrast the then-current interpretation of romances produced by trained literary critics with that produced by fans of the genre.[15] Thus, in going into the field, I still conceived of reading in a limited fashion *as interpretation* and saw the project largely as one focusing on the differential interpretation of texts. It was only when the Smithton women repeatedly answered my questions about the meaning of romances by talking about the meaning of romance *reading* as an activity and a social event in a familial context that the study began to intersect with work being done in Britain.

What is so striking to me now is the way in which the romance readers themselves and their articulation of their concerns pushed me into a consideration of many of the same issues then preoccupying Paul Willis, David Morley, Charlotte Brunsdon, Angela McRobbie, Dorothy Hobson, Dick Hebdige, and many others.[16] Indeed, it was the women readers' construction of the act of romance reading as a "declaration of independence" that surprised me into the realization that the meaning of their media use was multiply determined and internally contradictory and that to get at its complexity, it would be helpful to distinguish analytically between the significance of the *event* of reading and the meaning of the *text* constructed as its consequence. Although I did not then formulate it in so many words, this notion of the event of reading directed me toward a series of questions about the uses "to which a particular text is put, its function within a particular conjuncture, in particular institutional spaces, and in relation to particular audiences."[17] What the book gradually became, then, was less an account of the way romances as texts were interpreted than of the way romance reading as a form of behavior operated as a complex intervention in the ongoing social life of actual social subjects, women who saw themselves first as wives and mothers.

As a consequence, *Reading the Romance* bears striking similarities to Dorothy Hobson's *Crossroads*, to the work on "Nationwide" by David Morley and Charlotte Brunsdon, and to Angela McRobbie's work on the culture of working-class girls. Although the central problematic of the book is not formulated in the languages they employ, nor is their work cited specifically, *Reading the Romance* shares their preoccupation with questions about the degree of freedom audiences demonstrate in their interaction with media messages and their interest in the way such cultural forms are embedded in the social life of their users. The theoretical position taken in the book is quite close to Dorothy Hobson's conclusion that "there is no overall intrinsic message or meaning in the work," and that "it comes alive and communicates when the viewers add their own interpretation and understanding to the programme."[18] Indeed, because I agreed at the outset with Stanley Fish's claim that textual features are not an essential structure upon which an interpretation is hung but rather are produced *through* the interpretive process, I think the theoretical position of *Reading the Romance* is also close to Hobson's additional observation that "there can be as many interpretations of a programme [or text] as the individual viewers bring to it."[19] Importantly, however, the book argues additionally that whatever the theoretical possibility of an infinite number of readings, in fact, there are patterns or regularities to what viewers and readers bring to texts in large part because they acquire specific cultural competencies as a consequence of their particular social location. Similar readings are produced, I argue, because similarly located readers learn a similar set of reading strategies and interpretive codes that they bring to bear upon the texts they encounter.

Reading the Romance turns to Fish's notion of "interpretive communities" to theorize these regularities and then attempts to determine whether the Smithton women operate on romances as an interpretive community in some way different from the community of trained literary scholars. However, because Fish developed the notion of the interpretive community only to account for varying modes of literary criticism within the academy, that is, interpretations produced by Freudian, Jungian, mythic, or Marxist critics, the concept is insufficiently theorized to deal with the complexities of social groups or to explain how, when, and why they are constituted precisely *as* interpretive communities. In other words, the theorization of "community" in *Reading the Romance* is itself somewhat anemic in that it fails to specify precisely how membership in the romance-reading community is constituted. Thus it cannot do complete justice to the nature of the connection between social location and the complex process of interpretation. It is inadequate finally to the task of explaining how social determination operates with respect to the larger activity of romance reading in Smithton.

Whatever the inadequacies of the treatment, however, the question of determination and regularities was nonetheless crucial to my research in large part because the group I examined was relatively homogeneous. Not only did the women give remarkably similar answers to my questions about romances, but they referred constantly and *voluntarily* to the connection between their reading and their daily social situation as wives and mothers. I thus theorized the correlation between their patterned answers and their similar social location by resorting to the explanatory constructs of feminist theory, to the notion of "patriarchal marriage" in particular. Not only have I used the concept to account for the social situation within which their reading occurs and thus employed it to make sense of their reading as an intervention within that situation, but I have also projected it back in time as a social form and, with the help of the psychoanalytic theories of Nancy Chodorow, used it to explain the construction of desire responsible for their location and their partial dissatisfaction with it, which itself leads ultimately to repetitive romance reading.

While I now feel this reification of patriarchal marriage was helpful in generating detailed knowledge about the ways in which romances engage these women, I also think it permitted me to avoid certain crucial theoretical questions about the precise mechanisms of determination. Had I designed the study comparatively, perhaps some of the issues David Morley has raised in his critical postscript to *The 'Nationwide' Audience* might have come more prominently to the fore.[20] He points there in particular to the inadequacies he sees in his own earlier discussion of the determinations upon meaning produced by the effectivity of the traditional sociological/structural variables—age, sex, race, and class. Many of the problems Morley identifies in his work with respect to this problem are also present in mine. Whereas he notes his excessive concentration on the single variable of class and the rather simple way in which the concept itself was constructed, so I might point in my own study to the exclusive preoccupation with gender and to the use of a fairly rigid notion of patriarchy. Indeed, I would now want to organize an ethnography of romance reading comparatively in order to make some effort to ascertain how other social variables like age, class location, education, and race intersect with gender to produce varying, even conflicting, engagements with the romance form. It might also be interesting to study similarly situated women who are non-romance readers in an effort to locate the absence (or perhaps the addition) of certain discursive competencies that renders the romance incomprehensible, uninteresting, or irrelevant.

Whatever the sociological weaknesses of *Reading the Romance*, I continue to feel that the particular method (or aggregate of methods) employed there to map the complexities of the romance's "purchase" on this small group of women can serve as a starting point for further discussion and perhaps for future analysis. I think this true, in part, because the understanding of reading that is worked out in the course of the discussion is close to the very useful generic or discursive model Morley has recommended in place of the encoding-decoding formulation that dominated early cultural studies work. I don't mean simply to imply here that *Reading the Romance* does what Morley calls for, although there are some striking similarities between what he recommends and the set of procedures the Smithton women's observations eventually pushed me toward. Rather, I want to suggest that his thoughtful comments in the postscript can usefully be employed to identify some of the other insufficiently theorized steps in my own analysis and thus might be used to extend and to improve it.

Having identified what he takes to be the principal sociological problems with his earlier work on the "Nationwide" audience, Morley suggests that audience research might be more successful if it turned to a genre-based theory of interpretation and interaction in place of a simple encoding-decoding model. Such a theory, he observes, might more adequately theorize the process of reading as a complex and interrelated series of actions that involves questions of relevance/irrelevance and comprehension/incomprehension in addition to that of ideological agreement. A theory in which genre is conceived as a set of rules for the production of meaning, operable both through writing and reading, might therefore be able to explain why certain sets of texts are especially interesting to particular groups of people (and not to others) because it would direct one's attention to the question of how and where a given set of generic rules had been created, learned, and used. This genre framework would focus attention on interdiscursive formations, that is, on questions about the kinds of cultural competencies that are learned as a consequence of certain social formations and how those are activated and perpetuated within and through multiple, related genres or discourses. Thus, just as one might want to ask what sorts of social grammars prepare adolescent boys to understand and take interest in slasher films like those in the *Halloween* series, so one might also want to ask what competencies prepare certain women to recognize romances as relevant to their experience and as potential routes to pleasure.

Although *Reading the Romance* does not use Morley's terms, it does work toward a kind of genre theory as he conceives it. To begin with, it attempts to understand how the Smithton women's social and material situation prepares them to find the act of reading attractive and even necessary. Secondly, through detailed questioning of the women about their own definition of romance and their criteria for distinguishing between ideal and failed versions of the genre, the study attempts to characterize the structure of the particular narrative the women have chosen to engage because they find it especially enjoyable. Finally, through its use of psycho-analytic theory, the book attempts to explain how and why such a struc-tured "story" might be experienced as pleasurable by those women as a consequence of their socialization within a particular family unit. I would like to elaborate briefly on each of these moments in *Reading the Ro-mance* in order to prepare the reader for what she or he will find in the subsequent pages and point to issues that would repay further explora-tion.

Most of the first half of *Reading the Romance* is devoted to a discussion of the social and material situation within which romance reading occurs. Thus I initially survey the collection of social forces resulting in the mass production of romances in the 1970s and 1980s, which were marketed in ways particularly appropriate to women, that is, through mail order and at commercial outlets largely frequented by them.[21] Although my method is analogous to Dorothy Hobson's detailed effort to explore the production of *Crossroads*, I have not gone so far as to investigate the professional ide-ologies informing the writing and editing of romances as she has done with the soap opera. The text does, however, recognize the importance of the romance-writing community even to readers, because the Smithton women made it absolutely clear that they understood themselves to be reading particular and individual authors, whose special marks of style they could recount in detail, rather than identical, factory-produced commodities. Despite the mediations of the publishing industry, romance reading was seen by the women as a way of participating in a large, ex-clusively female community. Were I conducting this study today, however, I would want to compare the meaning and significance of the romance as it is inserted in the day-to-day existence of writers, editors, readers, and even feminist critics, for such a move might demonstrate the problems inherent in a simple reading off of cultural meaning or ideology from a single text.[22]

Turning from the particular processes impinging on production that create the conditions of possibility for regular romance purchases, *Read-ing the Romance* then attempts a parallel look at the conditions organizing women's private lives that likewise contribute to the possibility of regular romance reading. It is in this context that I distinguish analytically be-tween the event of reading and the text encountered through that pro-cess. I found it necessary to do so, the reader will discover, because the Smithton women so insistently and articulately explained that their read-ing was a way of temporarily refusing the demands associated with their social role as wives and mothers. As they observed, it functioned as a "declaration of independence," as a way of securing privacy while at the same time providing companionship and conversation. In effect, what Chapters 2 and 3 try to do as a result is to unpack the significance of the

phrase "escape" by taking it somewhat more literally than have most analysts of the media in order to specify the origin and character of the distance the women find it necessary to maintain between their "ordinary"
lives and their fantasies.[23] I have therefore tried to take seriously the dual
implications of the word "escape," that is, its reference to conditions left
behind and its intentional projection of a utopian future.

It is this move, I think, that specifically relates *Reading the Romance* to
Hobson's *Crossroads* work, to her work on housewives, and to
McRobbie's work on the culture of working-class girls. Indeed, there are
remarkable similarities to the way all the women who contributed to these
studies use traditionally female forms to resist their situation *as women* by
enabling them to cope with the features of the situation that oppress
them. Thus, just as the adolescent girls studied by McRobbie manipulate
the culture of femininity to "combat the class-based and oppressive features of the school" and the housewives in Hobson's study rely on radio
and television to address their extreme loneliness, so the romance readers
of Smithton use their books to erect a barrier between themselves and
their families in order to declare themselves temporarily off-limits to those
who would mine them for emotional support and material care. What the
reader will find in Chapter 3, then, is an effort to explore the myriad ways
in which the simple act of taking up a book addresses the personal costs
hidden within the social role of wife and mother. I try to make a case for
seeing romance reading as a form of individual resistance to a situation
predicated on the assumption that it is women alone who are responsible
for the care and emotional nurturance of others. Romance reading buys
time and privacy for women even as it addresses the corollary consequence
of their situation, the physical exhaustion and emotional depletion
brought about by the fact that no one within the patriarchal family is
charged with *their* care. Given the Smithton women's highly specific references to such costs, I found it impossible to ignore their equally fervent
insistence that romance reading creates a feeling of hope, provides emotional sustenance, and produces a fully visceral sense of well-being.

It was the effort to account for the ability of romance reading to address the women's longing for emotional replenishment that subsequently
directed my attention to the cultural conditions that had prepared the
women to choose romances from among all the other books available to
them. Thus I found myself wondering how, given the particular "needs"
the event of reading seemed to address for the Smithton women, the romance story itself figured in this conjuncture. I began to wonder what it
was about the romance heroine's experience that fostered the readers'
ability to see her story as interesting and accounted for their willingness to
seek their own pleasure through hers precisely at the moment when they
were most directly confronting their dissatisfaction with traditionally

structured heterosexual relationships. What contribution did the narration of a romance make to their experience of pleasure? Why didn't the Smithton women choose to read detective stories, westerns, or best-sellers in their precious private moments?

In thus searching for a way to link a specific desire with a particularly chosen route to the fulfillment of that desire, I turned to psychoanalytic theory in general and to Nancy Chodorow's feminist revision of Freud in particular. Her work seemed relevant in this context because it insistently focused on the precise manner in which the social fact of parenting by women constitutes a female child with an ongoing need for the style of care associated originally with her primary parent, that is, her mother. What I was trying to explain was the fact that the Smithton women apparently felt an intense need to be nurtured and cared for and that despite their universal claim to being happily married (a claim I did not doubt), that need was not being met adequately in their day-to-day existence. Romance reading, it appeared, addressed needs, desires, and wishes that a male partner could not. Chodorow's work looked useful precisely because it theorized an asymmetrical engendering process constituting women and men in profoundly mismatched ways. That work appeared additionally relevant when an investigation of the romances the Smithton women liked best revealed that the heroines they most appreciated were virtually always provided with the kind of attention and care the Smithton women claimed to desire and further that the hero's ministrations were nearly always linked metaphorically with maternal concern and nurturance. Thus I found Chodorow's theories attractive; they provided a language that seemed potentially capable of articulating the Smithton readers' apparent desires as an ongoing search for the *mother* and her characteristic care.

Chodorow's revision of the psychoanalytic account of the family romance was interesting to me, in other words, because it postulated in women an ongoing, unfulfilled longing for the mother even after the oedipal turn to the father and heterosexuality had been negotiated. Although Chodorow's principal argument was that the tripartite internal object configuration with which women are therefore endowed is addressed by a woman's subsequent turn to mothering and to her child (an argument that might be taken to imply that the constructed desire for the preoedipal mother may be met through particular social arrangements), it seemed to me that what the Smithton readers were saying about romance reading indicated that in fact not even the activity of mothering could satisfy that lack or desire for the mother, at least for some women.[24] I thought this might be true because so much of what the women consciously said and unconsciously revealed through their evaluative procedures pointed to the centrality of the fact that in ideal romances the hero is constructed androgynously. Although the women were clearly taken with his spectacularly masculine phallic power, in their voluntary comments and in their revealed preferences they emphasized equally that his capacity for tenderness and attentive concern was essential as well. Chodorow's theories seemed helpful because of their capacity to explain what I thought of as the twin objects of desire underlying romance reading, that is, the desire for the nurturance represented and promised by the preoedipal mother and for the power and autonomy associated with the oedipal father. Romance reading, it seemed to me, permitted the ritual retelling of the psychic process by which traditional heterosexuality was constructed for women, but it also seemed to exist as a protest against the fundamental inability of heterosexuality to satisfy the very desires with which it engendered women.[25] Later I would come to see the romance as a symptom of the ongoing instability of the heterosexual solution to the oedipal dilemma, that is, as a ritual effort to convince its readers that heterosexuality is both inevitable and natural and that it is necessarily satisfying as well.[26]

Reading the Romance turns to Chodorow's revision of psychoanalytic theory in order to explain the construction of the particular desires that seem to be met by the *act* of romance reading. However, it additionally uses that theory to explore the psychological resonance of the romantic narrative itself for readers so constructed and engendered, a narrative that is itself precisely about the process by which female subjectivity is brought into being within the patriarchal family. Psychoanalysis is thus used also to explain why the story hails these readers, why they believe it possible to pursue their own pleasure by serving as witness to the romantic heroine's achievement of hers. What the psychoanalytically based interpretation reveals is the deep irony hidden in the fact that women who are experiencing the consequences of patriarchal marriage's failure to address their needs turn to a story that ritually recites the history of the process by which those needs are constituted. They do so, it appears, because the fantasy resolution of the tale ensures the heroine's achievement of the very pleasure the readers endlessly long for. In thus reading the story of a woman who is granted adult autonomy, a secure social position, and the completion produced by maternal nurturance, all in the person of the romantic hero, the Smithton women are repetitively asserting to be true what their still-unfulfilled desire demonstrates to be false, that is, that heterosexuality can create a fully coherent, fully satisfied, female subjectivity.[27]

In the end, *Reading the Romance* argues that romance reading is a profoundly conflicted activity centered upon a profoundly conflicted form. Thus the view of the romance developed here is similar to Valerie Walkerdine's account of girls' comics as a practice that channels psychic conflicts and contradictions in particular ways. It is also close to the view developed by Valerie Hey[28] as well as to that of Alison Light, who argues in her conclusion to her analysis of Daphne du Maurier's *Rebecca* that women's romance reading is "as much a measure of their deep dissatisfaction with heterosexual options as of any desire to be fully identified with the submissive versions of femininity the texts endorse. Romance imagines peace, security and ease precisely because there is dissension, insecurity and difficulty."[29] Light herself points to the crucial question raised by these fundamental ambiguities surrounding and infusing the act of romance reading, that is, to the crucial question of the ultimate effects the fantasy resolution has on the women who seek it out again and again. Does the romance's endless rediscovery of the virtues of a passive female sexuality merely stitch the reader ever more resolutely into the fabric of patriarchal culture? Or, alternatively, does the satisfaction a reader derives from the act of reading itself, an act she chooses, often in explicit defiance of others' opposition, lead to a new sense of strength and independence? *Reading the Romance* ends without managing to resolve these questions, asserting that an adequate answer will come only with time and careful investigation of the developmental trajectory of the lives of adult romance readers. However much I would like to resolve the issue here, once and forever, I continue to believe that such a resolution is theoretically impossible simply because the practices of reading and writing romances continue, and their effects, even now, are not fully realized.

Subsequent critical work on the romance that focuses both on developments within the genre and within the changing profession of romance writing itself has suggested that the recontainment of protest and the channeling of desire staged by the form have not been perfect enough to thwart all change. Indeed, Ann Jones has shown in an analysis of Mills & Boon romances that the genre has found it increasingly necessary to engage specifically with feminism.[30] She demonstrates that the contradictions within the genre have been intensified by a tendency to consolidate certain feminist agendas for women in the character of a working, independent heroine even while disparaging the women's movement itself, usually through the speeches of the hero. This "conflict between feminism as emergent ideology and romance as a residual genre," contends Jones, produces three kinds of contradiction, including narrative discontinuity, irreconcilable settings, and inconsistency in realist dialogue.

I have found similar contradictions in recent American romances and have been struck by the urgency, indeed by the near hysteria, with which romance authors assert that the newly active, more insistent female sexuality displayed in the genre is still most adequately fulfilled in an intimate, monogamous relationship characterized by love and permanence. Endless assertions of this claim are necessary because many of the more sexually explicit romances in lines such as Candelight Ecstasy, Silhouette Desire,

and Harlequin Temptation have come very close to validating female desire and even to locating its origins within the woman herself. Many of the
books in these lines, in fact, contain explicit depictions of premarital
sexual relationships between hero and heroine and acknowledge that the
heroine desires the hero as much as he does her and that she derives equal
pleasure from the encounter. Yet in every case, these romances refuse
finally to unravel the connection between female sexual desire and monogamous heterosexuality. The stories therefore close off the vista they
open up by virtue of their greater willingness to foreground the sexual
fantasy at the heart of the genre. The editorial guidelines concerning the
treatment of sex in Harlequin Temptations are illuminating in this context:

> Because this series mirrors the lives of contemporary women, realistic
> descriptions of love scenes should be included, provided they are
> taste-fully handled. Each book should sustain a high level of sexual
> tension throughout, balanced by a strong story line. Sensuous en-
> counters should concentrate on passion and the emotional sensations
> aroused by kisses and caresses rather than the mechanics of sex. Of
> course, the couple have to be obviously in love, with emphasis put on
> all that being in love entails. They should definitely consummate
> their relationship before the end of the story, at whatever point fits
> naturally into the plot. The love scenes may be frequent, but not
> overwhelming, and should never be gratuitously included.

It seems clear that while the sexually explicit romance of the eighties may
have begun positively to valorize female sexuality and thus to question the
equation of femininity with virtue and virginity, it nevertheless continued
to motivate sexual activity through love. It did so by retaining the notion
of passion as the natural and inevitable expression of a prior *emotional* attachment, itself dependent on a natural, biologically based sexual difference. Thus, as Jones has suggested, "critiques of the double standard are
now admissible; the notion that sexuality is socially constructed, variable,
re-inventable rather than instinctive is not."[31] Consequently, even the
most progressive of recent romances continue to bind female desire to a
heterosexuality constructed as the only natural sexual alliance, and thus
continue to prescribe patriarchal marriage as the ultimate route to the realization of a mature female subjectivity.

The recuperation is clearly important , but again I feel that we must not
allow it to blind us to the fact that the romance *is* being changed and
struggled over by the women who write them. Indeed, it is essential to
note that in response to the creation of these sexually explicit romances,
publishers have found it necessary to retain the more traditional "sweet"
romance and to create other new forms such as the "evangelical," or "in-

spirational," romance as it is called, for women who still cannot incorporate a more explicit sexuality into the ideology of love. Thus while some romance writers are perfectly willing to identify themselves as feminists, as Catherine Kirkland found in her study of a local chapter of the Romance Writers of America, others vociferously assert that the romance is in fact the proper response to the havoc wrought by feminism on gender relations.[32] Furthermore, it cannot be said with any certainty whether the writers who are trying to incorporate feminist demands into the genre have been moved to do so by their recognition of the contradictions within the form itself or by the pressures exerted by developments in the larger culture. What does seem clear, however, is that the struggle over the romance is itself part of the larger struggle for the right to define and to control female sexuality. Thus, it matters enormously what the cumulative effects of the act of romance reading are on actual readers. Unfortunately, those effects are extraordinarily difficult to trace.

That the problem might be even more complicated than we think is suggested by Kirkland's discovery that most of the women in the group of romance writers she studied had been avid readers *before* they tried their hand at romance writing. Some of those women suggested that they turned to writing in order to intensify the fantasy experience they associated with the act of romance reading. Others, however, did so out of newfound confidence, which they attributed to romance reading, and which led to a desire to provide pleasure for other women. Romance reading, it would seem, profoundly changes at least some women by moving them to act and speak in a public forum. Prompted to purchase their own word processor, to convert the former sewing room into a study, and to demand time, not now for pleasure but for their own work, such women clearly begin to challenge in a fundamental way the balance of power in the traditional family. Of course this does not happen to all romance readers, but we should not discount it as an insignificant phenomenon since the cross-over rate from consumer to producer seems to be unusually high within this genre. Indeed, the romance boom could not continue to the extent it has were not thousands of women producing their own manuscripts and mailing them off regularly to Harlequin editors. Whether the satisfaction they derive from this activity ever prompts them to demand changes outside the privatized family environment is impossible to say, but I am not willing to rule out the possibility. Indeed, positive political strategies might be developed from the recognition that the practices of romance writing and reading continue, that they are fluid and actively being changed by both writers and readers, and that their final effects can neither be foreseen nor guaranteed in advance.

Such open-endedness, of course, immediately raises questions about specific modes of intervention, about how romance writers and readers themselves, as well as feminist intellectuals, might contribute to the re-writing of the romance in an effort to articulate its founding fantasy to a politics that would be progressive for more women. However, as many feminist theorists and their critics have pointed out, to call for such a project from within the privileged space of the academy is highly prob-lematic, since that call is almost inevitably grounded on a residual elitism that assumes that feminist intellectuals alone know what is best for all women. In this context, Angela McRobbie's admonition that academic feminists tend to "underestimate the resources and capacities of 'ordinary' women and girls . . . to participate in their own struggles as women but quite autonomously" is well taken.[33] What is needed, I have come to feel, is a recognition that romance writers and readers are themselves strug-gling with gender definitions and sexual politics *on their own terms* and that what they may need most from those of us struggling in other arenas is our support rather than our criticism or direction. To find a way to provide such support, however, or alternatively to learn from romance writers and readers is not easy, for we lack the space and channels for in-tegrating our practices with theirs. Our segregation by class, occupation, and race, once again, works against us.

I am drawn finally to McRobbie's exciting suggestion that it might be our traditional restriction to the arena of personal relations and our re-sultant penchant for talk about them that will enable us to come together as women and to explore both our common cause and our divergent agendas.[34] What we perhaps need most, then, is a place and a vocabulary with which to carry on a conversation about the meaning of such personal relations and the seemingly endless renewal of their primacy through the genre of romance. If we could begin to talk to each other from within our culture's "pink ghetto," we might indeed learn how "to make talk walk."[35] We might learn how to activate the critical power that even now lies buried in the romance as one of the few widely shared womanly com-mentaries on the contradictions and costs of patriarchy.

Durham, North Carolina
1991

The Institutional Matrix
Publishing Romantic Fiction

Like all other commercial commodities in our industrial culture, literary texts are the result of a complicated and lengthy process of production that is itself controlled by a host of material and social factors. Indeed, the modern mass-market paperback was made possible by such technological innovations as the rotary magazine press and synthetic glue as well as by organizational changes in the publishing and bookselling industries. One of the major weaknesses of the earlier romance critique has been its failure to recognize and take account of these indisputable facts in its effort to explain the genre's growing popularity. Because literary critics tend to move immediately from textual interpretation to sociological explanation, they conclude easily that changes in textual features or generic popularity must be the simple and direct result of ideological shifts in the surrounding culture. Thus because she detects a more overtly misogynist message at the heart of the genre, Ann Douglas can argue in her widely quoted article, "Soft-Porn Culture," that the coincidence of the romance's increasing popularity with the rise of the women's movement must point to a new and developing backlash against feminism. Because that new message is there in the text, she reasons, those who repetitively buy romances must experience a more insistent need to receive it again and again.[1]

Although this kind of argument sounds logical enough, it rests on a series of tenuous assumptions about the equivalence of critics and readers and ignores the basic facts about the changing nature of book production and distribution in contemporary America. Douglas's explanatory strategy assumes that purchasing decisions are a function *only* of the content of a given text and of the needs of readers. In fact, they are deeply affected by a book's appearance and availability as well as by potential readers' awareness and expectations. Book buying, then, cannot be reduced to a simple interaction between a book and a reader. It is an event that is affected and at least partially controlled by the material nature of book publishing as a socially organized technology of production and distribution.

The apparent increase in the romance's popularity may well be attributable to women's changing beliefs and needs. However, it is conceivable that it is equally a function of other factors as well, precisely because the romance's recent success *also* coincides with important changes in book production, distribution, advertising, and marketing techniques. In fact, it may be true that Harlequin Enterprises can sell 168 million romances not because women suddenly have a greater need for the romantic fantasy but because the corporation has learned to address and overcome certain recurring problems in the production and distribution of books for a mass audience.[2] If it can be shown that romance sales have been increased by particular practices newly adopted within the publishing industry, then we must entertain the alternate possibility that the apparent need of the female audience for this type of fiction may have been generated or at least augmented artificially. If so, the astonishing success of the romance may constitute evidence for the effectiveness of commodity packaging and advertising and not for actual changes in readers' beliefs or in the surrounding culture. The decision about what the romance's popularity constitutes evidence for cannot be made until we know something more about recent changes in paperback marketing strategies, which differ substantially from those that have been used by the industry for almost 150 years.

Standard book-marketing practices can be traced, in fact, to particular conceptions of the book and of the act of publication itself, both of which developed initially as a consequence of the early organization of the industry. The output of the first American press, established at Cambridge, Massachusetts, in 1639, was largely the ecclesiastical work of learned gentlemen of independent means who could afford to pay the printer to issue their books.[3] Limitation of authorship to those with sufficient capital occurred generally throughout the colonies because most of the early presses were owned by combined printer-publishers who charged authors a flat fee for typesetting and distribution and a royalty for each book sold.[4] Because it was the author who financed publication and thus shouldered the risk of unsold copies, the printer-publisher had relatively little interest in seeing that the book appealed to previously known audience taste. As a result, authors exerted almost total control over their works, which were then conceived as the unique products of their own individual intellects. Publication was concomitantly envisioned as the act of publicly issuing an author's ideas, an act that could be accomplished by the formal presentation of even one copy of those ideas for public review. In the early years of the printing industry, therefore, the *idea* of publication was not tied to the issue of sales or readership. As long as the work was presented in the public domain, it was considered published, regardless of whether it was read or not.

Of course, authors did concern themselves with readers, not least because they stood to lose a good deal if their books failed to sell. However, the problem was not a major one because the literate reading community was small and because publication itself was carried out on a local scale. The author very often knew who his readers were likely to be and could tailor his offering to their interests and tastes. Indeed, it was not uncommon for an early American writer to finance publication by soliciting contributions from specific, known subscribers whom he made every effort to please.[5] It was thus relatively easy to match individual books with the readers most likely to appreciate the sentiments expressed within them.

Thus the concept of the book as a unique configuration of ideas conceived with a unique hypothetical audience in mind developed as the governing conception of the industry. Publishers prided themselves on the diversity of their offerings and conceived the strength of an individual house to be its ability to supply the American reading public with a constant stream of unique and different books. In addition, they reasoned further that because publishing houses issued so many different kinds of works, each of which was intended for an entirely different public, it was futile to advertise the house name itself or to publicize a single book for a heterogeneous national audience. In place of national advertising, then, publishers relied on editors' intuitive abilities to identify the theoretical audiences for which books had been conceived and on their skills at locating real readers who corresponded to those hypothetical groups. Throughout the nineteenth century and indeed well into the twentieth, authors, editors, and publishers alike continued to think of the process of publication as a personal, discrete, and limited act because they believed that the very particularity and individuality of books destined them for equally particular and individual publics.

Despite the continuing domination of this attitude, the traditional view of book publishing was challenged, even if only tentatively, in the early years of the nineteenth century by an alternate view which held that certain series of books could be sold successfully and continuously to a huge, heterogeneous, preconstituted public. Made possible by revolutionary de-

velopments in technology and distribution and by the changing character
of the reading audience itself, this new idea of the book as a salable
commodity gradually began to alter the organization of the editorial process and eventually the conception of publishing itself. Although this new
view of the book and of the proper way to distribute it was at first associated only with a certain kind of printer-publisher, it was gradually acknowledged and later grudgingly used by more traditional houses when it
became clear that readers could be induced to buy quite similar books
again and again.

The specific technological developments that prepared the way for the
early rationalization of the book industry included the improvement of
machine-made paper, the introduction of mechanical typesetting and
more sophisticated flatbed presses, and the invention of the Napier and
Hoe cylinder press. The inventions of the steamboat and the railroad and
the extension of literacy—especially to women—combined to establish
publishing as a commercial industry with the technical capacity to produce for a mass audience by 1830.[6] What this meant was that commercially
minded individuals began to enter the business with the sole purpose of
turning a profit.

Lacking the interest of their literary confreres in the quality of the
material they produced, men like the Beadle brothers, Theophilus B.
Peterson, and later Street and Smith determined to publish what the general American public wanted in the way of diversionary reading material.
Their concern with profit further prompted the first literary entrepreneurs
to search for ways to sell their books not merely effectively but predictably
as well. These men reasoned that if they could take the traditional risk out
of book publication by identifying their potential audiences more successfully, they might avoid the common losses that came with overproduction
and poorly directed distribution. As a consequence, they experimented
with many varied schemes, all of which were designed to establish a permanent channel of communication between the publishing house and an
already identified, constantly available audience of readers. This view of
the relationship between a publisher and a book-buying public was vastly
different from the more traditional view held by men like Mathew Carey
of Philadelphia and the Harper Brothers of New York.

The extent of the gap between these two views of the publishing process can be illustrated easily by considering the two most commonly employed schemes used by literary entrepreneurs of the mid-nineteenth century to rationalize their production. In commodity exchange, which is
exactly what these men were proposing, the producer attempts to convince the largest number of individuals to part with relatively small
amounts of capital in return for some specially designed thing. Unless that
producer wishes to go out of business rather quickly after having initially

supplied the available audience, it becomes necessary to extend demand for the commodity either by enlarging the purchasing public or by convincing it to consume that commodity repetitively. Although the early commercial publishers attempted to do both, they tended to concentrate their efforts on the task of inducing repetitive consumption, either by closely duplicating earlier literary successes or by establishing newspaper-like subscription operations.

The first technique—the imitation of an earlier bestseller—led to the practice of publishing particular types or categories of books such as the domestic novels associated with Peterson or the dime-novel Westerns created by the Beadle brothers after the initial success of Ann Stephens's *Maleska.*[7] Peterson and the Beadles reasoned that once they had loosely identified an actual audience by inducing it to buy a specific kind of book, it would not be difficult to keep that audience permanently constituted and available for further sales by supplying it with endless imitations of the first success. Although a good idea, the technique failed as often as it worked. Because they lacked a formal way of maintaining contact with the audience they created, these publishers simply had to trust that continuous feeding would mean continuous buying. Furthermore, Peterson and the Beadles could determine audience preference only experimentally by issuing new material in the hope that some of it would ferret out new readers and thereby enlarge the market as needed. Nevertheless, in relying on repetitive formulas as a result of their primary interest in profit, they managed to create America's first mass-produced fiction in book form. We will see that the contemporary romance is nothing more than a highly sophisticated version of this prototypical category literature and that its publishers are, if anything, even more interested in profit than were their nineteenth-century counterparts.

Just as contemporary romance publishing is guided by this entrepreneurial vision of the book as an endlessly replicable commodity, so also does it rely on another distribution practice engineered in nineteenth-century America specifically to rationalize the sale of books. In depending heavily on highly predictable subscription sales to distribute their romances, Harlequin Enterprises and Silhouette Books, in fact, have merely realized the potential of a scheme adopted first in American book publishing in 1839 by New York journalists, Park Benjamin and Rufus Wilmot Griswold.[8] At first looking only for a way to enlarge newspaper sales, these two journalists created a "story" newspaper called *Brother Jonathan* whose pirated British serials, they hoped, would appeal to a larger audience than did the usual daily fare of political and criminal news. Although *Brother Jonathan* was essentially a magazine, it qualified for free distribution through the United States mail as a newspaper because Benjamin and Griswold deliberately combined their serials with a minimum of "news."

As a consequence, they managed to keep their prices well below those of the competing magazines that were the traditional channels for story and novel distribution.

The venture prospered so well that the newly enlarged serial audience often refused to wait for the concluding installments in *Brother Jonathan*. Many readers chose instead to purchase the complete novel in book form issued, of course, by a traditional printer-publisher. To combat their own self-subversion, Benjamin and Griswold then created the "supplement," a complete novel printed on cheap paper, priced at fifty cents, and disguised, still, as a newspaper. This all-important disguise permitted the inexpensive circulation of the *Brother Jonathan* supplements through the mail to an audience of permanent subscribers. Despite the disguise, however, these supplements were really the first mass-marketed paperbound books to be distributed in the United States.

Unfortunately for Benjamin and Griswold, other newspaper publishers caught on quickly and soon began to issue their own paperbound extras. The ensuing competition lowered prices even further, placing books well within the financial reach of a significant portion of the American population for the first time. Traditional book publishers, to be sure, were dismayed by this challenge to their control of book distribution. In retaliation, they, too, began issuing cheap reprints at twenty-five cents and then, later, at twelve and a half cents. By 1842, book charges had dropped so low that Bulwer's newly published *Zanoni* could be purchased from one of three sources for as little as six cents.

The situation did not improve for trade publishers until 1843 when, with the book market apparently saturated, the postal service ruled that the supplements could no longer be carried at newspaper rates. This decision effectively closed off the first real channel for mass distribution of books ever used in America. Deprived of its way to reach its thousands of readers regularly but cheaply, *Brother Jonathan* collapsed almost immediately; its many imitators disappeared soon thereafter. During their short lives, however, they had performed the important function of proving that a large and diverse audience, sometimes the size of thirty thousand individuals, could be persuaded to buy not only a single novel but the *regularly issued* fictional offerings of a single firm. They demonstrated, in fact, that it was possible to make book sales predictable and more profitable if one could establish a permanent conduit between a publishing source and a consuming audience and keep that conduit constantly filled with material that would continue to satisfy individual readers.

Despite the disappearance of the story newspapers, the new reading audience continued to support the sale of cheap books, which never again disappeared totally from the American book market. In fact, the story-paper public and its newly discovered appetite for book-length reading matter seems to have prompted what William Charvat has called "America's first great literary boom."[9] Running its course between 1845 and 1857, this boom was characterized by the fission of literary production and publication into two distinct practices.[10] The first, which was modeled after the category and story-paper concept of filling a permanently open channel of communication, aimed to sell remarkably similar novels and gift books to the same audience over and over again. The second, governed by the more traditional notion of book production as a discrete event initiated by an author, aimed to constitute for each work a temporary audience of like-minded individuals for whom the work had been theoretically conceived. Because few editors and publishers fully understood the revolutionary implications of the first procedure, both practices were often carried out within the same firm. Thus the goals of maximizing sales and pleasing already-identified audiences were imposed tacitly on writers who could never have appealed to a mass audience even if they had so wished. Hawthorne, Melville, and James were only a few of those who suffered as a result of this early conceptual confusion in the publishing industry.

Nevertheless, while it is true that cheap books never disappeared completely from the American publishing scene after the creation of the supplements, mass-produced and mass-marketed literary fare constituted only a very small portion of book production for almost the next one hundred years. Publishing continued to be dominated by the ideas and practices of the literary gentlemen in part because it was difficult to put the new commercial schemes into practice on a large scale. Publishers had not yet developed systematic ways to survey public taste, and they were often forced to experiment and to rely on intuition. Moreover, distribution networks themselves were inadequate, not only because the few book outlets that existed were concentrated on the East Coast but also because the newspaper and magazine distribution systems were localized and fragmented. Even if book publishers had learned to rely parasitically on the distribution networks of the few national magazines, which had, after all, relatively constant readerships, it is doubtful that the size of the audience they could thus have reached would have been large enough to make a book-production venture profitable. The mass-market portion of the industry languished, consequently, even throughout the first third of this century. It revived only with the invention of even more efficient presses and with the creation of more extensive and effective distribution networks.[11]

The first production scheme designed specifically to mass produce cheap paperbound books and to utilize the magazine distribution system was not mounted until 1937 when Mercury Publications created American Mercury Books. In fact, according to Frank Schick, American Mercury was the first paperbound book series to employ magazine distribution successfully.[12] Packaged to look like magazines, these books were sold at newsstands and, like periodicals, remained available only for a month. American Mercury's practices, which stressed the ephemerality of this literature, clearly differentiated this publishing venture from more traditional book production, which continued to focus on the establishment of a line of diverse books of lasting worth to be kept constantly in print on a backlist and in stock at the better retail establishments. Although the company at first published a variety of titles, by 1940 the editors had decided to concentrate on mysteries in the interest of establishing better control over their market. The new series, called Mercury Mysteries, differentiated its remarkably similar covers and titles by numbering each book for the reader's convenience.

To emphasize the significance of this particular editorial decision to concentrate on a single literary subgenre, it is worth pointing out that the American Mercury venture was really the first mass-distribution scheme to perfect the category method of production, which has been labeled by literary sociologist, Robert Escarpit, as "semi-programmed issue."[13] In noting the problem of locating a real audience of readers for a particular book within the modern, anonymous, reading public, Escarpit has observed that "[n]o one publishing a book can forsee exactly how much attention potential readers will give it."[14] Furthermore, because the publisher "cannot establish a programme" for a book because "he cannot determine the stages and limits of its distribution," Escarpit reasons that publication must be thought of as "non-programmed issuing."[15] Having made such an assertion, however, he subsequently admits that the problem is often ingeniously circumvented by semiprogrammed issue whereby books are "distributed within a small circle [of regular readers] whose requirements are known and whose preferences have been thoroughly established."[16] Determinations of this sort are made most often, he points out, in connection with related fan magazines that foster the creation of a generic formula or orthodoxy. Semiprogrammed issue differs, then, from the kind of publishing operation run by Peterson and the Beadles only in its utilization of more formalized and hence more reliable ways of determining audience preference.

The publishers of American Mercury Books were attempting exactly this sort of controlled production when they made the decision to restrict their list to a single type of fiction. They hoped thereby to sell their paperbacks in large quantities to readers who already knew their mystery magazines. Those magazines enabled the editors to take note of reader opinion and to gauge preferences that they then sought to match in their manuscript selection. In effect, American Mercury tried to control both its audience *and* the books produced especially for that group. Despite this successful formalization of category publishing, the relatively small size of the American Mercury venture has prevented it from being credited with the mass-market paperback revolution.[17] Although that honor is usually awarded to Robert de Graff for his founding of Pocket Books in 1939, his scheme introduced no new conceptual innovations to the industry.[18] Like the editors at American Mercury, de Graff thought of the book as a commodity to be sold, relied on the magazine system of distribution, and gradually turned to category publication.[19] Still, it was de Graff's ability to institute this system on a large scale that set the stage for the romance's rise to dominance within the mass-market industry. To understand exactly how and why the romance has become so important in commodity publishing, it is neceessary to understand first how the economics of paperback publishing and distribution created the industry's interest in the predictability of sales.[20]

In the years immediately preceding de Graff's entry into the field, major improvements had been made in both printing and binding techniques. The invention of magazine rotary presses made high-speed production runs possible and profitable. Although the new machinery was very expensive, the cost was born largely by the printers themselves who were, by tradition, independent from publishing firms. Because the printers had to keep the costly presses operating twenty-four hours a day to guarantee a return on their initial investment, they pressured de Graff and his competitors at Avon, Popular Library, and Dell to schedule production tightly and regularly. This practice led to a magazine-like monthly production schedule similar to American Mercury's, a practice that fit nicely with de Graff's intention to distribute his books through the magazine network. The regularization of production further enabled the printers to buy large quantities of paper at lower rates without also having to pay to store it indefinitely. The publishers benefited in turn because they could sell their books at much lower prices.[21]

Surprisingly enough, the invention of synthetic glue also helped to add speed to the publication of the mass-market paperback.[22] Traditional book binding is accomplished by hand or machine sewing of folded signatures of paper to create the finished book. Even when carried out mechanically, the process is both expensive and time-consuming. "Perfect" binding is an alternate procedure in which single leaves of paper are gathered together, cut uniformly, and then glued to the spine of the cover. The first adhesives used in the process of perfect binding were animal glues that were not only slow to dry, but once dried, were so inflexible that bindings often cracked, releasing individual pages. The glues made it necessary for a printer to obtain sufficient storage space for drying the perfect-bound books. The invention of quick-drying synthetic glues eliminated most of these problems. Fast-setting adhesives necessitated assembly-line procedures that simultaneously accelerated the whole production process and obviated the need for costly storage. The new binding machines were expensive but, once again, the printers shouldered the enormous costs and passed much of the benefit on to the publishers.

Together with the rotary presses, then, perfect binding and synthetic glues made possible the production of huge quantities of books at a very low cost per unit and contributed to the acceleration and regularization of the acquisition and editorial processes. The consequent emphasis on speed caused the paperback publishers to look with favor on category books that could be written to a fairly rigid formula. By directing their potential writers to create in this way, mass-market houses saved the time and expense of editing unique books that had as yet not demonstrated their ability to attract large numbers of readers.

The particular step taken by de Graff that made this production of vast numbers of books financially feasible was his decision to utilize the extensive magazine distribution network that had developed during the past thirty years. De Graff reasoned that if he was actually to sell the large quantities of books he could now produce so effortlessly, he would have to place books in the daily paths of many more Americans. Because he was aware of the relative lack of bookstores in the United States and of the general population's feeling that those establishments were intimidating and inhospitable, he concluded that books would have to be marketed somewhere else if they were to be sold on a grand scale. He turned to the American News Company, which had a virtual monopoly on the national distribution of magazines and newspapers, because it counted among its clients many thousands of newsstands, drugstores, candy stores, and even food outlets. De Graff felt sure that if confronted with attractively packaged and very inexpensive books at these establishments, the American magazine reader could be persuaded to become a paperback book purchaser. The phenomenal sales of his first ten titles proved him right.[23]

Despite the advantages it offered, however, magazine distribution also posed substantial problems. De Graff and his early competitors soon discovered that few of their new book retailers knew anything about books. Uneasy about purchasing materials they might not be able to sell, these individuals at first resisted efforts to get them to stock paperback books. To overcome their hesitation, de Graff and his counterparts at other houses proposed that the entire risk of unsold books be shouldered by the publishing firms themselves. As a result, they permitted all retail outlets to return any unsold books or to certify that the books themselves had been destroyed.

The returns policy had the desired effect in that it convinced retailers that they could not be harmed by stocking paperbacks, but it proved extremely troublesome to the publishers themselves. Because they had no way to track simultaneously progressing returns and new print orders or to shift the returns from one outlet to another, many publishers found themselves sending a book through a second printing to accommodate demand, only to discover later, after all returns were completed, that eventual total sales were less than the first print order.[24] The resulting overproduction was very costly and caused the mass-market publishers to search for ways to make book sales more predictable. It was thus that category literature suggested itself as a means of gauging how a new version of an already-proved type of book might perform in the market.

It might accurately be said that the high cost of paperback book production increased the importance of the ability to predict precisely the pattern and extent of sales. A subtle but nonetheless powerful inducement to identify and fulfill audience expectations was therefore built into the mass-market editorial process because editors became responsible for acquiring titles that would make money. Category literature became a useful tool for publishing houses whose success depended on their ability to predict demand so exactly that the product not only sold but sold in the identical quantities projected at the beginning of the entire process. Because of the cost of overproduction, a sense of the size of the potential audience, an understanding of the preferences its individual members held in common, and the ability to embody those preferences in a product they would buy became essential to the editorial process. Success, in effect, became a function of accurate prediction. That prediction was ultimately dependent on the capacity to control the interaction between an identifiable audience and a product designed especially for it.

Category or formulaic literature has been defined most often by its standard reliance on a recipe that dictates the essential ingredients to be included in each new version of the form. It therefore permits an editor to direct and control book creation in highly specific ways. It is worth emphasizing, however, that category literature is *also* characterized by its consistent appeal to a regular audience. Indeed, Escarpit's treatment of formulaic literature as "semi-programmed issue" is helpful here because it acknowledges its status as a unique mode of literary *production* and thus highlights the fact that such publishing enables the firm to control its audience as well. Whereas fully programmed issue is characterized by the conscious creation of literary material for an already formally identified audience, usually through the mechanism of advance subscription, semi-programmed issue involves the selection of texts from a large variety of offered material with the idea that those texts will be distributed to informally identified readers whose requirements and preferences have been determined partially in advance. The determinations are usually made on the basis of audience response to specialized magazines or newsletters devoted to the subject that constitutes the "content" of the category.

Not only does this kind of semiprogrammed production obviate the need to set print orders solely on the basis of blind intuition, but it also reduces the difficulties of designing a proper advertising campaign. By relying on the subscription lists of related periodicals and on sales figures of earlier offerings in the genre, category publishers can project potential sales with some certainty. At the same time, they can use the periodicals for a specific advertising strategy and thus avoid the difficulty and expense of mounting a national effort in the hope of ferreting out the proper audience by chance. As Escarpit has observed, semiprogrammed issue, "from the publisher's point of view . . . is financially safe."[25] At the distribution level, moreover, category publishing takes on the appearance of a subscription sale because each dealer knows the usual number of copies he sells and can order fairly accurately.[26]

To understand the importance of the fact that category publishing makes book advertising manageable, it is necessary to know that publishers have argued for years that books cannot be marketed or advertised as are other commodities. Because every book is individual and unique, the industry has maintained, all publishers must "start from scratch" in the effort to build an audience for them. Benjamin Compaine, for instance, has commented acidly that "the toothpaste equivalent [of what publishers attempt] would be if Lever Bros. came out with a different brand each month, changing the flavor, packaging and price, with each new brand having a maximum potential sale to only 4% of the adult population."[27] Assuming, therefore, that the discreteness of books necessitated that each be advertised individually, publishers concluded that the enormous expense of advertising an entire month's offering ruled out the process entirely. Furthermore, because they believed that the variety of books offered by each firm made the creation of a single image of the house impossible, they also concluded that potentially less expensive national advertising of the house imprint would do nothing for the sales of individual books. Thus the publishing industry's advertising budget has been remarkably small for many years. The situation did not change until the 1970s when corporate takeovers of independent houses by large communications conglomerates resulted in the infusion of huge amounts of capital, some of which was directed to advertising budgets. However, before explaining how and why this has occurred and its relevance for our investigation of the romance, it is necessary to return to the early years of the third paperback revolution to trace the growing importance of the romance genre within the mass-market industry.

Although the early paperback publishers relied initially on proven hardcover bestsellers to guarantee large sales, they soon found that an insufficient number of these were available to supply the demand for cheap, paper-covered books. Wary of producing huge quantities of a title that had not yet demonstrated its salability, these mass-market houses slowly began to rely on books that were examples of categories already proven to be popular with the reading public. The trend really began with the mystery or detective story that developed as the first dominant category in modern mass-market publishing.[28] The genre was particularly well suited for semiprogrammed issue because the writer-publisher-audience relationship had been formalized in the 1920s with the establishment of the pulps like *Black Mask, Dime Detective, Detective Story*, and *Detective Fiction Weekly*.[29] They helped to establish a generic orthodoxy which would then guide continuous novel production in hardcover format. Paperback mystery publishing developed simply as an extension of an already established literary practice.

Unfortunately, mystery popularity declined throughout the 1950s. Although the genre occasionally gained back the readers it lost, several publishers nonetheless began to look elsewhere for new material that they could sell on an even more regular and predictable basis.[30] Troubled by this variability in mystery sales, Gerald Gross at Ace Books recalled the consistent reprint success of Daphne du Maurier's *Rebecca*. Wondering whether its long-standing popularity (it had been published first in 1938) indicated that it struck a universal chord in female readers, he attempted to locate previously published titles resembling du Maurier's novel, which he hoped to issue in a "gothic" series. He settled upon Phyllis Whitney's *Thunder Heights*, which he then published in 1960 as the first title in his "gothic" line.[31]

Whitney had already written several similar novels published apparently because Appleton editor Patricia Myrer also recognized their similarity to *Rebecca*. In an interview, Myrer has stated that "this [1955] was a time when mysteries were not selling well. . . . Women didn't want to read Mickey Spillane. . . . I believed they wanted to read emotional stories about a woman in peril."[32] On the basis of her intuition, she established herself as Whitney's literary agent and as Victoria Holt's, whose similar novels had met with considerable success in England. It is no accident, then, that at the same time that Gross was issuing *Thunder Heights* at Ace, Doubleday was also releasing Holt's *Mistress of Mellyn*, which quickly developed into a bestseller. When it was reissued as a Fawcett Crest paperback only a year later, it performed even more successfully. Eventually, *Mistress of Mellyn* sold more than a million copies. When other publishers caught on, the boom in gothic sales began.

Since Myrer, Gross, and other gothic publishers were not simply inserting mass-produced reading matter into a previously formalized channel of communication as had been done with paperback mysteries, it is necessary to ask why they were almost immediately successful in establishing the gothic romance as a particular category and in creating a growing demand for new titles. Their success cannot be attributed to the mere act of offering a new product to an audience already identified and therefore "controlled" by the fact of its common subscription to the same magazines. Although confession and romance periodicals had been supplying love stories for faithful readers since their first appearance in the 1920s, these pulps were designed for a working-class audience. Because book reading has always been correlated with high education and income levels, it seems probable that the gothic's extraordinary paperback success was the result of the publishers' ability to convert and then repetitively reach middle-class women. Although one might suspect that these publishers relied on the middle-class trade magazines—such as *Good Housekeeping* or the *Ladies' Home Journal*—to identify and retain its new audience, in fact, this does not appear to have been the case. Publishers used very little advertising to promote the sales of the early gothics.

What, then, accounts for the immediate success of the category? The achievement has much to do with the special characteristics of its audience, that is, with the unique situation of women in American society. The principal problem facing the publisher in a heterogeneous, modern society is finding an audience for each new book and developing a method for getting that book to its potential readers. By utilizing the magazine distribution network, paperback publishers substantially increased their chances of finding buyers. But the use of this network proved especially significant for those paperback houses that were newly interested in female readers because it made available for book distribution two outlets almost always visited on a regular basis by women, the local drugstore and the food supermarket. Even the growing number of women who went to work in the 1960s continued to be held responsible for child care and basic family maintenance, as were their counterparts who remained wholly within the home.[33] Consequently, the publishers could be sure of regularly reaching a large segment of the adult female population simply by placing the gothics in drug and food stores. At the same time, they could limit advertising expenditures because the potential or theoretical audience they hoped to attract already had been gathered for them. The early success of the gothic genre is a function of the de facto but nonetheless effective concentration of women brought about by social constraints on their placement within society. This concentration had the overall effect of limiting their diffusion throughout social space. In turn, this limitation guaranteed that as a potential book-buying public, American women were remarkably easy to reach.

The popularity of gothic romances increased throughout the decade of the 1960s. While American college students were beginning to protest American involvement in Vietnam and a gradually increasing number of feminists vociferously challenged female oppression, more and more women purchased novels whose plots centered about developing love relationships between wealthy, handsome men and "spunky" but vulnerable women. The audience for gothics grew to such proportions that by the early 1970s works of top gothic authors outsold the works of equivalent writers in all other categories of paperback fiction, including mysteries, science fiction, and Westerns. A typical Whitney or Holt paperback issued by Fawcett began with a first printing of 800,000 copies. Although most of the category's authors sold nowhere near that number, when taken together the gothic novels released by no less than eight paperback houses constituted an enormous total output.

At the peak of their popularity, from about 1969 to 1972, gothics were issued at the rate of thirty-five titles a month, over four hundred per year.[34] In the peak year of 1971, gothics constituted 24 percent of Dell's paperback sales. At that time, Dell was publishing four to five titles every month.[35] This extraordinary sales success of gothics established them as a true cultural phenomenon and qualified them for endless analysis and satire in the news media. Many articles on "How to Write a Gothic" can be found in the Sunday supplements and popular magazines of the period, attesting to widespread awareness of the phenomenon, if less than universal approbation of it.

The increased publicity notwithstanding, sales of gothic romances dropped off gradually between 1972 and 1974. Returns increased to such an extent that many houses cut back their gothic output. When asked to explain the decline in popularity, former publishers of gothics equivocate. Some feel that the market had simply been saturated, while others suspect that the growing visibility of the feminist movement and increasing openness about female sexuality led to a greater tolerance if not desire for stories with explicit sexual encounters. All seem to agree, however, that the nature of romance publishing changed dramatically in April 1972, when Avon Books issued *The Flame and the Flower* by Kathleen Woodiwiss.

Because Woodiwiss had sent her unsolicited manuscript to Avon without the usual agent introduction, it landed on the "slush pile," usually considered an absolute dead end in contemporary publishing. Inexplicably, it was picked up by executive editor Nancy Coffey, who was looking for something to get her through a long weekend. As she tells the story, she could not put the manuscript down.[36] She returned to Avon enthusiastically determined to get the book into print. Coffey eventually convinced others and the book was released in April as an Avon Spectacular. Although Woodiwiss's novel, like the gothics, followed the fortunes of a pert but feminine heroine, it was nearly three times as long as the typical gothic, included more explicit descriptions of sexual encounters and near rapes, and described much travel from place to place. Despite the differences, it ended, as did all gothics, with the heroine safely returned to the hero's arms.

A paperback original, *The Flame and the Flower* was given all the publicity, advertising, and promotion usually reserved for proven bestsellers.[37] Such originals had been issued continuously in small quantities throughout the early years of mass-market history, but concentration on them was not widespread for the simple reason that it cost more to pay out an advance to an author and to advertise an unknown book than to buy reprint rights to an already moderately successful hardback. Avon, however, under the direction of Peter Meyer, had begun to experiment with originals and different advertising campaigns in the mid-1960s.[38] When Coffey agreed to publish *The Flame and the Flower* without previous hardcover exposure, she was simply following a practice that had become fairly common within her firm. The house's extraordinary success with Woodiwiss's novel soon caused industry-wide reconsideration of the possibilities of paperback originals as potential bestsellers. When Avon followed this success with two more bestseller romances in 1974, the industry was convinced not only of the viability of the original but also of the fact that a new category had been created. Within the trade, the genre was dubbed the "sweet savage romance" after the second entrant in the field, Rosemary Rogers's *Sweet Savage Love*.[39]

Once Avon had demonstrated that original romances could be parlayed into ready money, nearly every other mass-market house developed plans to issue its own "sweet savage romances," "erotic historicals," "bodice-rippers," or "slave sagas," as they were variously known throughout the industry. Virtually all recognized, as Yvonne McManus of Major Books did, that "Avon ha[d] smartly created a demand through heavy advertising and promotion." As she commented further, "it . . . invented its own new trend, which is clever paperback publishing."[40]

Although a few houses have developed bestsellers in the "sweet savage" category, Avon has been most successful at identifying the house imprint with this kind of romance and has established close ties with its audience by compiling a mailing list from its fan letters. Several publishers have attempted to develop other sorts of romances with the idea of creating a series or "line" that they hope to associate in readers' minds with the house name. The creation of "line" fiction is one more example of the familiar attempt to identify a permanent base audience in order to make better predictions about sales and to increase profit. The growing proliferation and success of such schemes, often modeled after Avon's informal techniques or the more elaborate operations of Harlequin Enterprises, makes them an extremely important development in romance publishing specifically and in mass-market paperback publishing generally. Before assessing several of the most important of these, it will be helpful to mention two further developments, one in general publishing, the other in bookselling, that help to explain why so many paperback houses not only have found the romance market attractive but also have been able to appeal to it successfully.

The most significant development in American publishing in the twentieth century has been the assumption of control of once privately owned houses by vast communications conglomerates. Begun in 1960 with the Random House "absorption" of Knopf and continued in 1967 when the Radio Corporation of America (RCA) purchased Random House, the merger trend has left only a few houses intact.[41] In 1967, for instance, the Columbia Broadcasting System (CBS) acquired Holt, Rinehart and Winston and then later purchased Praeger Publishers, Popular Library, and Fawcett Publications. Xerox has assumed control of Ginn and Company, R. R. Bowker, and the trade periodical, *Publishers Weekly.* Dell is owned by Doubleday and Company, as is the Literary Guild. Gulf and Western has acquired both Simon and Schuster and Pocket Books.[42] Although by no means exhaustive, this litany at least makes clear that the first impact of the merger trend has been the union of hardcover and mass-market paperback companies within a single corporate structure. Despite the fact that most individual houses have retained editorial control over what they produce, it is also apparently true that greater attention is paid to their profit-and-loss statements by corporate headquarters than the houses used to devote to them themselves.

It is not hard to understand why "attention to the bottom line" has begun to dominate the publishing process when one considers that despite increased profit consciousness within the mass-market segment of the industry, publishing remained a small, informally organized business well into the 1970s.[43] Once referred to as "seat-of-the-pants" publishing by its critics and supporters alike, the American industry continued to make decisions about manuscript selection, print orders, and advertising campaigns on the basis of editors' intuitions, ignoring the availability of the computer and the development of sophisticated market-research techniques. Much of the reluctance to adopt these highly mechanical procedures can be traced to the lingering vision of publishing as the province of literary gentlemen seriously devoted to the "cause" of humane letters. Editors worried that if profit became the principal goal, publishers would be reluctant to sponsor the first novel of a promising young writer because its financial failure would be virtually guaranteed.

In recently assessing the impact of corporate takeovers on publishing, Thomas Whiteside has observed that the "business was indeed riddled with inefficiency."[44] "Sluggish management, agonizingly slow editorial and printing processes, creaky and ill-coordinated systems of book distribution and sales, skimpy advertising budgets, and . . . inadequate systems of financing," he claims, "prevented many publishers from undertaking major long-range editorial projects that they knew were necessary to their companies' future well-being."[45] Traditionally a low-profit industry, trade-book publishing was also characterized by widely varying profits because each house's fortunes fluctuated rapidly in concert with its failure or success at selling its monthly list. When the corporate managers of the new conglomerates began to scrutinize the houses' financial practices and performances, they were appalled. Most responded by forcing the publishers to adopt the procedures long familiar to the corporate world: "efficient accounting systems, long-range planning, elimination of waste, and unnecessary duplication of services."[46]

Although it seems obvious that conglomerate control has had the effect of forcing trade publishers to do away almost completely with "mid-level" books—those that perform only moderately well in both the market and in critical opinion—it has had the additional effect of providing the paperback houses with large sums of money. This has enabled them to pay huge fees for the reprint rights to bestselling novels; it has also permitted them to devote a great deal of financial attention to planning category sales by commissioning market-research studies and to the advertising of the new "lines" created as their consequence. The logic behind this kind of financial maneuver is grounded on the assumption that if paperback sales can be made more predictable and steady, the newly acquired mass-market section of a conglomerate can be used to balance out the necessarily unpredictable operation of the trade process. "The hardcover publishers," Whiteside explains, "calculated that by adding a paperback branch to their corporate organizations they could smooth out some of the ups and downs of their business, making up on the swings what they might lose on the roundabouts."[47]

Corporate takeovers have had the effect, then, of adding to the pressure on paperback houses to devote increasing amounts of time and money to category sales.[48] At the same time, because reprint rights have grown enormously expensive, it has been necessary for them to place even more emphasis on the acquisition of original manuscripts.[49] To avoid the difficulties of training inexperienced writers and the expense of introducing their works on an individual basis to new audiences, paperback publishers have consequently tended to seek out originals that fit closely within category patterns. They believe it is easier to introduce a new author by fitting his or her work into a previously formalized chain of communication than to establish its uniqueness by locating a special audience for it. The trend has proven so powerful, in fact, that as of 1980, 40 to 50 percent of nearly every house's monthly releases were paperback originals.[50] The conglomerates' quest for financial accountability has had another effect besides that of increasing the emphasis on category publishing with its steady, nearly guaranteed sales. Their overwhelming interest in predictability has also helped to forge an important link between the now more profit-minded paperback houses and the increasingly successful bookstore chains, B. Dalton, Bookseller, and Waldenbooks. Together, these two developments have led to even greater industry interest in romantic novels and the women who purchase them.

Owned by the Dayton-Hudson department store chain, B. Dalton opened its first store in Edina, Minnesota, in 1966.[51] After exploring the future of bookselling in the United States, the parent chain had concluded that Americans would continue to increase their education level, their desire for knowledge, and their need for books. Cognizant also of the lack of book outlets throughout the country and of their concentration on the East Coast, Dayton-Hudson proposed, therefore, to make books available to more Americans by establishing fully stocked bookstores in suburban mall locations near mid-size cities.

The company began by designing impressive stores with parquet floors and leather armchairs, but it soon discovered that the "hands-off" atmosphere did not prove inviting in a mall location. In short order, it switched to the "jazzy" approach for which it is now well known. Dalton introduced angled book racks to force browsers to pass more shelf space than usual, raised the light level, dangled cheerful signs from the ceiling about the pleasures of book-reading, and added the point-of-purchase displays so common in supermarkets. The company hoped that the resulting clutter would increase impulse buying. As a Dalton promotion executive explained to Thomas Whiteside, "[W]e look for multiple purchases all the time. We work the impulse areas very hard. We use table displays and dump bins . . . for bestsellers, and you have to walk by different displays of the same books two or three times when you go through the store."[52]

Dayton-Hudson's move has undoubtedly helped to sell romance fiction. As Dalton opened more and more outlets—nearly all in shopping-mall locations—throughout the 1970s, it obligingly increased the number of potential outlets likely to be visited on a regular basis by American women. Richard Snyder, president of Simon and Schuster, has commented on the connections between the growth of the chains, their female clientele, and changing publishing practices. His remarks are worth quoting at length:

> In my opinion, what is really changing the face of publishing in America is not the conglomerates but the giant book chains. It's not that as publishers we get the advantage of big accounts with the chains; it's the fact that the chains serve a different community of book readers from any that the book business has ever had before— book readers with different tastes. The elitism of the book market

doesn't exist anymore. A lot of publishers are having great difficulty dealing with that. The minute you get into the suburbs, where ninety percent of the chain stores are located, you serve the customers, mainly women, the way you would serve them in a drugstore or a supermarket. You have new dynamics coming into play, affecting what people buy and affecting publishers who wish to satisfy the needs of these customers.[53]

Not only do the chains make books even easier for American women to obtain, but they also set up their stores so that the experience of buying a book in a bookstore seems no more threatening or out-of-the-ordinary than that of picking up a paperback while waiting for groceries to move down the conveyor at the market. Although publishers will not release figures about the percentage of romances sold in the chains or in other kinds of retail outlets, it seems clear that when more than 1,200 Dalton or Walden bookstores have opened in the last fifteen years in suburban shopping malls,[54] we ought to acknowledge that the romance's extraordinary popularity is a partial function of its increased incidence *and* accessibility to the audience for which it has been created.

Dalton's computerized operations have also worked to benefit romance publishers if not romance readers as well. Every outlet is tied to a central computer at corporate headquarters in Minneapolis, which registers all weekly receipts by author, title, and by more than one hundred subject categories.[55] Every store is then ranked by sales performance within each category. Dalton's managers can predict both individual outlet and general-category sales with astonishing success. In fact, they have one of the lowest returns rates in the industry. Moreover, Dalton's accuracy in ordering has taught many publishers to rely on its original order to set the size of further printings and even to make editorial decisions about the kinds of manuscripts that satisfy a given audience's preferences.[56] Through Dalton's feedback procedures, which are given great credence by the industry not only because of their accuracy but because Dalton's share of any given house's monthly releases is often close to 10 percent, readers can indirectly affect the editorial selection process and "force" publishers to take their tastes into account. This kind of corrective cycle seems to have led to a better, although by no means perfect, fit between the romance audience's desires and the books the audience is given by the industry.

Furthermore, because Dalton's computer can keep track of slow-moving items, since all books are given a code and followed for sales performance, the company is able to determine very quickly which books have not pleased their typical audience. These can be removed promptly from the shelves and replaced with other potentially more successful items. The entire procedure leads to rapid turnover in B. Dalton stock, just as it places a high premium on fast-moving titles. While this might seem detrimental to both reader and publisher at first glance, because books are not kept on hand long enough for readers to find them, in the case of the romance it works to both their advantages. Romance readers apparently read more titles than do other category readers over a similar period of time,[57] and thus the rapid turnover in Dalton stock well satisfies these readers.

As a result of all these practices, it seems clear that the approximately 500 Dalton stores represent a significant increase in potential purchase outlets for publishers who desire to make contact with the romance audience. In fact, Dalton and Walden stores together now account for one-fifth of all trade-book and mass-market paperback sales.[58] Growing chain domination of bookselling activity in the United States should be added, then, to the list of material factors contributing to the extraordinary popularity of romance fiction in the 1970s.

Several publishing houses have further perfected sales techniques for delivering category fiction to the right public. These techniques are even more sophisticated than those employed by Avon. The obvious lead in this trend has been taken by the Canadian firm, Harlequin Enterprises, whose incredible financial success has recently spawned many imitators of its operations. That operation is a highly sophisticated version of semi-programmed issue whereby books are produced especially for an already identified, codified, and partially analyzed audience. In fact, Harlequin operates on the assumption that a book can be marketed like a can of beans or a box of soap powder. Its extraordinary profit figures convincingly demonstrate that books do not necessarily have to be thought of and marketed as unique objects but can be sold regularly and repetitively to a permanent audience on the basis of brand-name identification alone.[59]

Like most mass-market paperback houses, Harlequin began as a reprint operation in 1949, issuing cheap versions of material it had purchased from a wide variety of sources. In its early years, the company published mysteries, adventure stories, Westerns, cookbooks, and, apparently, even some pornography, in addition to the romances it bought from the British firm of Mills and Boon.[60] In 1954, Mary Bonnycastle, the wife of the company's founder, noticed that the Mills and Boon romances seemed to be doing exceptionally well. Although she suggested that the firm concentrate on stories that ended happily and were in good taste, the decision to focus production on romance fiction alone did not occur until 1957.[61] Harlequin became a public company in 1968 upon the death of its founder. By 1971, the Canadian reprinter had enjoyed such success with its romances that it was able to merge with its early supplier, Mills and Boon.

In 1971, Harlequin hired W. Lawrence Heisey, a Harvard M.B.A. and self-described "soap salesman" for Proctor and Gamble.[62] Heisey de-

signed and perfected the marketing techniques responsible for Harlequin's current success. Prior to his takeover, the company marketed few
books in the United States, sold just under 19,000,000 copies, and netted
only $110,000 on sales of $7.7 million.[63] Within a year, profits had
climbed to $1.6 million. Within eight years, its sales had increased 800
percent. Phyllis Berman has estimated that in 1977, when Harlequin's sales
totaled $75 million, its profits were probably about $11 million. That year,
Harlequin accounted for 10 percent of the United States paperback market. In addition, the company distributed more than 100,000,000 copies
of its titles over North America. By 1979, the total distribution figure had
risen to 168,000,000 copies, largely because the books were being issued
in ninety-eight countries around the world. Harlequin now claims that it
"enjoys a regular readership of over 16 million women in North America"
alone.[64] Even if these figures are inflated, it seems clear that a substantial
measure of the romance category's popularity and visibility must be attributed to Harlequin's unusual but highly successful marketing strategies.

Those strategies, it should be pointed out, are unusual only because
Heisey has applied them to bookselling. In actuality, they are little different from the techniques that have been employed for years in various
consumer-product industries. Discounting the traditional wisdom of the
publishing business, Heisey set out in 1971 to prove that books could be
sold like any other commodity. *The qualities of the product itself,* he argued,
are unimportant in designing sales campaigns. Of greater significance is the
ability to identify an audience or consuming public, the discovery of a way
to reach that audience, and, finally, the forging of an association in the
consumer's mind between a generic product like soap, facial tissue, or
romantic fiction and the company name through the mediation of a deliberately created image.[65] Heisey began by conducting market research on
the audience for romance fiction.[66] Not only did he identify and locate his
readers in order to design specific strategies for contacting them, but he
also sought to discover their motives for reading and their preferences in
characters and plot in order to incorporate them all in a carefully elaborated advertising appeal.

Heisey decided that the audience could not be reached successfully
through traditional book outlets. He proposed to concentrate sales in
supermarkets and to expand the company's subscription service. He designed book covers and advertising materials to feature the Harlequin
name more prominently than either book titles or authors' names and
made extensive use of television promotion. In this way, he was able to
spread advertising costs across the entire series, thus avoiding the expense
of creating a different audience for each title. To introduce his carefully
standardized product, which he also assumed created reader addiction, he
even went so far as to include sample copies in boxes of Bio-Ad laundry

detergent and, in another gimmick, to offer one title for fifteen cents.[67] The latter was part of a 1973 campaign to capture a million new readers for the company's romances.[68] Heisey also promoted the subscription service within the books themselves by listing other titles on the inside front cover and suggesting that readers who had missed them write for a free catalog. Thus he acquired names and addresses for the service, which then attempted to sign readers up on a permanent basis. Together, the strategies proved so successful that even now they are the basis of the company's approach.

That approach is still dominated by subscription sales, although the books are also distributed in more than 100,000 supermarkets, variety stores, and drugstores throughout the United States alone.[69] Harlequin now issues twelve romances a month—six each in its standard "Romance" category and in the "spicier," more sexually explicit "Presents" series. Readers may contract to receive either or both of these Harlequin lines. When they do, they get their books earlier than if they wait for them to appear in the stores, though they still acquire them at newsstand prices as a consequence of Harlequin's absorption of the shipping costs. Because the subscription lists and market-research analyses have helped the company to predict sales with great precision, Harlequin is rarely saddled with overproduction costs. Whereas other publishing houses distribute 12,000 copies of an average paperback and expect 35 to 40 percent of the first run to be returned, Harlequin generally prints 500,000 copies, of which less than 25 percent are ever returned.[70] Indeed, some dealers report selling 80 percent of their allotment within ten days.[71] Heisey has observed that while "other companies print ten books to sell six, [Harlequin] print[s] seven and a half" to sell those same six.[72]

Once ignored within the industry, Harlequin is now followed with care by book people who have little respect for the company's editorial product but who would dearly love to duplicate its financial success. In fact, many houses have acted deliberately to establish their own "lines" of romance fiction. Ray Walters, who writes regularly about paperback publishing for the *New York Times Book Review*, has commented that this trend seems to have begun when the findings of the Yankelovich, Skelly and White reader survey became generally known in 1978. Just as publishing executives discovered that three-fifths of the American book-reading public was composed of women under fifty, he writes, "reports started circulating along Publishers' Row about the extraordinary success being enjoyed by the 'contemporary romances with exotic settings' produced by . . . Harlequin Enterprises."[73] Newly impressed by the size of the female audience and by Harlequin's ability to take advantage of its purchasing capacity, Fawcett, Dell, and Warner each proceeded to duplicate the Harlequin approach by presenting romances as products in a specially designed series or line. In explaining the reasoning behind Dell's move, company executive Ross Claiborne has identified the particular aspect of the Harlequin phenomenon that has impressed the industry most. "The profit figures from Harlequin are so staggering," he admits, "that every publisher is dying to get in. It's a small investment and few books are returned. Clearly, it's a license to print money."[74]

Although Dell was the first to launch a Harlequin-type line with its "Candlelight Romance" series, which first appeared in May 1979, it did not back the new venture with the same kind of market-research effort mounted by the Canadian firm.[75] Dell merely proposed to imitate Harlequin's packaging and advertising rather than its expensive processes for determining and satisfying reader tastes. Fawcett, on the other hand, entered the contest for the female audience by duplicating both Harlequin's research techniques and its marketing strategies. All aspects of its "Coventry Romance" line were researched and pretested before the series' appearance in November 1979. Conducted by its advertising agency, Grey 2, Fawcett's reader studies were designed to discover preferences not only for certain kinds of characters and plots but also for likely imprints and possible advertising campaigns.[76]

The company began, for instance, with five possible choices for the series imprint—including Regent Court, Clarion, Cotillion, Sovereign, and Coventry—which it then pretested in focus interviews with potential readers to determine the kinds of associations and expectations each imprint conjured up for them. Because they understood that the success of brand-name category publishing is entirely dependent on the ability to establish an exact congruence between what the audience anticipates from a product and what the product actually delivers, Fawcett executives wanted to avoid creating expectations they did not intend to fulfill. As Vice-President James Young has explained, "The most important aspect of this test was to check if the imprint resulted in any misassociations regarding the content and genre. As a result of consumer testing, Sovereign was scrapped because of its high association with kings and queens, Cotillion conveyed antebellum South, Regent Court also conjured up kings and queens plus legal associations, Clarion seemed to have no clear associations."[77] In the end, the most compelling reason for choosing the name Coventry was that readers attached no misassociations to it. It also seemed to help them correctly identify the probable period of the novels and the kinds of characters they were likely to contain.

Because Fawcett also wanted to determine why people read romances, one segment of the focus interview asked women to draw pictures of romance readers. When most of those pictures emphasized happy, smiling women who were reading even as they engaged in other activities, the company decided to center its advertising campaign around television spots and newspaper displays depicting women reading "Coventry Romances" while happily tending to their families and homes. In effect, Fawcett installed the reader-consumer at the heart of the entire publishing enterprise, including both the marketing and editorial aspects of the process, as Harlequin had before it. Authorial initiative and decision-making power were curtailed by both Harlequin and Fawcett as much as they had been encouraged earlier by more traditional trade houses. Concomitantly, the principal activity of these publishers changed significantly from that of locating or even creating an audience for an existing manuscript to that of locating or creating a manuscript for an already-constituted reading public.

The next series or line venture in the romance field was an elaborate and carefully conceived imitation of the Harlequin system. It testified to the then almost total acceptance of category publishing as a potentially lucrative operation and of commodity packaging as a way of achieving mass sales. Sponsored by Simon and Schuster, Silhouette Books were almost identical to their Canadian cousins. In fact, this particular venture was directed in its early stages by P. J. Fennell, previously Harlequin's vice-president of marketing and sales in North America. Fennell has indicated that, like Dell, Simon and Schuster decided to enter the competition for the female audience because it believed the market was "under-utilized" and therefore could support several new competitors. As Fawcett had, however, Simon and Schuster also understood the crucial importance of market research for this kind of category publishing. The key to building brand-name loyalty, Fennell has observed, is the ability "to deliver exactly what the customer expects." He adds, "Readers of books of this kind ask not, 'Have I heard of this book?' but, 'Did I enjoy the last dozen Silhouettes I read?' "[78]

To insure that all Silhouettes do indeed appeal to their audience, Simon and Schuster went further even than Harlequin or Fawcett in its conferral of status and power upon the reader, at least within the publishing process. Not only did the company initially survey potential readers in Dallas, San Diego, and Oklahoma City to help develop an imprint, standard plots and characterizations, and advertising approaches, but it has also established a system whereby all books were to be pretested before publication by two hundred readers from a preselected group.[79] Those readers were queried about plot and character and asked to answer open-ended questions about "the overall quality of the book." When any book was given a low rating, it was removed from the list.

In creating this process, Simon and Schuster shrewdly combined a limited-subscription editorial operation with the mass-distribution characteristic of semiprogrammed issue. By consulting a group of representative readers and accepting its judgment, the firm programmed its publications as completely as possible to serve an already constituted desire and taste. It was then free to distribute the resulting product in large quantities, knowing full well that it would probably find the audience represented by that small group. In effect, Simon and Schuster learned to avoid the very difficult problem of finding a real audience to match the theoretical one that usually guides the publication process through its early stages. Richard Snyder recently admitted that the desire for predictability prompted the creation of these procedures when he commented to *New York Times* reporter Michiko Kakutani, "We didn't want to leave anything to the guesswork that usually goes on in publishing."[80]

Indeed, while the recent history of paperback publishing has been dominated by the rise to prominence of the blockbuster bestseller, it has also been characterized by this slow but inexorable transformation of the business from a relatively small, informally run enterprise still focused on the figure of the author and the event of book *reading* into a consumer-oriented industry making use of the most sophisticated marketing and advertising techniques to facilitate simple commodity exchange. The extraordinary popularity of the romance is in part a function of this transformation, since those very techniques have been applied most energetically to this kind of category literature. Although publishers cannot explain adequately why marketing research was applied to romances rather than to spy thrillers or Westerns, it seems likely that the decision was influenced by two factors.

First, female readers constitute more than half of the book-reading public.[81] More money is to be made, it seems, by capturing a sizable portion of that large audience than by trying to reach nearly all of a smaller one. At the same time, women are remarkably available as a book-buying public in the sense that their social duties and habits make them accessible to publishers on a regular basis. The possibility of easy and extensive distribution to an audience inadvertently gathered for them by other forces thus tends to justify the mass production of romances.[82] Currently, one-quarter to one-third of the approximately 400 paperback titles issued each month are original romances of one kind or another.[83] Almost all of the ten largest paperback houses include a fair proportion of romance fiction as part of their monthly releases. In addition, Harlequin now claims that its million-dollar advertising campaigns reach one out of every ten women in America and that 40 percent of those reached can usually be converted into Harlequin readers.[84] The huge sales figures associated with romance fiction seem to be the result of this all-important ability to get at a potential audience.

Second, romance novels obviously provide a reading experience enjoyable enough for large numbers of women so that they wish to repeat that experience whenever they can. To conclude, however, that the increasing domination of the paperback market by the romance testifies automatically to some *greater* need for reassurance among American women is to make an unjustified leap in logic. It is also to ignore the other evidence demonstrating that the domination is the consequence of a calculated strategy to make the largest profit possible by appealing to the single most important segment of the book-buying public. The romance's popularity must be tied closely to these important historical changes in the book publishing industry as a whole.

Nonetheless, that popularity is also clearly attributable to the peculiar fact that much of book reading and book buying in America *is* carried on by women. Many observers of women and book publishing alike have concluded that middle-class women are book readers because they have both the necessary money and the time. They have the time, certainly, because, until recently, social custom kept them out of the full-time paid labor force and in the home where their primary duties involved the care and nurture of the family and, in particular, children. Because children are absent from the home for part of the day after the first several years, the reasoning proceeds, their mothers have blocks of time that can be devoted to the activity of reading.

Although not all women readers are represented by these conditions, it seems highly likely that they do provide the background for the majority of women who are romance readers. Actual demographic statistics are closely guarded within the competitive publishing industry by executives who often insist that romances are read by a broad cross section of the American female population. Still, both Harlequin and Silhouette have indicated repeatedly that the majority of their readers fall within the twenty-five to forty-five age group. If this is true, the meaning of the romance-reading experience may be closely tied to the way the act of reading fits within the middle-class mother's day and the way the story itself addresses anxieties, fears, and psychological needs resulting from her social and familial position. It is to these questions that we must turn in the following chapters, keeping in mind all the while that burgeoning sales do not necessarily imply increasing demand or need. Publishers and the profit motive must be given their due in any effort to explain the popularity of the romance or to understand its significance as a historical and cultural phenomenon. It should also be kept in mind that despite its relative success at gauging general audience interest, semiprogrammed issue cannot yet guarantee perfect fit between all readers' expectations and the publisher's product. In fact, we will see in the following chapter that the continuing discrepancy between the commodity offered by publishers and the desires of their customers has prompted the creation of at least one service designed to help readers choose books from monthly publishers' lists that they consider only partially acceptable.

The Readers and Their Romances

Surrounded by corn and hay fields, the midwestern community of Smithton, with its meticulously tended subdivisions of single-family homes, is nearly two thousand miles from the glass-and-steel office towers of New York City where most of the American publishing industry is housed. Despite the distance separating the two communities, many of the books readied for publication in New York by young women with master's degrees in literature are eagerly read in Smithton family rooms by women who find quiet moments to read in days devoted almost wholly to the care of others. Although Smithton's women are not pleased by every romance prepared for them by New York editors, with Dorothy Evans's help they have learned to circumvent the industry's still inexact understanding of what women want from romance fiction. They have managed to do so by learning to decode the iconography of romantic cover art and the jargon of back-cover blurbs and by repeatedly selecting works by authors who have pleased them in the past.

In fact, it is precisely because a fundamental lack of trust initially characterized the relationship between Smithton's romance readers and the New York publishers that Dorothy Evans was able to amass this loyal following of customers. Her willingness to give advice so endeared her to women bewildered by the increasing romance output of the New York houses in the 1970s that they returned again and again to her checkout counter to consult her about the "best buys" of the month. When she began writing her review newsletter for bookstores and editors, she did so because she felt other readers might find her "expert" advice useful in trying to select romance fiction. She was so successful at developing a national reputation that New York editors began to send her galley proofs of their latest titles to guarantee their books a review in her newsletter. She now also obligingly reads manuscripts for several well-known authors who have begun to seek her advice and support. Although her status in the industry does not necessarily guarantee the representivity of her opinions or those of her customers, it does suggest that some writers and editors believe that she is not only closely attuned to the romance audience's desires and needs but is especially able to articulate them. It should not be surprising to note, therefore, that she proved a willing, careful, and consistently perceptive informant.

I first wrote to Dot in December 1979 to ask whether she would be willing to talk about romances and her evaluative criteria. I asked further if she thought some of her customers might discuss their reading with someone who was interested in what they liked and why. In an open and enthusiastic reply, she said she would be glad to host a series of interviews and meetings in her home during her summer vacation. At first taken aback by such generosity, I soon learned that Dot's unconscious magnanimity is a product of a genuine interest in people. When I could not secure a hotel room for the first night of my planned visit to Smithton, she insisted that I stay with her. I would be able to recognize her at the airport, she assured me, because she would be wearing a lavender pants suit.

The trepidation I felt upon embarking for Smithton slowly dissipated on the drive from the airport as Dot talked freely and fluently about the romances that were clearly an important part of her life. When she explained the schedule of discussions and interviews she had established for the next week, it seemed clear that my time in Smithton would prove enjoyable and busy as well as productive. My concern about whether I could persuade Dot's customers to elaborate honestly about their motives for reading was unwarranted, for after an initial period of mutually felt awkwardness, we conversed frankly and with enthusiasm. Dot helped immensely, for when she introduced me to her customers, she announced, "Jan is just people!" Although it became clear that the women were not accustomed to examining their activity in any detail, they conscientiously tried to put their perceptions and judgments into words to help me understand why they find romance fiction enjoyable and useful.

During the first week I conducted two four-hour discussion sessions with a total of sixteen of Dot's most regular customers. After she informed them of my interest, they had all volunteered to participate. About six more wanted to attend but were away on family vacations. These first discussions were open-ended sessions characterized by general questions posed to the group at large (see Appendix 1 for the interview schedule). In the beginning, timidity seemed to hamper the responses as each reader took turns answering each question. When everyone relaxed, however, the conversation flowed more naturally as the participants disagreed among themselves, contradicted one another, and delightedly discovered that they still agreed about many things. Both sessions were tape-recorded. I also conducted individual taped interviews with five of Dot's most articulate and enthusiastic romance readers. In addition, I talked informally to Dot alone for hours at odd times during the day and interviewed her more formally on five separate occasions. Along with twenty-five others approached by Dot herself at the bookstore, these sixteen all filled out a pilot questionnaire designed before I had departed from Philadelphia (see Appendix 2).

Upon returning from my visit to Smithton, I read as many of the specific titles mentioned during the discussions and interviews that I could acquire, transcribed the tapes, and expanded a field-work journal I had kept while away. In reviewing all of the information and evaluations I had been given, it became clear that I had neither anticipated all of the potentially meaningful questions that might be asked nor had I always included the best potential answers for the directed-response questions. Accordingly, I redesigned the entire questionnaire and mailed fifty copies to Dot in mid-autumn of 1980 (see Appendix 3). I asked her to give the questionnaire to her "regular" customers (those who she recognized and had advised more than once about romance purchases) and to give no additional directions other than those on the questionnaire and in an attached explanatory letter. She returned forty-two completed questionnaires to me in early February 1981, during my second sojourn in Smithton.

At that time, I stayed with Dot and her family for a week, watched her daily routine, and talked with her constantly. I also spent three full days at the bookstore observing her interactions with her customers and conversing informally with them myself. I reinterviewed the same five readers during this period, checked points about which I was uneasy, and tested the hypotheses I had formulated already. I also talked at length with Maureen, one of Dot's most forthright readers who had recently begun writing her own romances.

It is clear that the Smithton group cannot be thought of as a scientifically designed random sample. The conclusions drawn from the study, therefore, should be extrapolated only with great caution to apply to other romance readers. In fact, this study's propositions ought to be considered hypotheses that now must be tested systematically by looking at a much broader and unrelated group of romance readers. Despite the obvious limitations of the group, however, I decided initially to conduct the study for two reasons.

The first had to do with Dot's indisputable success and developing reputation on the national romance scene. The second was that the group was already self-selected and stably constituted. Dot's regular customers had continued to return to her for advice *because* they believed her perceptions accorded reasonably well with theirs. They had all learned to trust her judgment and to rely on her for assistance in choosing a varied array of romance reading material. They found this congenial because it freed all of them from the need to rely solely on a single "line" of books like the Harlequins that had recently begun to offend and irritate them. It also enabled them to take back some measure of control from the publishers by selectively choosing only those books they had reason to suspect would satisfy their desires and needs. Although there are important variations in taste and habit within the Smithton group, all of the women agree that their preferences are adequately codified by Dorothy Evans.

The nature of the group's operation suggests that it is unsatisfactory for an analyst to select a sample of romances currently issued by American publishers, draw conclusions about the meaning of the form by analyzing the plots of the books in the sample, and then make general statements about the cultural significance of the "romance." Despite the industry's growing reliance on the techniques of semiprogrammed issue to reduce the disjunction between readers' desires and publishers' commodities, the production system is still characterized by a fundamental distance between the originators, producers, and consumers of the fantasies embodied in those romances. Consequently, it must be kept in mind that the people who read romance novels are *not* attending to stories they themselves have created to interpret their own experiences. Because the shift to professional production has reduced self-storytelling substantially, there is no sure way to know whether the narratives consumed by an anonymous public are in any way congruent with those they would have created for themselves and their peers had they not been able to buy them.

Although repeated purchase and consumption of a professionally produced and mass-marketed commodity hints that some kind of audience satisfaction has been achieved, this is not a guarantee that each individual text's interpretation of experience is endorsed by all buyers. In fact, what the Smithton group makes clear is that its members continue to possess very particular tastes in romance fiction that are not adequately addressed by publishers. However, because these corporations have designed their products to appeal to a huge audience by meeting the few preferences that all individuals within the group have in common, they have successfully managed to create texts that are minimally acceptable to Dot and her readers. Moreover, because the Smithton women feel an admittedly intense need to indulge in the romantic fantasy and, for the most part, cannot fulfill that need with their own imaginative activity, they often buy and read books they do not really like or fully endorse. As one reader explained, "Sometimes even a bad book is better than nothing." The act of purchase, then, does not always signify approval of the product selected; with a mass-production system it can just as easily testify to the existence of an ongoing, still only partially met, need.

Precisely because romance publishers have not engineered a perfect fit between the product they offer and all of their readers' desires, the Smithton women have discovered that their tastes are better served when the exchange process is mediated by a trusted selector who assembles a more suitable body of texts from which they can safely make their choices. This particular reliance on a mediator to guide the process of selection suggests that to understand what the romance means, it is first essential to characterize the different groups that find it meaningful and then to determine what each group identifies as its "romance" before attempting any assessment of the significance of the form. Despite the overtly formulaic appearance of the category, there are important differences among novels *for those who read them* that prompt individual decisions to reject or to read. We must begin to recognize this fact of selection within the mass-production process, make some effort to comprehend the principles governing such selection, and describe the content that gives rise to those principles.[1] The Smithton women comprise only one small, relatively homogeneous group that happens to read romances in a determinate way. While their preferences may be representative of those held by women similar to them in demographic characteristics and daily routine, it is not fair to assume that they use romance fiction in the same way as do women of different background, education, and social circumstance. Conclusions about the romance's meaning for highly educated women who work in male-dominated professions, for instance, must await further study.

The reading habits and preferences of the Smithton women are complexly tied to their daily routines, which are themselves a function of education, social role, and class position. Most Smithton readers are married mothers of children, living in single-family homes in a sprawling suburb of a central midwestern state's second largest city (population 850,000 in 1970).[2] Its surrounding cornfields notwithstanding, Smithton itself is an urbanized area. Its 1970 population, which was close to 112,000 inhabitants, represented a 70 percent increase over that recorded by the 1960 census. The community is essentially a "bedroom" community in that roughly 90 percent of those employed in 1970 worked outside Smithton itself. Although this has changed slightly in recent years with the building of the mall in which Dot herself works, the city is still largely residential and dominated by single-family homes, which account for 90 to 95 percent of the housing stock.

Dot and her family live on the fringe of one of Smithton's new housing developments in a large, split-level home. When I last visited Smithton, Dot, her husband, Dan, her eldest daughter, Kit, and her mother were living in the house, which is decorated with Dot's needlework and crafts, projects she enjoyed when her children were young. Dot's other two children, Dawn, who is nineteen and married, and Joe, who is twenty-one, do not live with the family. Dot herself was forty-eight years old at the time of the study. Dan, a journeyman plumber, seems both bemused by Dot's complete absorption in romances and proud of her success at the bookstore. Although he occasionally reads thrillers and some nonfiction, he spends his leisure time with fellow union members or working about the house.

Although she is now a self-confident and capable woman, Dot believes she was once very different. She claims that she has changed substantially in recent years, a change she attributes to her reading and her work with people in the bookstore. When asked how she first began reading romances, she responded that it was really at her doctor's instigation. Although he did not suggest reading specifically, he advised her about fifteen years ago that she needed to find an enjoyable leisure activity to which she could devote at least an hour a day. He was concerned about her physical and mental exhaustion, apparently brought on by her conscientious and diligent efforts to care for her husband, three small children, and her home. When he asked her what she did for herself all day and she could list *only* the tasks she performed for others, he insisted that she learn to spend some time on herself if she did not want to land in a hospital. Remembering that she loved to read as a child, she decided to try again. Thus began her interest in romance fiction. Dot read many kinds of books at first, but she soon began to concentrate on romances for reasons she cannot now explain. Her reading became so chronic that when she discovered that she could not rely on a single shop to provide all of the latest releases by her favorite authors, she found it necessary to check four different bookstores to get all of the romances she wanted. Most of her customers commented that before they discovered Dot they did the same thing. Some still attend garage sales and flea markets religiously to find out-of-print books by authors whose more recent works they have enjoyed.

Dot would have continued as one of the legion of "silent" readers had not one of her daughters encouraged her to look for a job in a bookstore to make use of her developing expertise. Although hesitant about moving out into the public world, she eventually mustered the courage to try, soon finding employment at the chain outlet where she still works. She discovered that she thoroughly enjoyed the contact with other "readers," and, as she developed more confidence, she began to make suggestions and selections for uncertain buyers. In the first edition of her newsletter, she explained the subsequent events that led to the creation of her romance review:

> Soon it became apparent that the women who were regular customers were searching me out for my opinions on their selections. Also, the Area Supervisor of our store had noticed a sharply marked increase in sales of the general category of romances. . . . So the interviews and articles in . . . periodicals began and brought more attention to my socalled expertise.
>
> The idea for a newsletter and rating of new releases every month . . . belongs to my daughter, who felt we could make this available to a much larger group of women readers. As most of them know the prices of books are rising and the covers are not always a good indicator of the content of the book.[3]

With the help of her daughter, Kit, she planned, executed, and wrote the first edition of "Dorothy's Diary of Romance Reading," in April 1980. Despite reservations about taking up the role of critical mediator, she explained in her inaugural editorial that she was persuaded to such an authoritarian act by the intensity of her customers' needs and by the inability of the production system to meet them. "I know many women," she commented, "who need to read as an escape as I have over the years and I believe this is good therapy and much cheaper than tranquilizers, alcohol or addictive T.V. serials which most of my readers say bores them." She added that she intended to separate "the best or better books from the less wellwritten, so as to save the reader money and time." "However," she concluded, "I would never want to take from the ladies the right to choose their own reading materials, only to suggest from my own experience."[4]

Still conscious of the hierarchy implicit in the critic-consumer relationship, Dot continues to be careful about offering evaluative suggestions at the store. Her first question to a woman who solicits her advice is calculated to determine the kinds of romances the reader has enjoyed in the past. "If they are in my category," she explained in one of our interviews, "I start saying, 'OK, what was the last good book you read?' And then if they tell me that, I usually can go from there." Her services, like semiprogrammed publication techniques, are designed to gauge already formulated but not fully expressed reader preferences, which she subsequently attempts to satisfy by selecting the proper material from a much larger corpus of published works. Dot can be more successful than distant publishing firms attempting the same service through market research because she personalizes selection at the moment of purchase in a way that the absent publishers cannot.

Dot's unusual success is a function of her participant's understanding of the different kinds of romances, acquired as the consequence of her voracious reading, and of her insistence on the individuality of her readers and their preferences. This is especially evident at the stage in her advising process when she finally displays a selection of books for her customers. "Sometimes," she laments, "I have people who say, 'Well, which one do *you* say is the best of these three?'" Her response indicates the depth of her respect for the singularity of readers and romances despite the fact that those readers are usually thought of as category readers and the romances considered formulaic performances:

> I will say, "They are not alike, they are not written by the same author, they are totally and completely different settings and I cannot say you will like this one better than this one because they are totally and completely different books." [But they always continue with] "Which one did you like best?" And I'll say, "Don't try to pin me down like that because it's not right." I won't go any further. They have to choose from there because otherwise you're getting sheep. See, I like it when some of my women say, "Hey, I didn't care for that book." And I say, "Hey, how come?"[5]

Because Dot is ever mindful of her readers' dissatisfaction with some of the material flowing from the New York publishers and simultaneously aware of their desire to maintain and satisfy their own personal tastes, she has created a role for herself by facilitating a commercial exchange that benefits the reader as much as it does the producer. At the same time, Dot continues to perpetuate generic distinctions within a category that the publishers themselves are trying to rationalize and standardize. Hers is a strategy which, if not consciously calculated to empower readers with a selective ability, at least tends to operate in that way. By carefully identifying a book's particular historical setting, by relating the amount of sexually explicit description it contains, by describing its use of violence and cruelty, and by remarking about its portrayal of the heroine/hero relationship, she alerts the reader to the book's treatment of the essential features that nearly all of her customers focus on in determining the quality of a romance.

In addition to recognizing individual tastes and respecting personal preferences, Dot also performs another essential function for her regular customers. Although I suspect she was not always as effective at this as she is now, she capably defends her readers' preferences for romance fiction *to themselves*. One would think this unnecessary because so many of her customers come to her expressly seeking romances, but Dot finds that many of her women feel guilty about spending money on books that are regularly ridiculed by the media, their husbands, and their children. Dot encourages her customers to feel proud of their regular reading and provides them with a model of indignant response that they can draw upon when challenged by men who claim superior taste. By questioning them rhetorically about whether their romance reading is any different from their husbands' endless attention to televised sports, she demonstrates an effective rejoinder that can be used in the battle to defend the leisure pursuit they enjoy so much but which the larger culture condemns as frivolous and vaguely, if not explicitly, pornographic.

Dot's vociferous defense of her customers' right to please themselves in any way that does not harm others is an expression of her deeply held belief that women are too often the object of others' criticisms and the butt of unjustified ridicule. Although she is not a feminist as most would understand that term, she is perfectly aware that women have been dismissed by men for centuries, and she can and does converse eloquently on the subject. During my second stay in Smithton, she admitted to me that she understands very well why women have pushed for liberal abortion laws and remarked that even though her devoutly held religious convictions would prevent her from seeking one herself, she believes all women should have the right to *choose* motherhood and to control their own bodies. She also feels women should have the right to work and certainly should be paid equally with men. Many of our conversations were punctuated by her expressions of anger and resentment at the way women are constantly "put down" as childish, ignorant, and incapable of anything but housework or watching soap operas.

At first glance, Dot's incipient feminism seems deeply at odds with her interest in a literary form whose ultimate message, one astute observer has noted, is that "pleasure for women is men."[6] The traditionalism of romance fiction will not be denied here, but it is essential to point out that Dot and many of the writers and readers of romances interpret these stories as chronicles of female triumph. Although the particular way they do so will be explored later, suffice it to say here that Dot believes a good romance focuses on an intelligent and able heroine who finds a man who recognizes her special qualities and is capable of loving and caring for her as she wants to be loved. Thus Dot understands such an ending to say that female independence and marriage are compatible rather than mutually exclusive. The romances she most values and recommends for her readers are those with "strong," "fiery" heroines who are capable of "defying the hero," softening him, and showing him the value of loving and caring for another.

It is essential to introduce this here in order to take account adequately of Dot's personal influence on her customers and on their preferences in romance fiction. Because she is an exceptionally strong woman convinced of her sex's capabilities, when she expresses her opinions about a woman's right to pleasure, Dot not only supports her customers but confers legitimacy on the preoccupation they share with her. I suspect that in providing this much-needed reinforcement Dot also exerts an important influence on them that must be taken into account. She encourages her customers to think well of themselves not only by demonstrating her interest in them and in their desires but also by presenting them with books whose heroines seem out of the ordinary. Therefore, while the members of the Smithton group share attitudes about good and bad romances that are similar to Dot's, it is impossible to say whether these opinions were formed by Dot or whether she is simply their most articulate advocate. Nonetheless, it must be emphasized that this group finds it possible to select and construct romances in such a way that their stories are experienced as a reversal of the oppression and emotional abandonment suffered by women in real life. For Dot and her customers, romances provide a utopian vision in which female individuality and a sense of self are shown to be compatible with nurturance and care by another.

All of the Smithton readers who answered the questionnaire were female. Dot reported that although she suspects some of the men who buy romances "for their wives" are in fact buying them for themselves, all of the people she regularly advises are women. While the few houses that have conducted market-research surveys will not give out exact figures, officials at Harlequin, Silhouette, and Fawcett have all indicated separately that the majority of romance readers are married women between the ages of twenty-five and fifty. Fred Kerner, Harlequin's vice-president for publishing, for instance, recently reported to Barbara Brotman, of the *Chicago Tribune*, that "Harlequin readers are overwhelmingly women of whom 49 percent work at least part-time. They range in age from 24 to 49, have average family incomes of $15,000–20,000 and have high school diplomas but haven't completed college."[7] Harlequin will reveal little else about its audience, but a company executive did tell Margaret Jensen that the Harlequin reading population matches the profile of the "North American English-speaking female population" in age, family income, employment status, and geographical location.[8] For example, he said that 22 percent of the female population and Harlequin readers are between the ages of twenty-five and thirty-four. Carol Reo, publicity director for Silhouette Romances, has also revealed that the romance audience is almost entirely female, but indicates that 65 percent of Silhouette's potential market is under the age of forty and that 45 percent attended college.[9] If these sketchy details are accurate, the Smithton readers may be more representative of the Silhouette audience than they are of Harlequin's.[10] Unfortunately, the lack of detailed information about the total American audience for Harlequins as well as for other kinds of romances makes it exceedingly difficult to judge the representivity of the Smithton group. Still, it appears evident that the Smithton readers are somewhat younger than either Jensen's Harlequin readers or the Mills and Boon audience.

The age differential may account for the fact that neither Dot nor many of her customers are Harlequin fans. Although Dot reviews Harlequins and slightly more than half of her customers (twenty-four) reported reading them, a full eighteen indicated that they *never* read a Harlequin romance. Moreover, only ten of Dot's customers indicated that Harlequins are among the kinds of romances they *most* like to read. The overwhelming preference of the group was for historicals, cited by twenty (48 percent) as their favorite subgenre within the romance category.[11] Because historicals typically include more explicit sex than the Harlequins and also tend to portray more independent and defiant heroines, we might expect that this particular subgenre would draw younger readers who are less offended by changing standards of gender behavior. This would seem to be corroborated by the fact that only two of the women who listed Harlequins as a favorite also listed historicals.

In addition, the Smithton group also seemed to like contemporary mystery romances and contemporary romances, which were cited by another twelve as being among their favorites. Silhouettes are contemporary romances and, like the historicals, are less conventional than the Harlequins. Not only is their sexual description more explicit but it is not unusual for them to include heroines with careers who expect to keep their jobs after marriage. The similarity between Smithton's tastes and the content of the Silhouettes may thus explain why both audiences are younger than that for the relatively staid Harlequins.

Despite the discrepancies in the various reports, romance reading apparently correlates strongly with the years of young adulthood and early middle age. This is further borne out in the present study by the Smithton women's responses to a question about when they first began to read romances. Although fifteen (36 percent) of the women reported that they began in adolescence between the ages of ten and nineteen, sixteen (38 percent) indicated that they picked up the habit between the ages of twenty and twenty-nine. Another ten (24 percent) adopted romance reading after age thirty.[12]

Thirty-two women (76 percent) in the Smithton group were married at the time of the survey, a proportion that compares almost exactly with the 75 percent of married women included in Jensen's group.[13] An additional three (7 percent) of the Smithton women were single, while five (12 percent) were either widowed, separated, or divorced and not remarried.

Moreover, most of the women in the Smithton group were mothers with children *under* age eighteen (70 percent). Indeed, within the group, only five (12 percent) reported having no children at all. Nine (21 percent) of the Smithton women reported only one child, twelve (29 percent) claimed two children, eleven (27 percent) had three children, and three (7 percent) had four children. Interestingly enough, only five (12 percent) reported children under the age of five, while twenty-four of the women indicated that they had at least one child under age eighteen. Eleven (27 percent), however, reported that all of their children were over age eighteen. Fifteen (36 percent) reported children between ten and eighteen, and another fifteen (36 percent) had at least one child over age eighteen. The relatively advanced age of the Smithton readers' children is not surprising if one takes into account the age distribution of the women themselves and the fact that the mean age at first marriage within the group was 19.9 years.

Once again, the limited size of the sample and the lack of corroborating data from other sources suggest caution in the formation of hypotheses. Nonetheless, it appears that within the Smithton group romance reading correlates with motherhood and the care of children *other* than infants and toddlers.[14] This seems logical because the fact of the older children's attendance at school would allow the women greater time to read even as the children themselves continued to make heavy emotional demands on them for nurturance, advice, and attentive care. It will be seen later that it is precisely this emotional drain caused by a woman's duty to nurture and care for her children and husband that is addressed directly by romance reading at least within the minds of the women themselves.

Given the fact that fifteen (36 percent) of the Smithton readers reported children age ten and under, it should not be surprising to note that sixteen of the women (38 percent) reported that in the preceding week they were keeping house and/or caring for children on a full-time basis. Another nine (21 percent) were working part-time, while still another nine (21 percent) were holding down full-time jobs. In addition, two women failed to respond, two stated that they were retired, one listed herself as a student, and three indicated that they were currently unemployed and looking for work. These statistics seem to parallel those of the Mills and Boon study which found that 33 percent of the sample was represented by full-time housewives, while another 30 percent included housewives with full- or part-time jobs. Both studies suggest that romance reading is very often squeezed into busy daily schedules.

Although Fred Kerner's comment about the average $15,000–$20,000 income of the Harlequin audience is not very illuminating, neither is it at odds with the details reported by Dot's customers. Although four (10 percent) did not answer the question, eighteen (43 percent) in the group indicated a family income of somewhere between $15,000 and $24,999. Another fourteen (33 percent) claimed a joint income of $25,000 to $49,-

999, while four (10 percent) listed family earnings of over $50,000. The greater affluence of the Smithton group is probably accounted for by the fact that Dot's bookstore is located in one of the twelve most affluent counties in a state with 115. The median family income in Smithton, as reported by the 1970 United States census, was almost $11,000, which compares with the state median income of just slightly less than $9,000.

Before turning to the group's reading history and patterns, it should be noted that exactly half of the Smithton readers indicated that they had earned a high school diploma. Ten (24 percent) of the women reported completing less than three years of college; eight (19 percent) claimed at least a college degree or better. Only one person in the group indicated that she had not finished high school, while two failed to answer the question. Once again, as the Smithton readers appear to be more affluent than Harlequin readers, so also do they seem better educated; the Harlequin corporation claims that its readers are educated below even the statistical norm for the North American female population.

One final detail about the personal history of the Smithton women ought to be mentioned here: attendance at religious services was relatively high among Dot's customers. Although eight (19 percent) of the women indicated that they had not been to a service in the last two years, fifteen (36 percent) reported attendance "once a week or more," while another eight (19 percent) indicated attendance "once or a few times a month." Another nine (21 percent) admitted going to services a few times a year, while two (5 percent) did not answer the question. The women reported membership in a wide variety of denominations. Eight (19 percent) of the women indicated that they were Methodists and eight (19 percent) checked "Christian but non-denominational." The next two groups most heavily represented in the sample were Catholics and Baptists, each with five (12 percent) of the Smithton women.

When the reading *histories* of these women are examined, it becomes clear that, for many of them, romance reading is simply a variation in a pattern of leisure activity they began early in life. Indeed, twenty-two of Dot's customers reported that they first began to read for pleasure before age ten. Another twelve (27 percent) adopted the habit between the ages of eleven and twenty. Only seven (17 percent) of the Smithton women indicated that they began pleasure reading after their teen years. These results parallel earlier findings about the adoption of the book habit. Phillip Ennis found in 1965, for instance, that of the 49 percent of the American population who were "current readers," 34 percent consisted of those who started reading early in life and 15 percent consisted of those who began reading at an advanced age.[15]

When *current* reading habits are examined, however, it becomes clear that the women think that it is the romances that are especially necessary to their daily routine. Their intense reliance on these books suggests strongly that they help to fulfill deeply felt psychological needs. Indeed, one of the most striking findings to come out of the Smithton study was that thirty-seven (88 percent) of Dot's readers indicated that they read religiously every day. Only five of her regular customers claimed to read more sporadically. Twenty-two of the women, in fact, reported reading more than sixteen hours per week, and another ten (24 percent) claimed to read between eleven and fifteen hours weekly.[16] When asked to describe their typical reading pattern once they have begun a new romance, eleven (26 percent) selected the statement, "I won't put it down until I've finished it unless it's absolutely necessary." Thirty more indicated reading "as much of it as I can until I'm interrupted or have something else to do." None of Dot's customers reported a systematic reading pattern of "a few pages a day until done," and only one admitted that she reads solely when she is in the mood. These figures suggest that the Smithton women become intensely involved in the stories they are reading and that once immersed in the romantic fantasy, Dot's customers do not like to return to reality without experiencing the resolution of the narrative.

This need to see the story and the emotions aroused by it resolved is so intense that many of the Smithton women have worked out an ingenious strategy to insure a regular and predictable arrival at the anticipated narrative conclusion. Although they categorize romances in several ways, one of the most basic distinctions they make is that between "quick reads" and "fat books." Quick reads contain less than 200 pages and require no more than two hours of reading time. Harlequins, Silhouettes, and most Regencies are considered quick reads for occasions when they know they will not be able to "make it through" a big book. If, for example, a woman has just finished one romance but still "is not ready to quit," as one of my informants put it, she will "grab a thin one" she knows she can finish before going to sleep. Fat books, on the other hand, tend to be saved for weekends or long evenings that promise to be uninterrupted, once again because the women dislike having to leave a story before it is concluded. This kind of uninterrupted reading is very highly valued within the Smithton group because it is associated with the pleasure of spending time alone.[17] Although a detailed exploration of the importance of this narrative and emotional resolution must be delayed until Chapter 4, where the structure of the romance story and its developing effect on the reader will be considered in detail, let it be said here that the Smithton readers' strategies for avoiding disruption or discontinuity in the story betoken a profound need to arrive at the *ending* of the tale and thus to achieve or acquire the emotional gratification they already can anticipate.

The remarkable extent of their familiarity with the genre is attested to by the number of romances these women read each week. Despite the fact that twenty-six (62 percent) of Dot's customers claimed to read somewhere between one and four books *other* than romances every week, more than a third (fifteen) reported reading from five to nine romances weekly. An additional twenty-two (55 percent) completed between one and four romances every week, while four women indicated that they consume anywhere from fifteen to twenty-five romances during that same period of time. This latter figure strikes me as somewhat implausible because it implies a reading rate of one hundred romances a month. I think this is unlikely given the fact that far fewer romances were issued monthly by publishers at the time of the study. Of course, the women could be reading old romances, but the figure still seems exaggerated. Nonetheless, it is evident that Dot's customers read extraordinary amounts of romance fiction.

Although their chronic reading of these books might sound unusual or idiosyncratic, the Yankelovich findings about romance reading, as noted before, indicate that romance readers are generally heavy consumers. Most, however, are probably not as obsessed as the Smithton readers seem to be. Unfortunately, the Yankelovich discovery that the average romance reader had read nine romances in the last six months does not tell us what proportion of the group read an even larger number of novels. Although 40 percent of the heavy readers (those who had read more than twenty-five books in the last six months) reported having read a romance, thus suggesting the possibility of a correlation between high levels of consumption and romance reading, the study gives no indication of how many of the romance readers actually read anywhere near the number the Smithton women report, which ranges from twenty-four to more than six hundred romances every six months.[18] I think it safe to say that the Smithton group's reliance on romances is not strictly comparable to that of the occasional reader. Rather, Dot's customers are women who spend a significant portion of every day participating vicariously in a fantasy world that they willingly admit bears little resemblance to the one they actually inhabit. Clearly, the experience must provide some form of required pleasure and reconstitution because it seems unlikely that so much time and money would be spent on an activity that functioned merely to fill otherwise unoccupied time.

The women confirmed this in their answers to a directed-response question about their reasons for reading romance fiction. When asked to rank order the three most important motives for romance reading out of a list of eight, nineteen (45 percent) of the women listed "simple relaxation" as the first choice. Another eight (19 percent) of the readers reported that they read romances "because reading is just for me; it is my time." Still another six (14 percent) said they read "to learn about faraway places and times"; while five (12 percent) insisted that their primary reason is "to escape my daily problems." When these first choices are added to the second and third most important reasons for reading, the totals are distributed as in Table 2.1:

TABLE 2.1
Question: Which of the Following Best Describes Why You Read Romances?

a. To escape my daily problems	13
b. To learn about faraway places and times	19
c. For simple relaxation	33
d. Because I wish I had a romance like the heroine's	5
e. Because reading is just for me; it is my time	28
f. Because I like to read about the strong, virile heroes	4
g. Because reading is at least better than other forms of escape	5
h. Because romantic stories are never sad or depressing	10

On the basis of these schematic answers alone I think it logical to conclude that romance reading is valued by the Smithton women because the experience itself is *different* from ordinary existence. Not only is it a relaxing release from the tension produced by daily problems and responsibilities, but it creates a time or space within which a woman can be entirely on her own, preoccupied with her personal needs, desires, and pleasure. It is also a means of transportation or escape to the exotic or, again, to that which is different.

It is important to point out here that the responses to the second questionnaire are different in important ways from the answers I received from the women in the face-to-face interviews and in the first survey. At the time of my initial visit in June 1980, our conversations about their reasons for romance reading were dominated by the words "escape" and "education." Similarly, when asked by the first questionnaire to describe briefly what romances do "better" than other books available today, of the thirty-one answering the undirected question, fourteen of the first respondents *volunteered* that they like romance fiction because it allows them to "escape." It should be noted that "relaxation" was given only once as an answer, while no woman mentioned the idea of personal space.

Both answers *c* and *e* on the second form were given initially in the course of the interviews by two unusually articulate readers who elaborated more fully than most of the women on the meaning of the word "escape." They considered these two answers synonymous with it, but they also seemed to prefer the alternate responses because they did not so clearly imply a desire to avoid duties and responsibilities in the "real" world. Although most of the other women settled for the word "escape" on the first questionnaire, they also liked their sister readers' terms better. Once these were introduced in the group interviews, the other women agreed that romance reading functions best as relaxation and as a time for self-indulgence. Because the switch seemed to hint at feelings of guilt, I decided to add the more acceptable choices to the second survey. Although both answers *c* and *e* also imply movement away from something distasteful in the real present to a somehow more satisfying universe, a feature that appears to testify to romance reading's principal function as a therapeutic release and as a provider of vicarious pleasure, the fact of the women's preference for these two terms over their first spontaneous response suggests again that the women harbor complex feelings about the worth and propriety of romance reading.[19]

The women provided additional proof of their reliance on romance reading as a kind of tranquilizer or restorative agent in their responses to questions about preferred reading times and the habit of rereading favorite romances. When asked to choose from among seven statements the one that best described their reading pattern, twenty-four (57 percent) eschewed specification of a particular time of day in order to select the more general assertion, "It's hard to say when I do most of my reading, since I read every chance I get." Another fourteen claimed to read mostly in the evenings, usually because days were occupied by employment outside the home. In the case of either pattern, however, romances are not picked up idly as an old magazine might be merely to fill otherwise unoccupied time. Rather, romance reading is considered so enjoyable and beneficial by the women that they deliberately work it into busy schedules as often and as consistently as they can.

Rereading is not only a widely practiced habit among the Smithton women but tends to occur most frequently during times of stress or depression. Three-fourths of Dot's customers reported that they reread favorite books either "sometimes" (twenty-one) or "often" (eleven). They do so, they explained in the interviews, when they feel sad or unhappy because they know exactly how the chosen book will affect their state of mind. Peter Mann similarly discovered that 46 percent of his Mills and Boon readers claimed to reread "very often," while another 38 percent reported repeat reading "now and then."[20] Unfortunately, he has provided no further information about why or when the women do so. Although it is possible that they may reread in order to savor the details of particular plots, it is clear that for the most part the Smithton women do not. For them, rereading is an activity engaged in expressly to lift the spirits. The following comment from one of the first questionnaires illustrates nicely the kind of correlation the Smithton women see between their daily needs and the effects of romance reading: "Romances are not depressing and very seldom leave you feeling sad inside. When I read for enjoyment I want to be entertained and feel lifted out of my daily routine. And romances are the best type of reading for this effect. Romances also revive my usually optimistic outlook which often is very strained in day-to-day living." Although all of Dot's customers know well that most romances end happily, when their own needs seem unusually pressing they often refuse even the relatively safe gamble of beginning a new romance. Instead, they turn to a romance they have completed previously because they already know how its final resolution will affect them. Romance reading, it would seem, can be valued as much for the sameness of the response it evokes as for the variety of the adventures it promises.[21]

Interestingly enough, the Smithton readers hold contradictory opinions about the repetitious or formulaic quality of the fiction they read. On the one hand, they are reluctant to admit that the characters appearing in romances are similar. As Dot's daughter, Kit, explained when asked to describe a typical heroine in the historical romance, "there isn't a typical one, they all have to be different or you'd be reading the same thing over and over." Her sentiments were echoed frequently by her mother's customers, all of whom claim to value the variety and diversity of romance fiction.

On the other hand, these same women exhibit fairly rigid expectations about what is permissible in a romantic tale and express disappointment and outrage when those conventions are violated. In my first interview with Dot, she discussed a particular author who had submitted a historical novel to her publisher. Although the author explained repeatedly that the book was not a romance, the publisher insisted on packaging it with a standard romance cover in the hope of attracting the huge romance market. The author knew this would anger that audience and, as Dot remarked, "she was not surprised when she got irate letters." Clearly, romances may not deviate too significantly if regular readers are to be pleased. They expect and, indeed, rely upon certain events, characters, and progressions to provide the desired experience.

Dot herself often finds it necessary but difficult to overcome her customers' fixed expectations when she discovers a romance she thinks they will enjoy even though it fails to follow the usual pattern. In the case of *The Fulfillment*, for example, which Dot loved and wanted to share with her women, she worked out an entire speech to get them to buy the book and to read it through. The following is a verbatim transcription of her re-creation of that speech: "Now this is a good book—but please don't think that it is the run of the mill. It isn't. At one point in this book, you're gonna want to put it down—and you're gonna say, 'Dot didn't tell me this'—and I said, 'Don't put it down. You keep reading.' Every one of them came back and said, 'You were right. I thought why did she give me this book?' They said, 'I kept reading like you said and it was great.' " The problem with this particular book was the fact that the hero died three-quarters of the way through the tale. However, because the author had worked out an unusually complex plot involving the heroine simultaneously with another equally attractive man in an acceptable way, the women did not find her sudden remarriage distasteful. Without Dot's skillful encouragement, however, most of the women would never have read the book past the hero's death.

Dot also tries to circumvent set expectations in her newsletter. She occasionally tells booksellers and readers about books classified by their publishers as something other than a romance. Erroneous categorization occurs, she believes, because the publishers really do not understand what a romance is and thus pay too much attention to meaningless, superficial details that lead to mistaken identifications. Because Jacqueline Marten's *Visions of the Damned* suffered this fate, Dot attempted to alert her readers to the problem classification. Her way of doing so provides an essential clue to the proper identification of a romance, which the women rely on despite their claim that all romantic novels are different. Of Marten's story, she wrote, "This book, because of cover and title, was classed as an occult. What a mistake! *Visions* is one of the best love stories I've read of late. Get it and read it. I loved it."[22] Although *Visions of the Damned* concerns itself with extrasensory perception and reincarnation, Dot believes that the book's proper plot structure is what makes it a romance. It is not the mere use of the romantic subject matter that qualifies Marten's book as a romance, she explained, but rather its manner of developing the loving relationship. As Dot remarked in a later interview, "Not all love stories are romances." Some are simply novels about love.

If the Smithton readers' stipulations are taken seriously, a romance is, first and foremost, a story about a woman. That woman, however, may not figure in a larger plot simply as the hero's prize, as Jenny Cavileri does, for instance in Erich Segal's *Love Story*, which the Smithton readers claim is not a romance. To qualify as a romance, the story must chronicle not merely the events of a courtship but *what it feels like* to be the *object* of one. Dot's customers insist that this need not be accomplished by telling the story solely from the heroine's point of view, although it is usually managed in this way. Although five of the women refuse to read first-person narratives because they want to be privy to the hero's thoughts and another ten indicate that they prefer to see both points of view, twenty-three of Dot's regular customers indicate that they have no preference about the identity of the narrator. However, all of the women I spoke to, regardless of their taste in narratives, admitted that they want to identify with the heroine as she attempts to comprehend, anticipate, and deal with the ambiguous attentions of a man who inevitably cannot understand her feelings at all. The point of the experience is the sense of exquisite tension, anticipation, and excitement created within the reader as she imagines the possible resolutions and consequences for a woman of an encounter with a member of the opposite sex and then observes that once again the heroine in question has avoided the ever-present potential for disaster because the hero has fallen helplessly in love with her.

In all of their comments about the nature of the romance, the Smithton women placed heavy emphasis on the importance of *development* in the romance's portrayal of love. The following two definitions were echoed again and again in other remarks:

> Generally there are two people who come together for one reason or another, *grow to love each other* and *work together solving problems* along the way—united for a purpose. They are light easy reading and always have a happy ending which makes one feel more light-hearted.

> I think [a romance] is a man and woman meeting, the growing awareness, the culmination of the love—*whether it's going to jell or if it's going to fall apart*—but they [the heroine and the hero] have recognized that they have fallen in love [emphasis added].

The women usually articulated this insistence on process and development during discussions about the genre's characteristic preoccupation with what is typically termed "a love-hate relationship." Because the middle of every romantic narrative must create some form of conflict to keep the romantic pair apart until the proper moment, many authors settle for misunderstanding or distrust as the cause of the intermediary delay of the couple's happy union. Hero and heroine are shown to despise each other overtly, even though they are "in love," primarily because each is jealous or suspicious of the other's motives and consequently fails to trust the other. Despite the frequency with which this pattern of conflict is suddenly explained away by the couple's mutual recognition that only misunderstanding is thwarting their relationship, the Smithton women are not convinced when a hero decides within two pages of the novel's conclusion that he has been mistaken about the heroine and that his apparent hatred is actually affection. Dot's customers dislike such "about faces"; they prefer to see a hero and heroine gradually overcome distrust and suspicion and grow to love each other.

Although this depiction of love as a gradual process cannot be considered the defining feature of the genre for all of the Smithton women, slightly more than half (twenty-three) believe it one of the "three most important ingredients" in the narrative. As might have been predicted, when responding to a request to rank order narrative features with respect to their importance to the genre, Dot's customers generally agreed that a happy ending is indispensable. Twenty-two of the women selected this as the essential ingredient in romance fiction out of a list of eleven choices, while a total of thirty-two listed it in first, second, or third place. The runner-up in the "most important" category, however, was "a slowly but consistently developing love between hero and heroine," placed by twenty-three of the women in first, second, or third place. Considered almost equally important by Dot's customers was the romance's inclusion of "some detail about the heroine and the hero after they have finally gotten together."[23] Twenty-two of the women thought this one of the three most important ingredients in the genre. Table 2.2 summarizes the ranking responses of the Smithton women.

The obvious importance of the happy ending lends credence to the suggestion that romances are valued most for their ability to raise the spirits of the reader. They manage to do so, the rankings imply, by involving that reader vicariously in the gradual evolution of a loving relationship whose culmination she is later permitted to enjoy in the best romances through a description of the heroine's and hero's life together after their necessary union. When combined with the relative unimportance of detailed reports about sexual encounters, it seems clear that the Smithton readers are interested in the verbal working out of a romance, that is, in the reinterpretation of misunderstood actions and in declarations of mutual love rather than in the portrayal of sexual contact through visual imagery.

Beatrice Faust has recently argued in *Women, Sex, and Pornography* that female sexuality is "tactile, verbal, intimate, nurturant, process-oriented and somewhat inclined to monogamy," traits she attributes to biological predisposition and social reinforcement through culture.[24] Although there are important problems with Faust's reliance on biology to account for female preferences in sexual encounters as well as with her assertion that such tastes characterize all women, her parallel claim that women are not excited by the kinds of visual displays and explicit description of physical contact that characterize male pornography is at least true of the Smithton readers. Dot and her customers are more interested in the affective responses of hero and heroine to each other than in a detailed account of their physical contact. Interestingly enough, the Smithton women also explained that they do not like explicit description because they prefer to imagine the scene in detail by themselves. Their wish to participate in the gradual growth of love and trust and to witness the way in which the heroine is eventually cared for by a man who also confesses that he "needs" her suggests that the Smithton women do indeed want to see a woman attended to sexually in a tender, nurturant, and emotionally open way. It should be added that these preferences also hint at the existence of an equally powerful wish to see a man dependent upon a woman.

TABLE 2.2
Question: What Are the Three Most Important Ingredients in a Romance?

Response	First Most Important Feature	Second Most Important Feature	Third Most Important Feature	Total Who Checked Response In One of Top Three Positions
a. A happy ending	22	4	6	32
b. Lots of scenes with explicit sexual description	0	0	0	0
c. Lots of details about faraway places and times	0	1	2	3
d. A long conflict between hero and heroine	2	1	1	4
e. Punishment of the villain	0	2	3	5
f. A slowly but consistently developing love between hero and heroine	8	9	6	23
g. A setting in a particular historical period	3	4	3	10
h. Lots of love scenes with some explicit sexual description	3	7	3	13
i. Lots of love scenes without explicit sexual description	0	3	1	4
j. Some detail about heroine and hero after they've gotten together	1	7	14	22
k. A very particular kind of hero and heroine	3	4	3	10

Although Dot's customers will not discuss in any detail whether they themselves are sexually excited by the escalation of sexual tension in a romance, they willingly acknowledge that what they enjoy most about romance reading is the opportunity to project themselves into the story, to become the heroine, and thus to share her surprise and slowly awakening pleasure at being so closely watched by someone who finds her valuable and worthy of love. They have elaborated this preference into a carefully articulated distinction between good and bad romances, which differ principally in the way they portray the hero's treatment of the heroine.

A substantial amount of popular and even scholarly writing about mass-produced entertainment makes the often correct assumption that such fare is cynically engineered to appeal to the tastes of the largest possible audience in the interest of maximum profit.[25] However, a certain portion of it is still written by sincere, well-meaning people who are themselves consumers of the form they work in and indeed proponents of the values it embodies. Despite publishers' efforts at rationalization of romance production through the use of carefully calculated "tip sheets to writers," the genre is not yet entirely written by men and women who do it only to make money. Although many of the most successful authors in the field are professional writers, a significant number of them are "amateurs" drawn to the genre by a desire to write the kind of material they love to read. More often than not, it is the work of *these* women that the Smithton readers like best.

In a letter to the readers of Dot's newsletter, for instance, LaVyrle Spencer has explained that her first book "was written because of one very special lady, Kathleen Woodiwiss," whose book, *The Flame and the Flower*, "possessed me to the point where I found I, too, wanted to write a book that would make ladies' hearts throb with anticipation." She continued, "I even got to the point where I told myself I wanted to do it for her, Kathleen, to give her a joyful reading experience like she'd given me."[26] *The Fulfillment* resulted from this inspiration.

Jude Deveraux, another successful author, also commented in Dot's newsletter on Woodiwiss's role in her decision to become a writer. She so enjoyed *The Flame and the Flower* that she dashed out to buy two more romances to re-create the pleasure Woodiwiss's book had provided. "I planned to stay up all night and read them," she explained to Dot's subscribers, but "by ten o'clock I was so disgusted I threw the books across the room. They were nothing but rape sagas." She gave up, turned off the light and thought, "If I read the perfect romance, what would the plot be?" Deveraux spent the night creating dialogue in her head and when she arose the next morning, she began writing. The book that resulted, *The Enchanted Land*, with its independent heroine and thoughtful hero, was mentioned often by Dot's customers as one of their favorites.[27]

Even the incredibly prolific and very professional Janet Dailey confesses that she too began the career that has made her a millionaire, by some obervers' reckoning, because she wanted to write the kinds of books she most enjoyed reading.[28] Convinced by her husband to go ahead and try, she set out to write a romance. Since that day in 1968, millions of readers have informally acknowledged through their repeat purchases of her books that she understands very well what her readers want.

Given the fact that many romance writers were romance readers before they set pen to paper, it seems logical to expect that their views of the romance might parallel those held by their readers. Of course, this is not universally the case because many romances are considered failures by readers. Some otherwise popular books do not please the entire audience, thus bearing witness to the possibility of a discrepancy between writers' and readers' definitions and conceptions. Rosemary Rogers, for example, is universally detested by the Smithton readers who consider her books "trashy," "filthy," and "perverted." Her views of the romance are at least not representative of this group of regular readers.

Despite exceptions like these, it is striking to note that there is a distinct similarity between the Smithton conception of the romance and that implied in comments about the form by writers who are themselves enthusiastic readers. In an article on "Writing the Gothic Novel," for instance, Phyllis Whitney has cautioned aspiring writers, "no feeling, no story—and that's a rule!"[29] She explains that even though explicit sexual description must never appear in a gothic, this prohibition does not mean sexual feeling should not figure in the stories. In fact, she goes on to say, anticipation and excitement *must* "smolder" beneath the surface in scenes that are "underplayed, suggested rather than stated." That way, Whitney elaborates, "the reader's imagination will work for you."[30] She understands that women like the Smithton readers project themselves into the story by identifying with the heroine as she responds to the hero with all of her "strongly passionate nature." Whitney also knows that those women wish to be shown repeatedly that men can attend to a woman in the manner she most desires. To clarify her point she explains finally that "in the true love scenes, there is always an underlying tenderness that, for a woman, can be an exciting factor in sex—James Bond to the contrary."[31] Like Beatrice Faust and the Smithton women, Phyllis Whitney seems to believe that "women want to love and be made love to as they love babies—that is, in a nurturant fashion."[32] Whitney closes with perhaps her most central piece of advice: "I doubt that you can write Gothic novels unless you like reading them. . . . While I am in the process of writing, I am submerged in my heroine and her problems—and having a wonderful time. Me and all those dark-browed heroes! I'm sure this is the first necessary ingredient, though I'm mentioning it last."[33]

Her attitude has been echoed by Jeanne Glass, an editor at Pyramid Publications, a house that attempts to specialize in the kinds of romances the Smithton readers like. She has written that the sex in romances must be "sensual, romantic, breathy—enough to make the pulse race, but not rough-guy, explicit, constantly brutal." She adds that the predominant flavor must be an "understanding of female *emotions*: hesitancy, doubt, anger, confusion, loss of control, exhilaration, etc."[34]

These comments suggest that some romance writers agree with the Smithton group that a romance is a love story whose gradually evolving course must be experienced from the heroine's point of view. These writers understand that the goal and raison d'être of the genre is its actual, though perhaps temporary, effect on readers like the Smithton women. While explicit description of sexual encounters may be included in some of the genre's variations, the writers agree with their readers that the emphasis in the encounters must be on the love that is being conveyed through sexual contact and not on its physical details.

If readers' and writers' interpretations of their own experiences are taken into account, then, the romance cannot be dismissed as a mere pretense for masturbatory titillation. The reading experience is valued for the way it makes the reader feel, but the feeling it creates is interpreted by the women themselves as a general sense of emotional well-being and visceral contentment. Such a feeling is brought on by the opportunity to participate vicariously in a relationship characterized by *mutual* love and by the hero's quite unusual ability to express his devotion gently and with concern for his heroine's pleasure. The question that needs to be asked, therefore, is *why* the readers find it essential and beneficial to seek out this particular kind of vicarious experience. That can perhaps best be answered by comparing good and bad romances. In explaining what they do when they have determined a particular text's quality, the Smithton women provide clues to both the *deprivation* that prompts their activity and the *fears* that are assuaged and managed in the reading experience.

The reactions of the Smithton women to books they are not enjoying are indicative of the intensity of their need to avoid offensive material and the feelings it typically evokes. Indeed, twenty-three (55 percent) reported that when they find themselves in the middle of a bad book, they put it down immediately and refuse to finish it. Some even make the symbolic gesture of discarding the book in the garbage, particularly if it has offended them seriously. This was the universal fate suffered by Lolah Burford's *Alyx* (1977), a book cited repeatedly as a perfect example of the pornographic trash distributed by publishers under the guise of the romance.

Another nine (21 percent) of the women indicated that although they do not read the rest of the book, they at least skip to the ending "to see how it came out." In responding to the question about why she must read the ending of a book even in the face of evidence that the book is insulting, Maureen explained that to cease following a story in the middle is to remain suspended in the heroine's nightmare while she *is* the heroine. Her comments were corroborated by every other woman I spoke to who engaged in this kind of behavior. In elaborating upon the problem, Maureen also mentioned the kind of books that most upset her:

Maureen: A lot of your thicker books—it's rape—sometimes gang rape. I could not handle that in my own life. And since I'm living as the heroine, I cannot handle it in a book. And I hate myself for reading them. But if I start it, I have to get myself out of there, so I have to read my way out.

Interviewer: So you must finish a book?

Maureen: Yes, I have to finish it. Even if it's only skimming, one word per page—or sometimes I just read the ending. I have to finish it. But it leaves a bad taste in my mouth forever.

Because nearly all romances end in the union of the two principal characters, regardless of the level of violence inflicted on the heroine during the course of the story, by reading that "happy" conclusion Maureen at least formally assures herself that all works out for the heroine as it should. She cannot simply dismiss the story as a badly managed fiction precisely because she becomes so involved in the tale that she lives it emotionally as her own. She and other readers like her feel it necessary to continue the imaginative pretense just long enough to share the heroine's achievement of mutual love that is the goal of all romance-reading experiences.

This need to read one's way out of a bad situation and to resolve or contain all of the unpleasant feelings aroused by it is so strong in some of the Smithton readers that they read the whole book even when they hate it. In fact, ten (24 percent) of Dot's customers indicated that they *always* finish a book no matter what its quality. Nevertheless, this habit does not testify to a wish or even a need to see women abused. Rather, it is the mark of the intensity with which they desire to be told that an ideal love is possible *even in the worst of circumstances* and that a woman can be nurtured and cared for even by a man who appears gruff and indifferent.

It is necessary to raise this issue of the romance readers' attitude toward the violence that undeniably exists in some romances because several commentators, including Ann Douglas, have recently suggested that women enjoy the experience of reading about others of their sex who are mistreated by men. In "Soft-Porn Culture," Douglas asserts that "the women who couldn't thrill to male nudity in *Playgirl* are *enjoying* the titillation of seeing themselves, not necessarily as they are, but as some men would like to see them: illogical, innocent, *magnetized by male sexuality and brutality.*"[35] Although it is hard to disagree with her point about traditional male sexuality, which is still treated as compelling, especially in the Harlequins about which Douglas writes, there is good reason to believe that male brutality is a concern in recent romances, not because women are magnetized or drawn to it, but because they find it increasingly prevalent and horribly frightening.

Clifford Geertz maintains that all art forms, like the Balinese cockfight, render "ordinary everyday experience comprehensible by presenting it in terms of acts and objects which have had their practical consequences removed and been reduced . . . to a level of sheer appearance, where the meaning can be more powerfully articulated and more exactly perceived."[36] If Geertz is correct, then it seems likely that the romance's preoccupation with male brutality is an attempt to understand the meaning of an event that has become almost unavoidable in the real world. The romance may express misogynistic attitudes not because women share them but because they increasingly need to know how to deal with them.

The romance also seems to be exploring the consequences of attempts to counter the increased threat of violence with some sort of defiance. While the final effect of such a display may be, as Douglas claims, the formulation of the message, "don't travel alone"; "men can't stand it," "men won't let you get away with it,"[37] the motive behind the message is less one of total assent than one of resignation born of fear about what might happen if the message was ignored. Romantic violence may also be the product of a continuing inability to imagine any situation in which a woman might acquire and use resources that would enable her to withstand male opposition and coercion.

When the Smithton readers' specific dislikes are examined in conjunction with their preferences in romance fiction, an especially clear view of the genre's function as an artistic "display" of contemporary cultural habits develops. In particular, when the events and features that the readers *most* detest are taken as indicators of their fears, it becomes possible to isolate the crucial characteristics and consequences of gender relations that prove most troubling to the Smithton women. In Chapter 4, through an examination of "the ideal romance," I shall demonstrate that the same awful possibilities of violence that dominate bad romances are always evoked as potential threats to female integrity even in good romances, simply because women are trying to *explain* this situation to themselves. Because the explanation finally advanced in the good romance remains a highly conservative one of traditional categories and definitions, when events that occur in reality are displayed in the text, they are always reinterpreted as mere threats. However, in those romances where the potential consequences of male-female relations are too convincingly imagined or permitted to control the tenor of the book by obscuring the developing love story, the art form's role as *safe* display is violated. In that case, the story treads too closely to the terrible real in ordinary existence that it is trying to explain. Then, the romance's role as conservator of the social structure and its legitimizing ideology is unmasked because the contradictions the form usually papers over and minimizes so skillfully render the romantic resolution untenable even for the women who are usually most convinced by it.

Dot first acquainted me with the features of such a "bad" romance during our initial interview when she informed me that her customers can tell the difference between romances written by women and those written by men. She agrees with their dismissal of male-authored romances, she explained, because very few men are "perceptive" or "sensitive" and because most cannot imagine the kind of "gentleness" that is essential to the good romance. When asked to elaborate on the distinction between a good romance and a bad one, she replied that the latter was "kinky, you know, filled with sado-masochism, cruelty, and all sorts of things." She concluded decisively, "I detest that!"

Her readers apparently do too for in response to a question requesting them to select the three things that "should never appear in a romance" from a list of eleven choices, rape was listed by eleven of the women as the most objectionable feature, while a sad ending was selected by an additional ten. The rest of the group divided almost evenly over explicit sex, physical torture of the heroine or hero, and bed-hopping. Despite the apparent range of dislikes, when their rankings are summarized, clear objections emerge. The women generally agree that bed-hopping or promiscuous sex, a sad ending, rape, physical torture, and weak heroes have no place in the romance. Their choices here are entirely consistent with their belief in the therapeutic value of romance reading. The sad ending logically ranks high on their list of objections because its presence would negate the romance's difference and distance from day-to-day existence, dominated as it so often is by small failures, minor catastrophes, and ongoing disappointments. In addition, without its happy ending, the romance could not hold out the utopian promise that male-female relations can be managed successfully.

I suspect bed-hopping is so objectionable in a romance because the genre is exploring the possibilities and consequences for women of the American middle class of adopting what has been dubbed "the new morality." Most students of the romance have observed that after the 1972 appearance of Woodiwiss's unusually explicit *The Flame and the Flower*, romance authors were free to treat their heroines as sexual creatures capable of arousal and carnal desire. Indeed, the extraordinary popularity of Woodiwiss's novel and its rapid imitation by others seem to suggest that large numbers of American women had been affected by feminism and the sexual revolution of the 1960s. The strong reader distaste for bed-hopping or promiscuous sex suggests, however, that this change in sexual mores

TABLE 2.3

Question: Which of the Following Do You Feel Should Never Be Included in a Romance?

Response	First Most Objectionable	Second Most Objectionable	Third Most Objectionable	Total
a. Rape	11	6	2	19
b. Explicit sex	6	2	1	9
c. Sad ending	10	4	6	20
d. Physical torture	5	6	7	18
e. An ordinary heroine	1	1	1	3
f. Bed-hopping	4	12	6	22
g. Premarital sex	0	0	1	1
h. A cruel hero	1	5	6	12
i. A weak hero	4	5	7	16
j. A hero stronger than the heroine	0	0	0	0
k. A heroine stronger than the hero	0	1	3	4

was and still is tolerable only within very strict limits. Hence, the "good" romance continues to maintain that a woman acknowledge and realize her feelings *only* within traditional, monogamous marriage. When another text portrays a heroine who is neither harmed nor disturbed by her ability to have sex with several men, I suspect it is classified as "bad" because it makes explicit the threatening implications of an unleashed feminine sexuality capable of satisfying itself outside the structures of patriarchal domination that are still perpetuated most effectively through marriage.[38] Such a portrayal also strays too close to the suggestion that men do not care for women as individuals but, as the saying goes, are interested only in one thing.

In fact, the Smithton women revealed that they suspected as much when they voiced their anger about male promiscuity and repeatedly complained about romances that advance the double standard. "We do not want to be told," one of Dot's customers explained, "that if you love a man you'll forgive him." Neither do they wish to adopt male standards; Dot and her customers would prefer that men learn to adhere to theirs. The Smithton women overwhelmingly believe that sex is a wonderful form of intimate communication that should be explored only by two people who care for each other deeply and intend to formalize their relationship through the contract of marriage. For them, the romance is neither a recommendation for female revolt nor a strictly conservative refusal to acknowledge any change. It is, rather, a cognitive exploration of the possibility of adopting and managing some attitude changes about feminine sexuality by making room for them within traditional institutions and structures that they understand to be protective of a woman's interests.

Rape and physical torture of the heroine and the hero are obviously objectionable because the readers are seeking an opportunity to be shown a happier, more trouble-free version of existence. Such features are probably also distasteful, however, because the romance, which is never simply a love story, is also an exploration of the meaning of patriarchy for women. As a result, it is concerned with the fact that men possess and regularly exercise power over them in all sorts of circumstances. By picturing the heroine in relative positions of weakness, romances are not necessarily endorsing her situation, but examining an all-too-common state of affairs in order to display possible strategies for coping with it. When a romance presents the story of a woman who is misunderstood by the hero, mistreated and manhandled as a consequence of his misreading, and then suddenly loved, protected, and cared for by him because he recognizes that he mistook the meaning of her behavior, the novel is informing its readers that the minor acts of violence they must contend with in their own lives can be similarly reinterpreted as the result of misunderstandings or of jealousy born of "true love." The readers are therefore assured that those acts do not warrant substantial changes or traumatic upheaval in a familiar way of life.[39]

Woodiwiss's handling of what one reader called "a little forceful persuasion" is acceptable to the Smithton women because they are fully convinced by her attempt to show that the hero's sexual sway over the heroine is always the product of his passion and her irresistibility. Indeed, one publishing house understands this quite well, for in its directions to potential writers it states that rape is not recommended but that one will be allowed under specific conditions if the author feels it is necessary to make a point.[40] Should that rape occur "between the heroine and the hero," the directions specify, it must "never be initiated with the violent motivation that exists in reality" because "a woman's fantasy is to lose control" with someone who really cares for her. "A true rape" can be included only if "it moves the story forward" and if it happens to someone other than the heroine.

Vicious or "true" rape upsets the tenuous balance for most of the Smithton readers because they feel they would not be able to forgive or explain away an overtly malicious act. They cannot understand how a heroine finds it within herself to ignore such an event, forgive the man who violated her, and then grow to love him. As Ann, one of Dot's most outspoken customers, put it, "I get tired of it if they [the heroes] keep grabbing and using sex as a weapon for domination because they want to win a struggle of the wills. I'm tending to get quite a few of these in Harlequins and I think they're terrible." Her comment prompted excited discussion among those in the interview group who had read the recent Harlequins. All of the women agreed that they found Harlequin's new, more explicit preoccupation with male violence nauseating, and several even admitted that they stopped buying them to avoid being subjected to this form of male power. The following explanation of several Harlequin plots was given by another of Dot's customers:

> Four of the eight in the last shipment—they're married and separated four to eight years and all of a sudden *he* decides that they should have stayed together and *he* punishes her. They're gonna get together and live happily ever after, after *he* punishes her! Right!

> That sounds terrible.

> Well, they were. He tricks her into coming back or meeting with him or whatever and he has some sort of powerhold over her either emotionally or physically—either he'll take her child away or ruin her father. He's determined to win her back. She's good enough to have him now.[41]

This reader's scorn for a typical pattern of explanation in romance fiction makes it clear that there are limits to what can be justified by evoking the irrationality of passionate love. Although opinions about acceptability probably vary tremendously within the entire romance audience, Dot's readers at least seem to agree about the conditions that must be met. Violence is acceptable to them only if it is described sparingly, if it is controlled carefully, or if it is *clearly* traceable to the passion or jealousy of the hero. On the other hand, if it is represented as brutal and vicious, if it is extensively detailed and carried out by many men, or if it is depicted as the product of an obvious desire for power, these same women find that violence offensive and objectionable. This curious and artificial distinction that they draw between "forceful persuasion" and "true rape" is a function of the very pressing need to know how to deal with the realities of male power and force in day-to-day existence.

I suspect their willingness to see male force interpreted as passion is also the product of a wish to be seen as so desirable to the "right" man that he will not take "no" for an answer. Because he finds her irresistible, the heroine need not take any responsibility for her own sexual feelings. She avoids the difficulty of choosing whether to act on them or not. Although female sexuality is thus approvingly incorporated into the romantic fantasy, the individual ultimately held responsible for it is not the woman herself but, once again, a man.

If the qualities of a bad romance reveal the fears and concerns that are troubling to the women who read them, the characteristics they identify with good romances point to the existence of important needs and desires that are met and fulfilled by the perfect romantic fantasy. According to Dot and her customers, the relative excellence of a romance is a function of its treatment of three different aspects of the story. These include the personality of the heroine, the character of the hero, and the particular manner in which the hero pursues and wins the affections of the heroine. If these individuals and relationships are not presented properly, not even ingenious plotting will rescue the novel from "the garbage dump."

On first discussing romances with the Smithton readers, I was struck by the fact that individual books were inevitably registered in their memories as the stories of particular *women*. When specific titles were volunteered to illustrate a point, they were always linked with a capsule plot summary beginning with a statement about the heroine and continuing with the principal events of what was, to the speaker, her tale. Because of her perceived centrality in the romance and because of their admitted tendency to project themselves into the heroine's being, the Smithton readers hold particularly exacting expectations about the qualities the heroine should have and the kinds of behavior she should exhibit.

So consistent are their feelings about heroines, in fact, that no discrepancy appears between their orally reported preferences and those acknowledged on the anonymous questionnaires. Dot's customers inevitably responded to my query about the characteristics of a good heroine with the statement that she must have three traits: intelligence, a sense of humor, and independence. On the questionnaire, nineteen (45 percent) of the women selected intelligence from a list of nine other possibilities as the characteristic they *most* liked to see in a heroine, while nine (21 percent) picked a sense of humor. The only other traits to score significantly were femininity and independence. When the group's rankings are totaled, intelligence joins independence and a sense of humor as the three traits that score significantly higher than all of the others. It seems especially important to note that three-fourths of the group selected intelligence (79 percent) and a sense of humor (74 percent) at least once, whereas independence was chosen by almost half (48 percent) of the Smithton women. Femininity, with its connotation of demure deference was, however, still a choice of fourteen of the Smithton readers.

It may seem curious to insist here on the importance of the heroine's intelligence and independence to the Smithton women when so many "objective" students of the genre have commented on her typical passivity and quivering helplessness.[42] This harsh analytical judgment, however, is often founded on an assessment of the heroine's ultimate success in solving a mystery, making her desires known, or in refusing to be cowed by the hero. The *results* of her actions, in short, are always measured on a scale whose highest value is accorded the autonomous woman capable of accomplishing productive work in a nondomestic sphere. While the romantic heroine understandably compares badly with this ideal woman, it is important to note that neither Dot nor her readers find such an ideal attractive nor do they scrutinize and evaluate the heroine's success in effecting change or in getting others to do what she wants in order to assess her character. The heroine's personality is, instead, inevitably and securely established for them at the beginning of the tale through a series of simple observations about her abilities, talents, and career choice. Because the Smithton women accept those assertions at face value, they search no further for incidents that might comment on or revise her early portrayal. Not only do they believe in the heroine's honest desire to take care of herself, but they also believe in the mimetic accuracy of the extenuating circumstances that always intervene to thwart her intended actions. The Smithton women are, in sum, significantly more inclined than their feminist critics to recognize the inevitability and reality of male power and the force of social convention to circumscribe a woman's ability to act in her own interests. It must also be said that they are comfortable with the belief that a woman should be willing to sacrifice extreme self-interest for a long-term relationship where mutually agreed-upon goals take precedence over selfish desire.

The point I want to make here is that when analysis proceeds from within the belief system actually brought to bear upon a text by its readers, the analytical interpretation of the meaning of a character's behavior is more likely to coincide with that meaning as it is constructed and understood by the readers themselves. Thus the account offered to explain the desire to experience this particular fantasy is also more likely to approximate the motives that actually initiate the readers' decisions to pick up a romance. While the romantic heroine may appear foolish, dependent, and even pathetic to a woman who has already accepted as given the equality of male and female abilities, she appears courageous, and even valiant, to another still unsure that such equality is a fact or that she herself might want to assent to it.

The Smithton women seem to be struggling simultaneously with the promise and threat of the women's movement as well as with their culture's now doubled capacity to belittle the intelligence and activities of "the ordinary housewife." Therefore, while they are still very conservative and likely to admit the rightness of traditional relations between men and women, at the same time they are angered by men who continue to make light of "woman's work" as well as by "women's libbers" whom they accuse of dismissing mothers and housewives as ignorant, inactive, and unimportant. Their desire to believe that the romantic heroine is as intelligent and independent as she is asserted to be even though she is also shown to be vulnerable and most interested in being loved is born of their apparently unconscious desire to realize some of the benefits of feminism within traditional institutions and relationships—hence, the high value attached to the simple *assertion* of the heroine's special abilities. With a few simple statements rather than with truly threatening action on the part of the heroine, the romance author demonstrates for the typical reader the compatibility of a changed sense of the female self and an unchanged social arrangement. In the utopia of romance fiction, "independence" and a secure individual "identity" are never compromised by the paternalistic care and protection of the male.

Although Chapter 4 will explore the particular strategies employed by Smithton's favorite romance authors to avoid the real contradictions between dependency and self-definition, I would like to quote here from a lengthy and exuberant discussion carried on in one of the interviews when I asked Dot, her daughter, Kit, and Ann to describe the "ideal" romantic heroine. Rather than list a series of abstract traits as others generally did, these women launched into a fifteen-minute, communally produced plot summary of Elsie Lee's *The Diplomatic Lover* (1971). The delight with which they described the heroine and what they perceived to be her constant control of her situation is as good an example as any of the desire they share with feminists to believe in the female sex's strength and capabilities and in themselves as well. When I asked them why they liked the book so much after they told me they had xeroxed the text for their own use (the book is now out of print), the extended reply began in the following way:

Dot: It's just classic.
Ann: She *decides* that she wants to lose her virginity and picks *him*.
Kit: Well, he's really nice looking; he's a movie star and he's . . .
Dot: Well, the thing is, actually, because she is in a modern workaday world. She's in Washington, D.C., in the diplomatic corps.
Kit: And *she* makes the decision, you know.
Dot: And she's the only one [in the diplomatic community] who's a virgin and her name is Nanny.
Ann: Yes.
Dot: And they call her Nanny-No-No because she's always saying no, no, no!
Ann: She knows, she's read all the textbooks; but she's just never found anyone that set her blood to boiling.
Dot: And she's known him for years.
Ann: But he walks into the room at this one party and all of a sudden

. . .

Kit: *She* makes the decision! It's her birthday.
Ann: She mentally licks her chops.
Kit: She's twenty-three. She decides, "Well, this is it!"
Ann: Yes.
Dot: But you know it's not distasteful. There's nothing . . . it was unusual.
Kit: It was very intimate.
Dot: It's not bold.[43]

In the midst of recounting the rest of the tale, they proudly exclaimed that Nanny "spoke six languages," was "a really good artist," and "did not want to marry him even though she was pregnant" because she believed he was an "elegant tomcat" and would not be faithful to her. These untraditional skills and unconventional attitudes are obviously not seen as fulfilling or quite proper by Lee herself because they are legitimated and rendered acceptable at the novel's conclusion when the hero convinces Nanny of his love, refuses to live without her, and promises to take care of her in the future. Here is the group's recitation of this moment:

Dot: He starts stalking her and this is visually . . .
Kit: It's hysterical.
Dot: You can see it.
Kit: She's backin' off.
Dot: She's trying to get to the stairway to get to her room.
Kit: And make a mad dash.
Ann: She's what they call a "petite pocket Venus type."
Dot: Yes, and he's stalking her and she's backing away and saying, "No, I won't marry you!"
Ann: "I ain't going!"
Kit: "No, just forget that!"
Dot: "No, I don't need you!"
Ann: "And he says I'll camp on your doorstep; I'll picket; unfair to, you know . . ."

As in all romances, female defiance is finally rendered ineffectual and childlike as well as unnecessary by Lee's conclusion. Nonetheless, if we are to understand the full meaning of the story for these women, it is essential to recognize that their temporary reveling in her intelligence, independence, self-sufficiency, and initiative is as important to their experiencing of the book as the fact of her final capture by a man who admits that he needs her. Indeed, after recounting the resolution of this tale, Dot, Kit, and Ann relived again her "seduction of him" by marveling over the moment "when she asks him, and he's drinking and he about chokes to death!"

In novels like *The Diplomatic Lover*, which the Smithton women like best, the happy ending restores the status quo in gender relations when the hero enfolds the heroine protectively in his arms. That ending, however, can also be interpreted as an occasion for the vicarious enjoyment of a woman's ultimate triumph. Dot's readers so interpret it because the heroine, they claim, maintains her integrity on her own terms by exacting a formal commitment from the hero and simultaneously provides for her own future in the only way acceptable to her culture.

The Smithton readers' interest in a strong but still traditional heroine is complemented by their desire to see that woman loved by a very special kind of hero. As noted earlier, these women will read many romances they do not especially like, even when the hero mistreats the heroine, because the experience of the happy ending is more important to them than anything else and because it successfully explains away many individual incidents they do not condone. Nevertheless, they prefer to see the heroine desired, needed, and loved by a man who is strong and masculine, but equally capable of unusual tenderness, gentleness, and concern for her pleasure. In fact, when asked to rank ten male personality traits as to desirability, not one of the Smithton readers listed independence in first, second, or third place. Although this might be explained by suggesting that the women felt no need to single this characteristic out because they assumed that men are, by nature, independent, their interview comments suggest otherwise. Throughout their discussions of particular books, they repeatedly insisted that what they remembered and liked most about favorite novels was the skill with which the author described the hero's recognition of his own deep feelings for the heroine and his realization that he could not live without her. While the women want to feel that the heroine will be protected by the hero, they also seem to want to see her dependency balanced by its opposite, that is, by the hero's dependence on her. In this context, the Smithton women's constant emphasis on the importance of mutuality in love makes enormous sense.

I do not want to suggest here that male protectiveness and strength are not important elements in the romantic fantasy; they are. Remember, sixteen (38 percent) of the women indicated that they think a weak hero is one of the three most objectionable features in a romance. In addition, almost 25 percent of Dot's customers agreed that out of nine traits strength is the third most important in a hero. Still, neither strength nor protectiveness is considered as important as intelligence, gentleness, and an ability to laugh at life, all of which were placed significantly more often by the readers in one of the three top positions on the questionnaire.

TABLE 2.4
Question: What Qualities Do You Like to See in a Hero?

Response	Most Important	Second Most Important	Third Most Important	Total
a. Intelligence	14	11	5	30
b. Tenderness	11	8	7	26
c. Protectiveness	3	4	7	14
d. Strength	3	3	9	15
e. Bravery	1	4	2	7
f. Sense of humor	8	5	6	19
g. Independence	0	0	0	0
h. Attractiveness	2	5	3	10
i. A good body	0	2	2	4
j. Other	0	0	0	0
Blank			1	1

However, because Dot and her customers rarely initiated discussion of the romantic hero and just as seldom volunteered opinions about specific male characters, it has been difficult to develop a complex picture of their ideal or of the motivation prompting its formation. Even when their responses are displayed in a graph, certain mysteries persist.

The principal difficulty involves the marked preference for an "intelligent" hero. Although it is hard to say why intelligence was ranked so high by the Smithton women, it is possible that the choice is both consistent with the high value they place on books, learning, and education and their own upward mobility as well as a way of reaffirming male excellence and agentivity without also automatically implying female inferiority. The word did appear in discussions of the ideal hero, but the women offered little that would explain its prominence in their questionnaire responses. A few oral comments seemed to hint at the existence of an expectation that an "intelligent" man would be more likely to appreciate and encourage the extraordinary abilities of the ideal heroine, but this link was not volunteered consistently enough to warrant its formulation as the motive behind the fantasy. Equally hard to explain is the emphasis on a sense of humor, although I suspect the interest in this trait masks a desire to see a hero who is up to a "verbal duel" with the heroine. Not only does this create the air of "lightness" so important to the Smithton women, but it also helps to show off the heroine's tart-tongued facility to advantage.

This vagueness about the actual content of the hero's personality persisted throughout many commentaries that tended to center instead on his ability to establish the proper relationship with the heroine. The Smithton women are less interested in the particularities of their heroes as individuals than in the roles the most desirable among them perform. Gentleness and tenderness figure often in their accounts of favorite novels not so much as character traits exhibited by particular men but as the distinguishing feature of the attention accorded the heroine by all good heroes in the outstanding novels. The focus never shifts for these readers away from the woman at the center of the romance. Moreover, men are rarely valued for their intrinsic characteristics but become remarkable by virtue of the special position they occupy vis-à-vis the heroine. The romantic fantasy is therefore not a fantasy about discovering a uniquely interesting life partner, but a ritual wish to be cared for, loved, and validated in a particular way.

In distinguishing the ideal romance from Rosemary Rogers's "perversions," one of the five customers I interviewed at length wondered whether her editor had been male because, she reasoned, "it's a man's type book." When pressed to elaborate, she retorted, "because a man likes the sex in it, you know, Matt Helm and all that type." The distinction she sees here between sex and romance was continually employed by the Smithton women to differentiate pornography, which they associate with men, from their own interest in "insightful love," which they wish men could manage. As Joy said of the recent Harlequins, "all they worry about is sex—that's the first thing on their minds. They don't worry about anything else." She continued, "they don't need that; they need humor and love and caring." Similarly, in one of our final discussions, Dot also elaborated on the differences between pornography and romance and between men and women and, in doing so, identified in a wistful tone the particular characteristic she and her customers believe all men should possess:

> I've always thought that women are more insightful into men's psyches than men are into women's. Well, men just don't take the time. They just don't. And it's always been interesting to me that psychiatrists are probably . . . 85 to 90 percent of the psychiatrists in this country are men and I'm sure they know the book. I'm sure they know the textbook. But as far as insightful, I think that is one of the most rare commodities that there is . . . is an insightful man. . . . I don't think men look deep. I think they take even a man at face value. Whatever they see—that's what the man is.

What the Smithton women are looking for in their search for the perfect romantic fantasy is a man who is capable of the same attentive observation and intuitive "understanding" that they believe women regularly accord to men. We will see in Chapter 4, in a more thorough examination of the Smithton group's favorite romances, that the fantasy generating the ideal romantic story thus fulfills two deeply felt needs that have been activated in women by early object-relations and cultural conditioning in patriarchal society. On the one hand, the story permits the reader to identify with the heroine at the moment of her greatest success, that is, when she secures the attention and recognition of her culture's most powerful and essential representative, a man. The happy ending is, at this level, a sign of a woman's attainment of legitimacy and personhood in a culture that locates both for her in the roles of lover, wife, and mother.

On the other hand, by emphasizing the intensity of the hero's uninterrupted gaze and the tenderness of his caress at the moment he encompasses his beloved in his still always "masculine" arms, the fantasy also evokes the memory of a period in the reader's life when she was the center of a profoundly nurturant individual's attention. Because this imaginative emotional regression is often denied women in ordinary existence because men have been prompted by the culture's asymmetrical conditioning to deny their own capacities for gentle nurturance, it becomes necessary to fulfill this never-ending need in other areas. Nancy Chodorow has suggested, in *The Reproduction of Mothering*, that one way for women to provide this essential sustenance for themselves is through the mothering of others. By taking care of a child in this intense emotional way and by identifying with her child, Chodorow reasons, a woman is able to nurture herself, albeit vicariously. However, Chodorow does not comment at any length about whether this vicarious care and attention prove a perfectly adequate substitute. The ideal romance, at least as it is conceived by the Smithton women, argues effectively that it is not. Its stress on the emotional bonding between hero and heroine suggests that women still desire to be loved, cared for, and understood by an adult who is singularly capable of self-abnegating preoccupation with a loved one's needs.

In the next chapter we will discover that it is the constant impulse and duty to mother others that is responsible for the sense of depletion that apparently sends some women to romance fiction. By immersing themselves in the romantic fantasy, women vicariously fulfill their needs for nurturance by identifying with a heroine whose principal accomplishment, if it can even be called that, is her success at drawing the hero's attention to herself, at establishing herself as the object of his concern and the recipient of his care. Because the reader experiences that care vicariously, her need is assuaged only as long as she can displace it onto a fictional character. When that character's story is completed, when the book must be closed, the reader is forced to return to herself and to her real situation. Although she may feel temporarily revived, she has done nothing to alter her relations with others. More often than not, those relations remain unchanged and in returning to them a woman is once again expected and willing to employ her emotional resources for the care of others. If she is then not herself reconstituted by another, romance reading may suggest itself again as a reasonable compensatory solution. Therefore, the romance's short-lived therapeutic value, which is made both possible and necessary by a culture that creates needs in women that it cannot fulfill, is finally the cause of its repetitive consumption.

The Act of Reading the Romance
Escape and Instruction

By the end of my first full day with Dorothy Evans and her customers, I had come to realize that although the Smithton women are not accustomed to thinking about what it is in the romance that gives them so much pleasure, they know perfectly well why they like to read. I understood this only when their remarkably consistent comments forced me to relinquish my inadvertent but continuing preoccupation with the text. Because the women always responded to my query about their reasons for reading with comments about the pleasures of the act itself rather than about their liking for the particulars of the romantic plot, I soon realized I would have to give up my obsession with textual features and narrative details if I wanted to understand their view of romance reading. Once I recognized this it became clear that romance reading was important to the Smithton women first because the simple event of picking up a book enabled them to deal with the particular pressures and tensions encountered in their daily round of activities. Although I learned later that certain aspects of the romance's story do help to make this event especially meaningful, the early interviews were interesting because they focused so resolutely on the significance of the *act of romance reading* rather than on the meaning of the romance.

The extent of the connection between romance reading and my informants' understanding of their roles as wives and mothers was impressed upon me first by Dot herself during our first two-hour interview which took place before I had seen her customers' responses to the pilot questionnaire. In posing the question, "What do romances do better than other novels today?," I expected her to concern herself in her answer with the characteristics of the plot and the manner in which the story evolved. To my surprise, Dot took my query about "doing" as a transitive question about the *effects* of romances on the people who read them. She responded to my question with a long and puzzling answer that I found difficult to interpret at this early stage of our discussions. It seems wise to let Dot speak for herself here because her response introduced a number of themes that appeared again and again in my subsequent talks with other readers. My question prompted the following careful meditation:

> It's an innocuous thing. If it had to be . . . pills or drinks, this is harmful. They're very aware of this. Most of the women are mothers. And they're aware of that kind of thing. And reading is something they would like to generate in their children also. Seeing the parents reading is . . . just something that I feel they think the children should see them doing. . . . I've got a woman with teenage boys here who says "you've got books like . . . you've just got oodles of da . . . da . . . da . . . [counting an imaginary stack of books]." She says, "Now when you ask Mother to buy you something, you don't stop and think how many things you have. So this is Mother's and it is my money." Very, almost defensive. But I think they get that from their fathers. I think they heard their fathers sometime or other saying, "Hey, you're spending an awful lot of money on books aren't you?" You know for a long time, my ladies hid' em. They would hide their books; literally hide their books. And they'd say, "Oh, if my husband [we have distinctive blue sacks], if my husband sees this blue sack coming in the house. . . ." And you know, I'd say, "Well really, you're a big girl. Do you really feel like you have to be very defensive?" A while ago, I would not have thought that way. I would have thought, "Oh, Dan is going to hit the ceiling." For a while Dan was not thrilled that I was reading a lot. Because I think men do feel threatened. They want their wife to be in the room with them. And I think my body is in the room but the rest of me is not (when I am reading).[1]

Only when Dot arrived at her last observation about reading and its ability to transport her out of her living room did I begin to understand that the real answer to my question, which she never mentioned and which was the link between reading, pills, and drinks, was actually the single word, "escape," a word that would later appear on so many of the questionnaires. She subsequently explained that romance novels provide escape just as Darvon and alcohol do for other women. Whereas the latter are harmful to both women and their families, Dot believes romance reading is "an innocuous thing." As she commented to me in another interview, romance reading is a habit that is not very different from "an addiction."

Although some of the other Smithton women expressed uneasiness about the suitability of the addiction analogy, as did Dot in another interview, nearly all of the original sixteen who participated in lengthy conversations agreed that one of their principal goals in reading was their desire to do something *different* from their daily routine. That claim was borne out by their answers to the open-ended question about the functions of romance reading. At this point, it seems worth quoting a few of those fourteen replies that expressly volunteered the ideas of escape and release. The Smithton readers explained the power of the romance in the following way:

> They are light reading—escape literature—I can put down and pick up effortlessly.

> Everyone is always under so much pressure. They like books that let them escape.

> Escapism.

> I guess I feel there is enough "reality" in the world and reading is a means of escape for me.

> Because it is an Escape [*sic*], and we can dream and pretend that it is our life.

> I'm able to escape the harsh world for a few hours a day.

> They always seem an escape and they usually turn out the way you wish life really was.

The response of the Smithton women is apparently not an unusual one. Indeed, the advertising campaigns of three of the houses that have conducted extensive market-research studies all emphasize the themes of relaxation and escape. Potential readers of Coventry Romances, for example, have been told in coupon ads that "month after month Coventry Romances offer you a beautiful new escape route into historical times when love and honor ruled the heart and mind."[2] Similarly, the Silhouette television advertisements featuring Ricardo Montalban asserted that "the beautiful ending makes you feel so good" and that romances "soothe away the tensions of the day." Montalban also touted the value of "escaping" into faraway places and exotic locales. Harlequin once mounted a travel sweepstakes campaign offering as prizes "escape vacations" to romantic places. In addition, they included within the books themselves an advertising page that described Harlequins as "the books that let you escape into the wonderful world of romance! Trips to exotic places . . . interesting places . . . meeting memorable people . . . the excitement of love. . . . These are integral parts of Harlequin Romances—the heartwarming novels read by women everywhere."[3] Fawcett, too, seems to have discovered the escape function of romance fiction, for Daisy Maryles has reported that the company found in in-depth interviewing that "romances were read for relaxation and to enable [women] to better cope with the routine aspects of life."[4]

Reading to escape the present is neither a new behavior nor one peculiar to women who read romances. In fact, as Richard Hoggart demonstrated in 1957, English working-class people have long "regarded art as escape, as something enjoyed but not assumed to have much connection with the matter of daily life."[5] Within this sort of aesthetic, he continues, art is conceived as "marginal, as 'fun,'" as something "for you to *use*." In further elaborating on this notion of fictional escape, D. W. Harding has made the related observation that the word is most often used in criticism as a term of disparagement to refer to an activity that the evaluator believes has no merit in and of itself. "If its intrinsic appeal is high," he remarks, "in relation to its compensatory appeal or the mere relief it promises, then the term escape is not generally used."[6] Harding argues, moreover, on the basis of studies conducted in the 1930s, that "the compensatory appeal predominates mainly in states of depression or irritation, whether they arise from work or other causes."[7] It is interesting to note that the explanations employed by Dot and her women to interpret their romance reading for themselves are thus representative in a general way of a form of behavior common in an industrialized society where work is clearly distinguished from and more highly valued than leisure despite the fact that individual labor is often routinized, regimented, and minimally challenging.[8] It is equally essential to add, however, that although the women will use the word "escape" to explain their reading behavior, if given another comparable choice that does not carry the connotations of disparagement, they will choose the more favorable sounding explanation. To understand why, it will be helpful to follow Dot's comments more closely.

In returning to her definition of the appeal of romance fiction—a definition that is a highly condensed version of a commonly experienced process of explanation, doubt, and defensive justification—it becomes clear that romance novels perform this compensatory function for women because they use them to diversify the pace and character of their habitual existence. Dot makes it clear, however, that the women are also troubled about the propriety of indulging in such an obviously pleasurable activity. Their doubts are often cultivated into a full-grown feeling of guilt by husbands and children who object to this activity because it draws the women's attention away from the immediate family circle. As Dot later noted, although some women can explain to their families that a desire for a new toy or gadget is no different from a desire to read a new romantic novel, a far greater number of them have found it necessary to hide the evidence of their self-indulgence. In an effort to combat both the resentment of others and their own feelings of shame about their "hedonist" behavior, the women have worked out a complex rationalization for romance reading that not only asserts their equal right to pleasure but also legitimates the books by linking them with values more widely approved within American culture. Before turning to the pattern, however, I want to elaborate on the concept of escape itself and the reasons for its ability to produce such resentment and guilt in the first place.

Both the escape response and the relaxation response on the second questionnaire immediately raise other questions. Relaxation implies a reduction in the state of tension produced by prior conditions, whereas escape obviously suggests flight from one state of being to another more desirable one.[9] To understand the sense of the romance experience, then, as it is enjoyed by those who consider it a welcome change in their day-to-day existence, it becomes necessary to situate it within a larger temporal context and to specify precisely how the act of reading manages to create that feeling of change and differentiation so highly valued by these readers.

In attending to the women's comments about the worth of romance reading, I was particularly struck by the fact that they tended to use the word escape in two distinct ways. On the one hand, they used the term literally to describe the act of denying the present, which they believe they accomplish each time they begin to read a book and are drawn into its story. On the other hand, they used the word in a more figurative fashion to give substance to the somewhat vague but nonetheless intense sense of relief they experience by identifying with a heroine whose life does not resemble their own in certain crucial aspects. I think it important to reproduce this subtle distinction as accurately as possible because it indicates that romance reading releases women from their present pressing concerns in two different but related ways.

Dot, for example, went on to elaborate more fully in the conversation quoted above about why so many husbands seem to feel threatened by their wives' reading activities. After declaring with delight that when she reads her body is in the room but she herself is not, she said, "I think this is the case with the other women." She continued, "I think men cannot do that unless they themselves are readers. I don't think men are *ever* a part of anything even if it's television." "They are never really out of their body either," she added. "I don't care if it's a football game; I think they are always consciously aware of where they are." Her triumphant conclusion, "but I think a woman in a book isn't," indicates that Dot is aware that reading not only demands a high level of attention but also draws the individual *into* the book because it requires her participation. Although she is not sure what it is about the book that prompts this absorption, she is quite sure that television viewing and film watching are different. In adding immediately that "for some reason, a lot of men feel threatened by this, very, very much threatened," Dot suggested that the men's resentment has little to do with the kinds of books their wives are reading and more to do with the simple fact of the activity itself and its capacity to absorb the participants' entire attention.

These tentative observations were later corroborated in the conversations I had with other readers. Ellen, for instance, a former airline stewardess, now married and taking care of her home, indicated that she also reads for "entertainment and escape." However, she added, her husband sometimes objects to her reading because he wants her to watch the same television show he has selected. She "hates" this, she said, because she does not like the kinds of programs on television today. She is delighted when he gets a business call in the evening because her husband's preoccupation with his caller permits her to go back to her book.

Penny, another housewife in her middle thirties, also indicated that her husband "resents it" if she reads too much. "He feels shut out," she explained, "but there is nothing on TV I enjoy." Like Ellen's husband, Penny's spouse also wants her to watch television with him. Susan, a woman in her fifties, also "read[s] to escape" and related with almost no bitterness that her husband will not permit her to continue reading when he is ready to go to sleep. She seems to regret rather than resent this only because it limits the amount of time she can spend in an activity she finds enjoyable. Indeed, she went on in our conversation to explain that she occasionally gives herself "a very special treat" when she is "tired of housework." "I take the whole day off," she said, "to read."

This theme of romance reading as a special gift a woman gives herself dominated most of the interviews. The Smithton women stressed the privacy of the act and the fact that it enables them to focus their attention on a single object that can provide pleasure for themselves alone. Interestingly enough, Robert Escarpit has noted in related fashion that reading is at once "social and asocial" because "it temporarily suppresses the individual's relations with his [*sic*] universe to construct new ones with the universe of the work."[10] Unlike television viewing, which is a very social activity undertaken in the presence of others and which permits simultaneous conversation and personal interaction, silent reading requires the reader to block out the surrounding world and to give consideration to other people and to another time. It might be said, then, that the characters and events of romance fiction populate the woman's consciousness even as she withdraws from the familiar social scene of her daily ministrations.

I use the word ministrations deliberately here because the Smithton women explained to me that they are not trying to escape their husbands and children "per se" when they read. Rather, what reading takes them away from, they believe, is the psychologically demanding and emotionally draining task of attending to the physical and affective needs of their families, a task that is solely and peculiarly theirs. In other words, these women, who have been educated to believe that females are especially and naturally attuned to the emotional requirements of others and who are very proud of their abilities to communicate with and to serve the members of their families, value reading precisely because it is an intensely private act. Not only is the activity private, however, but it also enables them to suspend temporarily those familial relationships and to throw up a screen between themselves and the arena where they are required to do most of their relating to others.

It was Dot who first advised me about this phenomenon. Her lengthy commentary, transcribed below, enabled me to listen carefully to the other readers' discussions of escape and to hear the distinction nearly all of them made between escape from their families, which they believe they do *not* do, and escape from the heavy responsibilities and duties of the roles of wife and mother, which they admit they do out of emotional need and necessity. Dot explained their activity, for instance, by paraphrasing the thought process she believes goes on in her customers' minds. "Hey," they say, "this is what I want to do and I'm gonna do it. This is for me. I'm doin' for you all the time. Now leave me, just leave me alone. Let me have my time, my space. Let me do what I want to do. This isn't hurting you. I'm not poaching on you in any way." She then went on to elaborate about her own duties as a mother and wife:

> As a mother, I have run 'em to the orthodontist. I have run 'em to the swimming pool. I have run 'em to baton twirling lessons. I have run up to school because they forgot their lunch. You know, I mean, really! And you do it. And it isn't that you begrudge it. That isn't it. Then my husband would walk in the door and he'd say, "Well, what did you do today?" You know, it was like, "Well, tell me how you spent the last eight hours, because I've been out working." And I finally got to the point where I would say, "Well, I read four books, and I did all the wash and got the meal on the table and the beds are all made, and the house is tidy." And I would get defensive like, "So

what do you call all this? Why should I have to tell you because I certainly don't ask you what you did for eight hours, step by step."— But their husbands do do that. We've compared notes. They hit the house and it's like "Well all right, I've been out earning a living. Now what have you been doin' with your time?" And you begin to be feeling, "Now really, why is he questioning me?"

Romance reading, it would seem, at least for Dot and many of her customers, is a strategy with a double purpose. As an activity, it so engages their attention that it enables them to deny their physical presence in an environment associated with responsibilities that are acutely felt and occasionally experienced as too onerous to bear. Reading, in this sense, connotes a free space where they feel liberated from the need to perform duties that they otherwise willingly accept as their own. At the same time, by carefully choosing stories that make them feel particularly happy, they escape figuratively into a fairy tale where a heroine's similar needs are adequately met. As a result, they vicariously attend to their own requirements as independent individuals who require emotional sustenance and solicitude.

Angie's account of her favorite reading time graphically represents the significance of romance reading as a tool to help insure a woman's sense of emotional well-being. "I like it," she says, "when my husband—he's an insurance salesman—goes out in the evening on house calls. Because then I have two hours just to totally relax." She continued, "I love to settle in a hot bath with a good book. That's really great." We might conclude, then, that reading a romance is a regressive experience for these women in the sense that for the duration of the time devoted to it they feel gratified and content. This feeling of pleasure seems to derive from their identification with a heroine whom they believe is deeply appreciated and tenderly cared for by another. Somewhat paradoxically, however, they also seem to value the sense of self-sufficiency they experience as a consequence of the knowledge that they are capable of making themselves feel good.

Nancy Chodorow's observations about the social structure of the American family in the twentieth century help to illuminate the context that creates both the feminine need for emotional support and validation and the varied strategies that have evolved to meet it. As Chodorow points out, most recent studies of the family agree that women traditionally reproduce people, as she says, "physically in their housework and child care, psychologically in their emotional support of husbands and their maternal relation to sons and daughters."[11] This state of affairs occurs, these studies maintain, because women alone are held responsible for home maintenance and early child care. Ann Oakley's 1971 study of forty London housewives, for instance, led her to the following conclusion: "In the housekeeping role the servicing function is far more central than the productive or creative one. In the roles of wife and mother, also, the image of women as servicers of men's and children's needs is prominent: women 'service' the labour force by catering to the physical needs of men (workers) and by raising children (the next generation of workers) so that the men are free *from* child-socialization and free *to* work outside the home."[12] This social fact, documented also by Mirra Komarovsky, Helena Lopata, and others, is reinforced ideologically by the widespread belief that females are *naturally* nurturant and generous, more selfless than men, and, therefore, cheerfully self-abnegating. A good wife and mother, it is assumed, will have no difficulty meeting the challenge of providing all of the labor necessary to maintain a family's physical existence including the cleaning of its quarters, the acquisition and preparation of its food, and the purchase, repair, and upkeep of its clothes, even while she masterfully discerns and supplies individual members' psychological needs.[13] A woman's interests, this version of "the female mystique" maintains, are exactly congruent with those of her husband and children. In serving them, she also serves herself.[14]

As Chodorow notes, not only are the women expected to perform this extraordinarily demanding task, but they are also supposed to be capable of executing it without being formally "reproduced" and supported themselves. "What is . . . often hidden, in generalizations about the family as an emotional refuge," she cautions, "is that in the family as it is currently constituted no one supports and reconstitutes women affectively and emotionally—either women working in the home or women working in the paid labor force."[15] Although she admits, of course, that the accident of individual marriage occasionally provides a woman with an unusually nurturant and "domestic" husband, her principal argument is that as a social institution the contemporary family contains no role whose principal task is the reproduction and emotional support of the wife and mother. "There is a fundamental asymmetry in daily reproduction," Chodorow concludes, "men are socially and psychologically reproduced by women, but women are reproduced (or not) largely by themselves."[16]

That this lack of emotional nurturance combined with the high costs of lavishing constant attention on others is the primary motivation behind the desire to lose the self in a book was made especially clear to me in a group conversation that occurred late in my stay in Smithton. The discussion involved Dot, one of her customers, Ann, who is married and in her thirties, and Dot's unmarried, twenty-three-year-old daughter, Kit. In response to my question, "Can you tell me what you escape from?," Dot and Ann together explained that reading keeps them from being overwhelmed by expectations and limitations. It seems advisable to include their entire conversation here, for it specifies rather precisely the source of those felt demands:

Dot: All right, there are pressures. Meeting your bills, meeting whatever standards or requirements your husband has for you or whatever your children have for you.

Ann: Or that you feel you should have. Like doing the housework just so.

Dot: And they do come to you with problems. Maybe they don't want you to—let's see—maybe they don't want you to solve it, but they certainly want to unload on you. You know. Or they say, "Hey, I've got this problem."

Ann: Those pressures build up.

Dot: Yeah, it's pressures.

Ann: You should be able to go to one of those good old—like the MGM musicals and just . . .

Dot: True.

Ann: Or one of those romantic stories and cry a little bit and relieve the pressure and—a legitimate excuse to cry and relieve some of the pressure build-up and not be laughed at.

Dot: That's true.

Ann: And you don't find that much anymore. I've had to go to books for it.

Dot: This is better than psychiatry.

Ann: Because I cry over books. I get wrapped up in them.

Dot: I do too. I sob in books! Oh yes. I think that's escape. Now I'm not gonna say I've got to escape my husband by reading. No.

Ann: No.

Dot: Or that I'm gonna escape my kids by getting my nose in a book. It isn't any one of those things. It's just—it's pressures that evolve from being what you are.

Kit: In this society.

Dot: And people do pressure you. Inadvertently, maybe.

Ann: Yes, it's being more and more restrictive. You can't do this and you can't do that.[17]

This conversation revealed that these women believe romance reading enables them to relieve tensions, to diffuse resentment, and to indulge in a fantasy that provides them with good feelings that seem to endure after they return to their roles as wives and mothers. Romance fiction, as they experience it, is, therefore, *compensatory literature*. It supplies them with an important emotional release that is proscribed in daily life because the social role with which they identify themselves leaves little room for guiltless, self-interested pursuit of individual pleasure. Indeed, the search for emotional gratification was the one theme common to all of the women's observations about the function of romance reading. Maureen, for instance, a young mother of two intellectually gifted children, volunteered, "I especially like to read when I'm depressed." When asked what usually caused her depression, she commented that it could be all kinds of things. Later she added that romances were comforting after her children had been especially demanding and she felt she needed time to herself.

In further discussing the lack of institutionalized emotional support suffered by contemporary American women, Chodorow has observed that in many preindustrial societies women formed their own social networks through which they supported and reconstituted one another.[18] Many of these networks found secondary institutional support in the local church while others simply operated as informal neighborhood societies. In either case, the networks provided individual women with the opportunity to abandon temporarily their stance as the family's self-sufficient emotional provider. They could then adopt a more passive role through which they received the attention, sympathy, and encouragement of other women. With the increasing suburbanization of women, however, and the concomitant secularization of the culture at large, these communities became exceedingly difficult to maintain. The principal effect was the even more resolute isolation of women within their domestic environment. Indeed, both Oakley in Great Britain and Lopata in the United States have discovered that one of the features housewives dislike most about their role is its isolation and resulting loneliness.[19]

I introduce Chodorow's observations here in order to suggest that through romance reading the Smithton women are providing themselves with another kind of female community capable of rendering the so desperately needed affective support. This community seems not to operate on an immediate local level although there are signs, both in Smithton and nationally, that romance readers are learning the pleasures of regular discussions of books with other women.[20] Nonetheless, during the early group discussions with Dot and her readers I was surprised to discover that very few of her customers knew each other. In fact, most of them had never been formally introduced although they recognized one another as customers of Dot. I soon learned that the women rarely, if ever, discussed romances with more than one or two individuals. Although many commented that they talked about the books with a sister, neighbor, or with their mothers, very few did so on a regular or extended basis. Indeed, the most striking feature of the interview sessions was the delight with which they discovered common experiences, preferences, and distastes. As one woman exclaimed in the middle of a discussion, "We were never stimulated before into thinking why we like [the novels]. Your asking makes us think why we do this. I had no idea other people had the same ideas I do."

The romance community, then, is not an actual group functioning at the local level. Rather, it is a huge, ill-defined network composed of readers on the one hand and authors on the other. Although it performs some of the same functions carried out by older neighborhood groups, this female community is mediated by the distances of modern mass publishing. Despite the distance, the Smithton women feel personally connected to their favorite authors because they are convinced that these writers know how to make them happy. Many volunteered information about favorite authors even before they would discuss specific books or heroines. All expressed admiration for their favorite writers and indicated that they were especially curious about their private lives. Three-fourths of the group of sixteen had made special trips to autographing sessions to see and express their gratitude to the women who had given them so much pleasure. The authors reciprocate this feeling of gratitude and seem genuinely interested in pleasing their readers. As has been noted in Chapter 2, many are themselves romance readers and, as a consequence, they, too, often have definite opinions about the particular writers who know how to make the reading experience truly enjoyable.[21]

It seems highly probable that in repetitively reading and writing romances, these women are participating in a collectively elaborated female fantasy that unfailingly ends at the precise moment when the heroine is gathered into the arms of the hero who declares his intention to protect her forever because of his desperate love and need for her. These women are telling themselves a story whose central vision is one of total surrender where all danger has been expunged, thus permitting the heroine to relinquish self-control. Passivity *is* at the heart of the romance experience in the sense that the final goal of each narrative is the creation of that perfect union where the ideal male, who is masculine and strong yet nurturant too, finally recognizes the intrinsic worth of the heroine. Thereafter, she is required to do nothing more than *exist* as the center of this paragon's attention. Romantic escape is, therefore, a temporary but literal denial of the demands women recognize as an integral part of their roles as nurturing wives and mothers. It is also a figurative journey to a utopian state of total receptiveness where the reader, as a result of her identification with the heroine, feels herself the *object* of someone else's attention and solicitude. Ultimately, the romance permits its reader the experience of feeling cared for and the sense of having been reconstituted affectively, even if both are lived only vicariously.

Dot's readers openly admit that parts of the romantic universe little resemble the world as they know it. When asked by the questionnaire how closely the fictional characters resemble the people they meet in real life, twenty-two answered "they are not at all similar," eighteen checked "they are somewhat similar," and two asserted that "they are very similar." None of Dot's customers believed that romantic characters are "almost identical" to those they meet daily.[22] In a related set of responses, twenty-three revealed that they consider the events in romances to be "not at all similar" to those occurring in real life. An additional eighteen said that the two sets of events are "somewhat similar," while only one checked "very similar."

It is interesting to note, however, that when the questionnaire asked them to compare the heroine's reactions and feelings with their own, only thirteen saw no resemblance whatsoever, while twenty-two believed that the heroine's feelings "are somewhat like mine." Five women did not answer the question. The general shift from perceptions of no similarity to detection of some resemblance suggests that Dot's readers believe that the heroine is more realistically portrayed than other characters. At the very least, they recognize something of themselves in her feelings and responses. Thus while the lack of similarity between events in the fantasy realm and those in the real world seems to guarantee a reading experience that is "escapist," emotional identification with the central character also insures that the experience will be an affectively significant one for the reader.

These conclusions are supported by comments about the nature of escape reading culled from the interviews. Jill, a very young mother of two, who had also begun to write her own romance, commented, for example, that "we read books so we won't cry." When asked to elaborate, she responded only that romances portray the world as "I would like it to be, not as it really is." In discussing why she preferred historicals to contemporary romances, Susan explained that "the characters shouldn't be like now because then you couldn't read to escape." "I don't want to read about people who have all the problems of today's world," she added. Her sentiments were echoed by Joy who mentioned in her discussion of "bad romances" that while "perfection's not the main thing," she still hates to see an author "dwelling on handicaps or disfigurements." "I find that distasteful and depressing," she explained. This sort of desire to encounter only idealized images is carried over even into meetings with romance authors. Several told of their disappointment at meeting a favorite writer at an autograph session who was neither pretty nor attractively dressed. All agreed, however, that Kathleen Woodiwiss is the ideal romance author because she is pretty, petite, feminine, and always elegantly turned out.

When I pursued this unwillingness to read about ugliness, despair, or serious human problems with Dot, she indignantly responded, "Why should we read depressing stuff when we have so much responsibility?"

Ann made a similar remark, mentioning that she particularly dislikes books that attribute the hero's "nastiness" toward the heroine to a bad love affair that soured him on other women. When I asked her for her reasons, she said, "because *we've* been through it, we've been ditched, and it didn't sour us!" This comment led immediately to the further observation, "Optimistic! That's what I like in a book. An optimistic plot. I get sick of pessimism all the time."

Her distinction between optimistic and pessimistic stories recurred during several of the interviews, especially during discussions of the difference between romances and other books. At least four of the women mentioned Colleen McCullough's best-selling novel, *The Thorn Birds*, as a good example of a tale that technically qualified as a romance but that all disliked because it was too "depressing." When urged to specify what made the story pessimistic, none cited specific events in the plot or the death of the hero. Rather, they referred to the general tenor of the story and to the fact that the characters were poor. "Too much suffering," one reader concluded. In similarly discussing a writer whose books she never enjoys, Dot also mentioned the problem of the depressing romance and elaborated on her usual response to such a story. She described her typical argument with herself as follows:

> "Well, Dorothy, you were absolutely, physically exhausted, mentally exhausted because everything was down—it was depressing." And I'd get through it and it was excellently written but everyone worked in the coal mines. They were poor as church mice. They couldn't make ends meet. Somebody was raped, an illegitimate kid. By the time I got through, I said, "What am I reading this for? This is dumb." So I quit.

Dot's sentiments were echoed by Ann when she volunteered the information that she dislikes historical romances set in Ireland, "because they always mention the potato famine" and "I tend to get depressed about that."

In a related discussion, Dot's daughter, Kit, observed that an unhappy ending is the most depressing thing that can happen in a romance. She believes, in fact, as does nearly everyone else, that an unhappy ending excludes a novel that is otherwise a romantic love story from the romance category. Kit is only one of the many who insist on reading the endings of the stories *before* they buy them to insure that they will not be saddened by emotionally investing in the tale of a heroine only to discover that events do not resolve themselves as they should. Although this latter kind of intolerance for ambiguity and unhappiness is particularly extreme, it is indicative of a tendency among Dot's customers to avoid any kind of reading matter that does not conform to their rigid requirements for "optimism" and escapist stories. Romances are valuable to them in proportion to their lack of resemblance to the real world. They choose their romances carefully in an attempt to assure themselves of a reading experience that will make them feel happy and hold out the promise of utopian bliss, a state they willingly acknowledge to be rare in the real world but one, nevertheless, that they do not want to relinquish as a conceptual possibility.

In discussing the therapeutic function of true fairy stories and folk tales, Bruno Bettelheim has argued that they perform the fundamental service for children of creating and maintaining *hope*.[23] Because he believes folk tales take as their true subject the psychosexual traumas of early childhood and that they are psychologically "true" in the sense that they symbolically demonstrate how these conflicts can be resolved, Bettelheim maintains that they act as emotional primers for the children who imaginatively participate in them. Not only do they indicate specific psychological solutions to problems such as separation anxiety and the Oedipal conflict, but they also hold out the promise of future solution for the child who cannot see the way to negotiate the necessary journey at the present moment. Bettelheim believes that children are actually encouraged by their experience of identification with a character whose remarkably similar problems are happily resolved. "We know," he writes, "that the more deeply unhappy and despairing we are, the more we need to be able to engage in optimistic fantasies."[24] He continues that "while the fantasy is *unreal*, the good feelings it gives us about ourselves and our future *are real*, and these good feelings are what we need to sustain us."

I want to argue similarly that by participating in a fantasy that they are willing to admit is unrealistic in some ways, the Smithton women are permitting themselves the luxury of self-indulgence while simultaneously providing themselves with the opportunity to experience the kind of care and attention they commonly give to others. Although this experience *is* vicarious, the pleasure it induces is nonetheless real. It seems to sustain them, at least temporarily, for they believe reading helps to make them happier people and endows them with renewed hope and greater energy to fulfill their duty to others. Later, it will be necessary to consider the question of whether romance fiction is actually deflecting or recontaining an indigenous impulse to express dissatisfaction with the traditional status quo in the family by persuading women to feel more content with their role. However, since that question can be addressed only after the entire reading experience has been assessed, a task that will be attempted in Chapters 4, 5, and 6, it is now time to return to the query posed earlier about why the act of romance reading is threatening to men. I also want to consider the subsequent justification process such male resentment sets in motion before moving on to an analysis of the larger significance of this entire explanation-guilt-justification process.

To begin with, it is evident that the Smithton women believe that their husbands object to the simple fact that reading draws their wives' attention away from the immediate familial context and from themselves more specifically. They may also feel unsettled by their wives' evident ability to satisfy themselves emotionally, a situation that perhaps suggests a reduction in their spouses' dependency upon them. This is merely speculation, however, for I neither asked questions of their husbands nor did I probe very deeply into the issue of whether romance reading *actually* changes a woman's behavior in her marriage. It is important to note, nonetheless, that the women themselves vehemently maintain that their reading has transformed them in important ways.

I accidentally stumbled across this belief in the course of observing the relish with which they described their favorite heroines whom they invariably characterized as "extremely intelligent," "spunky," "independent," and "unique." It occurred to me to ask whether reading about such heroines changed the women's perception of themselves. When I finally posed the query of whether romance reading ever changes women, it was met with gales of disbelieving laughter whose force cannot be conveyed on paper. Dot, Ann, and Kit answered at once and the overlapping exclamations on the tape include "Yes," "Oh, yes," "You better believe it," "Ask the men," and "Of course," which was shouted with happy indignation. They immediately came up with the names of three women who had been dramatically changed and then collectively told the story of June Anderson and her husband, Sam, who believed, my informants told me, "that the gods were talking to him!" I think it best to let them give their version of the transformation here:

Dot: She was such a sweet little thing. It's not that she isn't anymore. But she was under his thumb.
Ann: He was the ruler of the roost, the king of the domain; his word was all-seeing, all-knowing, all-omnipotent!
Dot: And now she knows all, sees all, hears all.
Ann: Yes.
Dot: She's just smart enough not to tell him all.
Kit: Now, the same gods are talking to her!
       [They collapse in laughter.]
Dot: And the thing is she was doing it *all*. She was makin' his life one slide, buttered well! And here he was, you know, thinkin', "boy my house is in tip-top shape."
Ann: Yup.

Dot: And then she got ahold of books and it's been really a shame!
[More laughter.]

They went on to tell the story of how June had her hair cut one day
despite the fact that Sam insisted she keep it long. Of course, it is not
possible to say for sure whether this act had anything to do with her
romance reading. The important point is that both she and her sister
readers believe that it did. Dot even concluded the story with the assertion
that June had gone out and secured a job in order to pay for her books.
She added that this is not uncommon because so many of her customers
have to justify book purchases to husbands who resent the expenditure of
"their" money on an activity that has no clear function or use, at least as
far as they are concerned.

Dot contended in a later conversation that, strangely enough, it is the
bad romances that most often start the women thinking. A bad romance,
the reader should recall, is often characterized by a weak or gullible heroine. In reading some of those "namby-pamby books about the women
who lets the man dominate them," Dot explained, the readers "are thinking 'they're nerds.' And they begin to reevaluate. 'Am I acting like that?'"
They begin to say to themselves, she added, "Hey, wait a minute—my old
man kinda tends to do this." And then, "because women are capable of
learning from what they read," they begin "to express what they want and
sometimes refuse to be ordered around any longer."

In attempting to corroborate Dot's assertion by questioning her customers about this issue, I found that most agree that romance reading
does change a woman, although very few would go beyond that simple
statement. I could not discern whether they could not articulate how they
had been affected or whether they did not want to talk about it for fear of
admitting something that might then lead to further change. They made it
clear, however, that they believe their self-perception has been favorably
transformed by their reading. They are convinced, in fact, that romance
fiction demonstrates that "intelligence" and "independence" in a woman
make her more attractive to a man. Although marriage is still the idealized
goal in all of the novels they like best, that marriage is always characterized
by the male partner's recognition and appreciation of the heroine's saucy
assertion of her right to defy outmoded conventions and manners. This
fiction encourages them to believe that marriage and motherhood do not
necessarily lead to loss of independence or identity.

Such feelings of hope and encouragement, it must be pointed out, are
never purchased cheaply. Dot and her readers understandably pay a substantial price in guilt and self-doubt as a result of their temporary refusal
to adopt the self-abnegating stance that is so integral a part of the roles of
wife, mother, and housewife which they otherwise embrace as acceptable

for themselves and other women. This guilt was conveyed most often in the earnestness with which the women insisted that they too have a right to do something for themselves always immediately after explaining that they read "to escape." Although this sort of evidence is difficult to pin down and certainly subject to varying interpretation, I found their extreme defensiveness about the amount of time and money spent on reading so compelling that I think it important not to ignore these only partially acknowledged feelings of culpability.

Guilt seems to arise over three specific aspects of romance reading. The Smithton readers are most troubled about the quantity of time they devote to their books. They are aware that this activity demands the attention that would otherwise be devoted to children, house, or husband, but they defend themselves with the assertion that they have a right to escape just as others do. Indeed, one of their most effective strategies for justification involves the equation of romance reading with other forms of escape, especially with participation in and attendance at sports events, which are activities enjoyed by most of their husbands. Dot commented with some irritation, for instance, that "women have been very tolerant of that in men. But, do you know, when a woman picks up a book, a man's not tolerant of it? Nine times out of ten he's not." Her customers confirm her assertion, but they also demonstrate, however, that they are not comfortable with their own unaccustomed defiance. They confess that they sometimes hide their books and usually acquiesce to their spouses' wishes if they specifically demand their complete attention. Romance reading, then, is an acceptable way of securing emotional sustenance not provided by others *only* if the activity can be accomplished without mounting a fundamental challenge to the previous balance of power in the marriage relationship. It is a method of garnering attention for the self that creates a minimum amount of dissonance between accepted role expectations and actual behavior precisely because the assertion of self-interest is temporary and expressed through leisure pursuits that are relatively less significant than other areas of concern.

A second difficulty seems to arise over the amount of money spent on books as many of the Smithton women report that they are often called to task by their husbands for their repetitive consumption. Their most common response is the astute observation that neither their husbands nor their children worry about duplicating tools, gadgets, toys, or clothes they already have when they express interest in acquiring new ones. The women wonder, then, why they should have to adhere to standards of thrift and parsimony with respect to books when other family members do not observe the same requirements. Despite this sense of fair play, however, many of the readers still seem ill at ease spending money that they did not earn on a pleasure that is at least questionable, if not downright objectionable, to their husbands. They are more comfortable with a picture of themselves as generous and giving mothers who would sooner spend money on other members of the family than on themselves. As Dot explained of her customers, "Not one of my women hankers after the beautiful clothes and jewels of the women in the Regencies. They're not like that." She believes that if it came down to choosing between something for themselves and something for their children, they would certainly spend their money on their children. I found nothing in my interviews with those customers to contradict her assertion. Indeed, the Smithton readers struck me as genuinely troubled by their simultaneous attempt to buy generously for their families and to admit their own need and right to spend on themselves. Every customer with whom I talked expressed some concern about whether she spent too much money on herself, and several even questioned me rhetorically about whether I agreed that they had a "right" to buy things that gave them pleasure.

This concern about expenditure is further exacerbated by a third worry concerning the subject matter of the books. Dot and her customers are aware that many critics label the books they love soft-core pornography. In fact, at the time of my first visit, Dot's success in the romance field had recently been the focus of a scornful feature in one of the local newspapers. Although the reporter had questioned her at length about why women read romances, he ignored her careful explanations in order to assert that housewives are getting their kicks in the afternoon from "pornographic" love stories. This article deeply offended Dot and her readers who were especially angered by the fact that the reporter was male. They insist that the books are not about sex but about romance and cite in conversation their preference for novels that lack explicit sexual description. Many of the women admit that they are especially embarrassed by the graphic representation of "cleavage and nudity" that publishers insist on attaching to the books. This has sometimes forced them to hide their books from their children or the public "so the public won't get the wrong idea." Dot's customers almost unanimously prefer covers that depict a tender caress between a fully clothed hero and heroine or one that includes small vignettes portraying key scenes in the novel.

However, if we also recall their answers to my question about the necessary features of ideal romances, it becomes clear that while the Smithton women are obviously interested in a story chronicling the development of a single romance, most are not offended by sexual description if the act occurs between two individuals whom the writer has established as already "in love." Remember, thirteen women did indicate that they like to see "lots of love scenes with some explicit sexual description." Still, the fact that so many of the women object to bed-hopping demonstrates that, in their minds at least, sex is unalterably linked with the idea of romantic love. They believe the act is rightly indulged in only by those who have made a monogamous commitment to each other. As discussed in the previous chapter, "bed-hopping" is a term employed by Dot and her customers to describe promiscuous sexual relations between a heroine and several men. They vehemently object to this sort of narrative. Indeed, the women ardently asserted again and again in the interviews that it is the "one woman–one man" kind of book that they prefer.

Despite their evident ability to tolerate certain kinds of sexual description, I think the readers' assertion that such detail ought to be subordinated, in the words of one woman, "to tenderness and the expression of emotional love," should be accepted as given. The women are not being disingenuous when they maintain that "the story is the main thing," for indeed what they want to experience above all else is the hero's protective concern and tender regard for the heroine. It matters little whether that care and attention are detailed in general terms or presented as overtly sexual as long as they are extensively described. However, this focus on his attention to her is in itself erotic, for even the most euphemistic descriptions of the heroine's reception of his regard convey the sensual, corporal pleasure she feels in anticipating, encouraging, and finally accepting those attentions of a hero who is always depicted as magnetic, powerful, and physically pleasing. While explicit description of his bodily reaction is offensive to the Smithton readers, attention to the heroine's response to his appreciation of her physical beauty is not only desirable but absolutely central to the entire event. Although the readers are themselves reluctant to admit this on a conscious level, romance reading seems to be valued primarily because it provides an occasion for them to experience good feelings. Those feelings appear to be remarkably close to the erotic anticipation, excitement, and contentment prompted when any individual is the object of another's total attention. In effect, romance reading provides a vicarious experience of emotional nurturance *and* erotic anticipation and excitation.

Guilt arises, then, as a result of the readers' own uneasiness about indulging in such an obviously pleasurable experience as much as it does as the consequence of others' disapproval. This guilt is the understandable result of their socialization within a culture that continues to value work above leisure and play, both of which still seem to carry connotations of frivolousness for the Smithton women. Their guilt can also be traced to a culture that remains uneasy about the free expression of female sexuality even as it unabashedly sells everything, from jeans to typewriters, with the aid of sexual imagery. On the one hand, American women are told by mass-media symbolism that their very worth as individuals is closely tied to their sexual allure and physical beauty. On the other hand, they are educated by their families and churches to believe that their sexual being may be activated only by and for one other individual. The double message effectively produces a conflicted response to sexual need and desire.

Because the implicit content of the cultural message linking female identity with sexual attractiveness stipulates that a woman's value is produced *only* when she is recognized by a man, women who accept this image of themselves must seek validation as sexually desirable partners. If, however, this validation is not regularly forthcoming in day-to-day existence, the search for it must be abandoned altogether or modified, either by accepting validation only when it is offered or by seeking it elsewhere. It seems evident that these obsessive romance readers have selected the latter course, searching for constant reassurance about their value through repetitive identification with a woman whose sexuality is only just being awakened and who discovers, as a consequence, that she is a truly valuable human being worthy of love and attention. Indeed, one of Dot's most articulate customers, who incidentally likes Civil War novels, confirmed this when she said, "I like the hero to be a gentlemanly Yankee soldier—a real lover-boy type who knows instantly what the heroine is like and is attracted to that." She believes that this instant recognition is a function of "love at first sight." "Isn't it weird," she asked, "how men *know* us—I mean—how they instantly know what we're like?" "Yes," she concluded, "I like a hero who can instantly pick out the woman as unique, special, as his *true* love!" Although she does not say so, it is clear that underlying her statement is the implicit assertion that what she finds enjoyable about Civil War romances is the pleasurable feeling *she* gets by identifying with a woman who is passionately loved, tenderly cared for, and carefully protected expressly because her intrinsic nature has been recognized by another.

In trying to satisfy culturally induced psychological needs and desires that can be met fully only through activities that are themselves illogically proscribed or limited, the Smithton readers have found it necessary to fill their needs vicariously. Yet even this ingenious solution to the cultural "catch 22" causes problems because in internalizing their culture's demand that female sexuality be realized only within the bonds of marriage, they accept a standard that brands their desire for an erotic and romantic literature as perverse and morally wrong. Of course, the women are neither, but the guilt remains. Fortunately for them, however, they have devised an explanation for why they read romantic novels based on values more acceptable to the culture at large and to men in particular. This explanation helps them to counteract the doubt they experience about the worth of romantic fiction. By claiming for it instructional value, they reassure themselves and their husbands that romance reading is not subversive of cultural standards or norms but an activity in conformity with them.

In embarking for Smithton, I was prepared to engage in detailed conversations about the connections between love and sex, the differences between romance and pornography, and the continued validity of traditional definitions of femininity. I was not, however, prepared to spend as much time as I did conversing about the encyclopedic nature of romance fiction. When I questioned Dot and her customers about why they like romances, I was surprised to find that immediately after extolling their benefits as an "escape," nearly every reader informed me that the novels teach them about faraway places and times and instruct them in the customs of other cultures. As Dot herself explained in our first formal interview, "These women [the authors] research the tar out of them. They go to great lengths. You don't feel like you've got a history lesson, but somewhere in there you have."

Throughout my stay, readers consistently referred to the "facts" and "truths" contained in the novels. Indeed, the tapes and transcripts of the interviews confirm that we spent more time discussing this aspect of romance reading than any other topic except its escape function and the nature of the romantic fantasy. Yet when these same women later filled out the extended questionnaire and rank ordered several sentences best explaining their reasons for reading romances, only nineteen checked the response "to learn about faraway places and times." Of those nineteen, only six selected this as their primary reason for reading. As I noted earlier, nineteen claimed that above all else they read romances to relax, eight answered "because reading is just for me—it is my time," and five said they read to escape their daily problems.

It seems necessary to explain this discrepancy between orally reported motives and those singled out as most significant under the guarantee of anonymity promised by the questionnaire form.[25] I think it likely that the "reading for instruction" explanation is a secondary justification for repetitive romance consumption that has been articulated by the women to convince skeptical husbands, friends, and interviewers that the novels are not merely frothy, purposeless entertainment but possess a certain intrinsic value that can be transferred to the reader. According to their theory, the value of the romance novel is a function of the information it is thought to *contain*. Because this information, which is a highly valued commodity in the advanced industrial society of which they are a part, can be imparted to these readers, their reading activity is transformed into a worthwhile pursuit precisely because its successful completion leaves them with something to show for their investment of time and money. When the reader can demonstrate to her husband or to an interviewer that an *exchange* has taken place, that she has acquired something in the process of reading, then her activity is defined retroactively as goal-directed work, as labor with a purpose, which is itself desirable in cultural terms.

In thus claiming that romance reading teaches them about the world, the Smithton women associate themselves with the long-standing, middle-class belief that education is closely connected with success and status. To read a romance, their informal theory implies, is to act deliberately to better one's self and thus, indirectly, one's social position. I might add that it is also an implicit declaration of faith in the ideologies of progress and democracy. Knowledge is not only the prerogative of the rich who can afford expensive educations, but it can be purchased by anyone in the form of a paperback book.

Dot's cryptic comment from that first interview should now make sense. When she responded to my question about what romances "do better than other reading matter available today" with a few apparently disconnected sentences, she was providing me with a glimpse of a quite logical thought process common among romance readers that moves from honest explanation to self-doubt to a more acceptable form of justification. It will be worthwhile to look briefly at her comments once again: "It's an innocuous thing. If it had to be pills or drinks—this is harmful. They're very aware of this. Most of the women are mothers. And they're aware of that kind of thing. And reading is something they would like to generate in their children also." At first, Dot contends that romance reading is an innocuous form of escape. It performs the same function as pills or drink but, unlike them, it is not harmful. She abruptly shifts, however, from the themes of escape reading and "addiction" to the thought that the women also want their children to see them reading, evidently because the activity itself is considered valuable. In Dot's case, it is clear that she has indeed conveyed this idea about reading to her children. Kit commented later in a discussion about the differences between reading and other forms of escape, that she, too, reads for "escape and entertainment." However, her very next statement indicated that she is not content with giving this as her only reason for romance reading. She continued, "The TV doesn't really have that much to offer—nothing that's intellectually stimulating—I mean—at least you learn something when you're reading books." Romance reading is "better" than other forms of escape in Kit's mind because, in addition to the enjoyment the activity gives her, it also provides her with information she would otherwise miss.

Dot and Kit are not unique in their tendency to resort to this kind of logic to justify their expenditures of time, money, and energy on romances. All of the Smithton women cited the educational value of romances in discussion as other readers apparently have when questioned by researchers for Harlequin, Fawcett, and Silhouette. Romance editors are all very aware of the romance reader's penchant for geographical and historical accuracy despite the usual restriction of information about audiences to the houses' marketing departments. When she was an editor at Dell, Vivien Stephens showed me the extensive research library she had compiled on the English Regency to help her check the accuracy of the manuscripts submitted to her for Dell's planned Candlelight series.[26] Her knowledge of reader preferences had come from letters written to authors as well as from the authors themselves who understand that instruction is one of the principal functions books can perform for their readers.

If it seems curious that the very same readers who willingly admit that romances are fairy tales or fantasies also insist that they contain accurate information about the real world, it should be noted that the contradictory assertions seem to result from a separation of plot and setting. When the Smithton women declare that romantic fiction is escapist because it isn't like real life, they are usually referring to their belief that reality is neither as just nor as happy as the romances would have it. Rewards do not always accrue to the good nor are events consistently resolved without ambiguity in the real world. A romance is a fantasy, they believe, because it portrays people who are happier and better than real individuals and because events occur as the women wish they would in day-to-day existence.

The fact that the story is fantastic, however, does not compromise the accuracy of the portrayal of the physical environment within which the idealized characters move. Even though the Smithton women know the stories are improbable, they also assume that the world that serves as the backdrop for those stories is exactly congruent with their own. Indeed, they believe so strongly in the autonomous reality of the fictional world that they are positively indignant if book covers inaccurately portray the heroine or the hero. A good cover, according to the Smithton readers, is one that implicitly confirms the validity of the imaginary universe by giving concrete form to that world *designated* by the book's language. As Ann patiently explained, a good cover is dependent on the artist's "having read the book and at least if you're going to draw the characters, have the right color hair." Favorite covers include several "factual" vignettes, again because these portrayals give credence to the separate, real existence of the fictive universe. That this belief in a parallel world is important to the women can also be seen in their commonly stated wish that more authors would write sequels to stories in order to follow the lives of particularly striking minor characters. The technique again continues the illusion that the romantic world is as real as the readers' world and that the characters' lives continue just as theirs do. As a consequence of this assumption about the congruence of the two worlds, anything the readers learn about the fictional universe is automatically coded as "fact" or "information" and mentally filed for later use as knowledge applicable to the world of day-to-day existence.

This faith in the reliability of the mimesis is the product of the widespread belief among readers that romance authors study a period and a place before they write about it. Not only are they thought to pore over historical "documents" and conduct "extensive research," but their readers also believe that the authors travel to the places they write about in order to give more realism to their descriptions.[27] The following stretch of conversation between Ann, Joy, and Dot gives a good indication of the intensity of their need to believe that their books are "factually correct." It is interesting to note as well that in response to my immediately preceding question, "Why do you read?" Ann followed the now-familiar pattern of explanation and justification:

Ann: To be entertained; escapism, armchair traveling. One of the things I enjoy about the Harlequins is that they are so geographically correct—in their facts. I had a friend who traveled to Ireland every year. She's the one who got me to read them. She had hers classified—her collection [of Harlequins]—she'd rip the front cover off and classify them by place.
　　　She'd travel to some of these places and she'd say, "I was there this time. It was just like so and so wrote. You turn that one corner and there's that well and that tree, and there's that . . ."
Dot: I'm sure that's true. I never questioned that for some reason.
Joy: I never *thought* of questioning it!
Dot: I wouldn't either, because I just assume they research like the devil. Every author does.
Ann: Remember the one about the eye hospital where you learn about the way they treat—the difference in nursing between the English and the American system?
Dot: How accurate they are in their descriptions . . .
Ann: Yes. You really learn something. The readers wrote in and asked for the recipes for some of these things—the way they described some of these fancy dishes.

Several of the other Smithton readers echoed Ann's interest in geography and her belief that romances are a good substitute for the traveling she would like to do but cannot afford. In a later conversation, for example, Joy discussed one of her favorite authors, Betty Neels, whose books she likes "because I like to go to Holland." She also explained that while she reads Regencies "for their humor and repartée," her mother reads them "for all the detail—furniture and costumes." Joy added, "She would love to see some of those carriages. She needs to know what sprig muslin looks like and things like that. You can't find those things now. She takes in as much detail [as she can]." Penny commented similarly, "I like descriptions of places and geography—you can feel like you're there then." Both Susan and Marie used the word "knowledge" in answering my question about their reasons for reading. Susan added, "Oh yes, you know all the authors faithfully research their periods."

The readers believe that research is such an integral part of romance writing that those who have begun to write their own romances all very proudly detail the amount of background reading they have completed. Lynn, who is planning to write a romantic story set in the American West, explained that she has already "researched Indian ways" and that she directs her husband, who is a truck driver, to pay particular attention to scenery in the western states so that he can describe accurately the locales she wants to write about.

Nearly all of the women indicated that they derive considerable enjoyment from surprising their husbands, in Ann's words, "with the little bits of information I get from my books." This is especially true of readers who concentrate on the long "historicals." These women all claim to enjoy "history" although they do not agree on the amount of factual detail that should be included in a narrative. Some, like Laurie, can tolerate long passages of exposition about such things as bread baking in the antebellum South, while others insist that history is more enjoyable if it is condensed into a few short sentences. Laurie, the Civil War buff mentioned earlier, reported that "I won't read anything after 1900. Somehow, you *feel* more when you're reading about detail. I don't know, somehow modern books don't get me to thinking as much." Her favorite book, she explained, is *Destiny's Woman*. Although she has many reasons for her preference, she especially appreciated the skill with which the author weaves historical detail into the narrative. Laurie explained that the heroine is forced by circumstances to run a plantation on her own. "Because that was unusual then," she added, "it let [the author] get all the details in." She commented later that those "details keep it from being a completely stupid fictional story."

In explaining their husbands' reactions to their reading, Dot's customers volunteered the information that despite initial resistance, the men could usually be convinced of the activity's value when their wives demonstrated that they learned from their books. Such a demonstration is not accomplished by explaining how much one has learned about human character, but rather by recounting a concrete "fact" about historical cooking practices, customs, or methods of transportation, by explaining word derivations, or by elaborating on the geographical features of a foreign country. Apparently, the more obscure and out-of-the-ordinary the information, the better. Several women delightedly told me that they had even heard their husbands pass on the information to others. Romances, then, connote change and progress for the women who read them because they believe the books expand their horizons and add to their knowledge about the world. They also provide these readers with an opportunity to "teach" skeptical family members and thus to assume temporarily a position of relative power.

My conversations with Dot's customers confirmed her claim in our first interview that although husbands usually object to their wives' reading at first, they generally change their minds if the women persist long enough. She has a theory, she tells her women, "that if you can hang in there for three years, [the fact that they are threatened] goes away as such." When she recounted her theory, she added, "it's true. It is weird. And before long, they get to the point where they're thinking, 'Oh well, you know my wife reads x amount of books a week.' And they're braggin about it." If they can shift perspectives, in other words, and rather than see romance reading as a pointless activity with no utilitarian purpose, consider the ability to read many books both an achievement in itself and a way to learn, they can then justify their wives' book expenses. Some of these men can even be persuaded that the form is interesting if their wives decide to try their hand at romance writing themselves. Dot observed, "Here we have some of these women who have decided, 'Well, I can write a book.' And now these very same husbands are so supportive that they are almost pushy. 'Well, get that book done. That's a good book. I've been reading it.' So you see, it can be a change if they just kind of push it in place." Romance reading can be justified to others, then, if the reader learns to stress the books' educational function, if she can demonstrate the extraordinary adeptness and speed with which she reads, or if she can turn the whole process around and write her own romance to be read and, of course, bought by others.

In maintaining that the "reading for instruction" argument helps to legitimate an activity that would otherwise be seen as self-indulgent and frivolous because it does not immediately appear to accomplish anything useful, I do not mean to imply that the Smithton women are being dishonest when they say they want to learn. Nor am I questioning whether they do, in fact, learn anything of value. I think it important to emphasize here that a genuine craving for knowledge of the world beyond the doors of their suburban homes is an important motivating factor in their decision to read rather than watch television, participate in craft activities, or involve themselves in physical recreation. They are cognizant that their lives have been limited by the need to stay close to home to care for children and to provide a supportive environment for their husbands. A common refrain in all of the conversations centered about the value of a book as a provider of "adult conversation" which they missed as a result of their confinement within their homes as the principal provider and companion for small children.

In summary, romances can be termed compensatory fiction because the act of reading them fulfills certain basic psychological needs for women that have been induced by the culture and its social structures but that often remain unmet in day-to-day existence as the result of concomitant restrictions on female activity. From the Smithton readers' experiences, in particular, it can be concluded that romance reading compensates women in two distinct ways. Most important, it provides vicarious emotional nurturance by prompting identification between the reader and a fictional heroine whose identity as a woman is always confirmed by the romantic and sexual attentions of an ideal male. When she successfully imagines herself in the heroine's position, the typical romance reader can relax momentarily and permit herself to wallow in the rapture of being the center of a powerful and important individual's attention. This attention not only provides her with the sensations evoked by emotional nurturance and physical satisfaction, but, equally significantly, reinforces her sense of self because in offering his care and attention to the woman with whom she identifies, the hero implicitly regards that woman and, by implication, the reader, as worthy of his concern. This fictional character thus teaches both his narrative counterpart and the reader to recognize the value they doubted they possessed.

Romance fiction is compensatory in a second sense because it fills a woman's mental world with the varied details of simulated travel and permits her to converse imaginatively with adults from a broad spectrum of social space. Moreover, the world-creating and instructional functions of romances provide the woman who believes in the value of individual achievement with the opportunity to feel that education has not ceased for her nor has the capacity to succeed in culturally approved terms been erased by her acceptance of the less-valued domestic roles. Because romance reading is coded as an instructional activity even as it is acknowledged to be entertaining, a woman can indulge herself by engaging in an activity that makes her feel good and simultaneously congratulate herself for acting to improve her awareness of the world by learning through books. Romance reading compensates, then, for a certain kind of emotional deprivation just as it creates the illusion of movement or change achieved through informal acquisition of factual "knowledge."

In populating her imagination with the attractive and exotically employed individuals found in romances, the woman whose intercourse with the community has been restricted in favor of her family widens her range of acquaintances and vicariously enriches the social space she inhabits. Like an individual prevented from dreaming who then begins to hallucinate in waking life to compensate for the reduction in symbolic activity, a woman who has been restricted by her relative isolation within the home turns to romances for the wealth of objects, people, and places they enable her to construct *within* her own imagination. The fact that she is reading and therefore learning functions for the romance reader as an assurance that she is not an example of that much-maligned cultural stereotype, the simpleminded housewife who can manage little more than to feed her children, iron a few shirts, and watch the afternoon soap operas. The Smithton women are all acutely aware that American culture does not value the role they perform and they indignantly protest that their employment as mothers and housewives does not mean that they are necessarily stupid. Their reading, finally, serves to confirm their image of themselves as intelligent individuals who are yet deserving of occasional pleasure and escape from responsibilities that are willingly accepted and dutifully performed.

In thus mediating between a desire to indulge the self emotionally through repetitive *consumption* and the contradictory need to exhibit the self as a hard-*working* achiever, the very act of romance reading seems to reconcile two opposing sets of values. Before elaborating on this further interpretation of the social factors contributing to the Smithton women's understanding of their own reading behavior, I would like to include one last conversation between Dot, Joy, and Kit. Not only does the exchange contain more references to the theme of escape and its connection to addiction, but it also provides a glimpse into the anger and indignation spawned by the culture's scorn for the fantasy that the women know they need. These comments developed out of a discussion about the publishers' belittlement of their own romances and the women who read them. The three were lamenting the publishers' inability to provide consistently the kinds of romances the women like to read.

Joy:	I hate these nonreaders that say what we will and will not read.
Dot:	But, you know, that is what I tell the—anyone that I come in contact with, the [publishers'] reps that I know. If they can go back and open their mouth, I say, "You know, you guys spend a heck of a lot of money on advertisement and all you'd have to do is come out and talk to the women." I said, "They're very voluble, they can converse. They read and they speak. They do all normal things. If you want—you know—a line of communication, it's here." They don't do it. Now I don't know whether they don't know anybody that can go out and handle the situation.
Joy:	Or if they're afraid of the Indian uprising [said with derision]. We *are* west of the Alleghenies!
Dot:	And I know that when this man [at the booksellers con-

vention] was so rather—made this statement, I took an immediate dislike to him. Kit was standing there and said, "You didn't like him, did you?" And I said, "You are right! . . ." He made the statement that—I said, "The women read for escapism." And he said, "Any reading is for escapism." And I said, "Well, I wouldn't call a textbook escapism." A mathematics textbook, I think, is probably what I said, something of that nature. He said, "Of course it is." And I said, "No, it isn't."

Kit: Well, then he made some rude comment about women's reading. I mean, he made a derogatory comment directly about woman's opium or something like that.

Dot: Oh yes, fix. Getting a fix—oh, when they get their romantic fix.

Interviewer: But you said to me that you think it's an addiction.

Dot: That's right. But I don't want *him* telling me it is. If *I* recognize that I need this, that's one thing. But for him to tell me in a disparaging manner . . .

Joy: Because there are well-written books and poorly written books in any group of any kind of reading and we can sift out what we think are the drivel.

Dot: Yes, we can tell the difference.

Joy: And we don't enjoy something that is poorly written either.

Kit: And a fix, you get the idea you'd go out and read just anything.

Joy: Yeah, anything in the romance section or the gothic section in the supermarket display.

Kit: Like you have no discretion.

Joy: And no mind—and no education.

Dot: Well, now, that's what most of them tend to think. The simpleminded housewife!

Joy: Hooked on her soap operas.

Kit: Yeah, they think that your intellectual level is nil and none.

Joy: I couldn't even tell you the names of the soap operas.

Dot: Well, it's actually almost as though he were speaking down to some two- or three-year-old child which—I resent that too—but the fact is, here is [the area representative] telling him that I'm selling books like there's no tomorrow—and he's standing there in his custom-made suit or whatever.

Joy:	Botany 500.
Dot:	Well, whatever it is he's standing there in—and it's like as though I'm probably paying for the suit on his back.
	[Here the conversation trails off and a new topic is picked up.]

Although Dot's anger here is focused specifically on a publisher's dismissal of her favorite books, it is still representative of a response common to all of her readers. The Smithton women believe very strongly that romance reading is worthwhile because the stories provide pleasure while the activity of reading challenges them to learn new words and information about a world they find intriguing and all too distant. Their anger is directed at those who would implicitly deny them, through "disinterested" criticism, the right to a temporary escape and to a fantasy they desire. In an effort to circumvent disapproval grounded in the attitude that fantasy and play are somehow unnecessary, useless, and unbecoming to adults, the Smithton readers have learned to defend their activity by boasting of all that it teaches them. The justification is a strategic one because it associates romances with a set of values that have been an integral part of American middle-class culture at least since the early days of industrialization. In effect, they establish themselves as hard-working, achievement-oriented individuals by claiming that romances are "factual" and therefore filled with information that can be extracted and used by the industrious reader.

In so defending their repetitive reading, the Smithton women appeal to a set of values that continues to serve as a powerful motivating force in the lives of middle-class Americans despite the elaboration of a new set of values displayed in mass-media advertisements proclaiming that the route to happiness and success entails not work but consumption. What we see reflected in their uneasy reliance on the contradictory assertions that romance fiction is a harmless but effective escape from psychological burdens and, at the same time, utilitarian instruction about the real world, is a clash between two value systems. One system serves to sustain a consumer-oriented economy, while the other, developed by an economy designed to accumulate and to concentrate capital, tacitly labels consumption for pure pleasure both wasteful and dangerous. By demonstrating that romance reading is work for the reader, the women are able to exorcise any lingering doubts they might have about the legitimacy of a consumption process that always exhausts its object even as it only temporarily satisfies the need that prompted the decision to buy in the first place. This return to the ideology of hard work or productive labor to justify pleasurable leisure activity seems to betoken an incomplete assimilation of the values of a consuming society whose very health depends on its members' continuous purchase of commodities.

It should not seem strange that romance readers' claims about the pleasures attendant upon completion of each book sound remarkably like the advertising claims made daily on television, in newspapers, and in glossy magazines that happiness, friendship, respect, and sexual pleasure can be had in the form of any number of mass-produced objects. Advertisements present the American population with an interminable parade of blissfully happy individuals whose extraordinary joy, excitement, satisfaction, beauty, and sense of power are linked by simple juxtaposition with the particular product being sold. Each individual addressed by an ad is told, in effect, that the emotional state represented in the picture by an always already transformed consumer can be purchased automatically, in tandem with the deodorant, designer jeans, gold-coin watch, or automobile that is the ostensible subject of the ad. Its concealed message, however, is the more significant one, for it legitimates through assertion the notion that commodity consumption is an adequate and effective way to negate the "pain" produced by the disappointments, imperfections, and small failures that are an inevitable part of human life. It is worth observing, however, that advertising's offer of happiness is nothing but a promise of vicarious experience. As a discursive form, it presents satisfaction, contentment, and pride, not as the result of an individual's actions or social intercourse with others, but as the natural consequence of the activity of consuming or displaying a particular product. Happiness is not an emotional condition one creates for oneself through action; in advertising, it is a thing that one can buy.[28]

Like the commodities constituted by advertising, romances also provide vicarious pleasure. Indeed, Harlequin, Fawcett, and Silhouette now publicly claim in their own advertising campaigns that certain "end emotional benefits" can be purchased along with the latest romance novel. These companies know well that when specific psychological needs, which they are not able to fully identify themselves, are inadequately addressed or left unfulfilled by a woman's daily round of activities and social contacts, she will turn to a romance and imagine what it feels like to have her needs met as are those of her alter ego, the heroine. Still, it must always be remembered that the good feelings this woman derives from reading romantic fiction are not experienced in the course of her habitual existence in the world of actual social relations, but in the separate, free realm of the imaginary. The happiness she permits herself is not only secondhand experience, but temporary as well. By resting satisfied with this form of vicarious pleasure, the romance reader may do nothing to transform her actual situation which itself gave rise to the need to seek out such pleasure in the first place. Consumption of one temporarily satisfying romance will lead in that case to the need and desire for another. The vicarious pleasure offered by romantic fiction finally may be satisfying enough to forestall the need for more substantial change in the reader's life. At the same time, its very ephemerality may guarantee a perpetual desire to repeat the experience. Consumption, in short, might result only in future consumption. Whether it in fact does so is open to some question. Because this issue can only be adequately addressed after the entire romance-reading experience has been assessed, I will delay further consideration of it until the conclusion of this book.

In summary, however, it is worth noting again that when Dot and her customers insist that they have a right to escape and to indulge themselves just as everyone else does, they are justifying their book purchases with arguments that are basic to a consuming society. In effect, they are insisting that they be permitted the same leisure, extravagance, and opportunities for immediate gratification that they help their husbands and children to realize. However, when they subsequently argue that romances are also edifying and that reading is a kind of productive labor, they forsake that ideology of perpetual consumption for a more traditional value system that enshrines hard work, performance of duty, and thrift. Romances are valuable according to this system because they enable the reader to accumulate information, to add to her worth, and thus to better herself. In so justifying the act of reading the romance, the Smithton women affirm their adherence to traditional values and, at the same time, engage in a form of behavior that is itself subversive of those values.

F O U R

The Ideal Romance
The Promise of Patriarchy

In examining the Smithton readers' conscious beliefs about the benefits of
romance reading, we have seen that an intensely felt but insufficiently met
need for emotional nurturance drives these women to repeated encounters
with romance fiction. Although Dot and her customers cannot formally
identify the particular features of the romantic fantasy that are the source
of its therapeutic value to them, they are certain, nonetheless, that the
activity of romance reading is pleasurable and restorative as well. We have
seen that their resulting emotional dependence on romantic fiction is at
least partially a function of their ability to restrict their reading to novels
that focus only on a particular kind of interaction between heroine and
hero. This ability, itself a function of their reliance on Dot's advice, guarantees the Smithton readers a vicarious experience that leaves them feeling
hopeful, happy, and content. In order to understand just how these books
actually provide this much-needed replenishment, it is now necessary to
look with some care at those they judge particularly successful. Such an
examination should enable us to pinpoint the characteristics that are the
essence of the romance's power and attraction for these readers. By locating the source of both, we should be able to explain why women turn
specifically to romances in their quest for vicarious pleasure.

Although the interpretation of the romantic fantasy that follows will be grounded in close textual analysis, more specifically, in a Proppian analysis of the romantic plot, it is essential to observe that even this more standard form of literary interpretation begins here in reader perceptions.[1] Instead of attempting to assemble an "objective," "representative" sample of the romance, I have relied on the Smithton readers' tendencies to separate their books into the categories of the "good" and the "bad." I have therefore departed from the usual procedure of focusing attention on a particular publisher's line or on a narrative subgenre, because virtually all of the Smithton women read more than one kind of romance in an effort to find the best books. I have also done so because I wanted to avoid uncritical acceptance of those assumptions discussed in the introduction that usually lie hidden within such an operation.

What the disparate texts in this sample have in common is that they have been identified by Dot and her customers as "excellent" or "favorite" examples of the genre. The women believe that they are perfect expressions of the romantic fantasy. Assuming, therefore, that an analysis of these twenty quintessentially romantic books would reveal the crucial generative matrix of the genre *as the readers understand it*, I attempted to determine whether the same sequence of narrative functions can be found in each of the texts.[2] In fact, a sequence of thirteen narrative functions does recur in the Smithton readers' favorite books. Consequently, I have used this set to probe into the psychological significance of the genre for its readers and to infer further unconscious needs that underpin and reinforce the more conscious motives investigated earlier that prompt them to seek out the romantic fantasy.

I should also point out here that I agree with Will Wright's argument, articulated in his critique of Propp, that a genre is never defined solely by its constitutive set of functions, but by interaction between characters and by their development as individuals.[3] As a result, I have assumed further that the romantic genre is additionally defined for the women by a set of characters whose personalities and behaviors can be "coded" or summarized through the course of the reading process in specific ways. Thus actual reader perceptions have also been used in this analysis to "name" or "code" the behaviors and personalities of the principal characters in the novels.[4] By pursuing similarities in the behaviors of these characters and by attempting to understand what those behaviors signify to these readers, I have sought to avoid summarizing them according to my own beliefs about and standards for gender behavior.

In assembling the sample for this chapter, I began with the Smithton readers' responses to an open-ended request that they list their three favorite romances and romance writers. Although an astonishing diversity characterized their responses, one shared preference clearly emerged. Despite the fact that fifty-five different titles and thirty-nine writers were cited by the Smithton readers, a Kathleen Woodiwiss novel was listed as the first, second, or third most-loved romance thirty-eight times. Indeed, her first romance, *The Flame and the Flower*, was the favorite book of ten of the Smithton women and was listed by six in second or third place. Only Celeste De Blasis's *The Proud Breed* and Laurie McBain's *Moonstruck Madness* came anywhere near Woodiwiss's work in the frequency with which it was cited. All of the other titles were mentioned much less often. The frequencies are summarized below:

First ranking:	*The Flame and the Flower* (Woodiwiss)	10
	Shanna (Woodiwiss)	8
	The Wolf and the Dove (Woodiwiss)	3
	The Proud Breed (De Blasis)	2
	(16 other titles received one vote each)	
Second ranking:	*Ashes in the Wind* (Woodiwiss)	4
	The Flame and the Flower (Woodiwiss)	3
	Moonstruck Madness (McBain)	3
	The Proud Breed (De Blasis)	3
	Ride the Thunder (Dailey)	2
	Gone with the Wind (Mitchell)	2
	Visions of the Damned (Marten)	2
	(17 other titles received one vote each)	
Third ranking:	*Shanna* (Woodiwiss)	5
	The Flame and the Flower (Woodiwiss)	3
	Ashes in the Wind (Woodiwiss)	2
	Fires of Winter (Lindsey)	2
	Blades of Passion (Williams)	2
	(23 other titles received one vote each)	

The Smithton group's response to the request for their favorite authors confirmed that Woodiwiss is the writer they hold in highest esteem. Indeed, of the thirty-nine women who listed a favorite author, seventeen gave that honor to Woodiwiss. The only other writers whose citations rivaled Woodiwiss's total of twenty-eight were Janet Dailey, with a total of thirteen, and Johanna Lindsey and Laurie McBain, each with six. Once again, frequency totals are summarized below:

First ranking:	Kathleen Woodiwiss	17
	Janet Dailey	6
	Elizabeth Peters	3
	(10 other authors received less than 3 votes each)	

Second ranking: Kathleen Woodiwiss   8
                Janet Dailey   4
                Laurie McBain   3
                (22 other authors received less than 3 votes each)

Third ranking: Johanna Lindsey   5
                Kathleen Woodiwiss   3
                Janet Dailey   3
                (21 other authors received less than 3 votes each)

To take account of the Smithton group's preferences, I have included all four Woodiwiss novels in the sample of texts to be analyzed in addition to *The Proud Breed* by Celeste De Blasis, *Moonstruck Madness* by Laurie McBain, *Visions of the Damned* by Jacqueline Marten, and *Fires of Winter* by Johanna Lindsey. I also added Janet Dailey's *Ride the Thunder* and *Nightway* and Elizabeth Peters's *Summer of the Dragon*. The rest of the sample was drawn up by relying on the frequency of citations in the interviews and on particularly enthusiastic newsletter reviews by Dot. Because Jude Deveraux's *The Black Lyon*, La Vyrle Spencer's *The Fulfillment*, and Elsie Lee's *The Diplomatic Lover* were each cited more than five times during oral interviewing, they were added to the list. Then, Dot's five-star recommendation insured the inclusion of the following: *Green Lady* by Leigh Ellis, *Dreamtide* by Katherine Kent, *Made for Each Other* by Parris Afton Bonds, *Miss Hungerford's Handsome Hero* by Noël Vreeland Carter (one of two five-star romances to which Dot gave a *gold* five-star rating), *The Sea Treasure* by Elisabeth Barr, and *Moonlight Variations* by Florence Stevenson.

When these twenty novels are compared with the "failed" romances discussed in Chapter 5 or a more random sample of the genre, essential differences emerge. Indeed, the most striking characteristic of the ideal romance—its resolute focus on a single, developing relationship between heroine and hero—is noticeably absent from those judged to be failures by the Smithton women. Although all romances eventually resolve the differences between two principal characters, as the ideal romances do, some also devote considerable attention to interim relationships between hero or heroine and rival individuals. Indeed, character foils are such a standard element in the genre that they have received much analytic attention. Margaret Jensen found that 98 percent of her sample of Harlequins, for instance, included either a male or female rival.[5]

Although the Smithton group's favorite romances also characteristically include such rival figures, few devote more than passing attention to them. Most simply introduce the foil figures as *suspected* rather than actual rivals by noting that the hero or heroine misunderstands the character's relation to the other partner. Never do they permit the reader to share the heroine's or hero's mistaken belief. Because the reader always knows that the principal in question is not attracted to the rival, that rival functions for her as a true foil, as a point of comparison and contrast for hero or heroine.

The lack of triangular relationships in ideal romances should not come as a surprise if we recall the Smithton readers' preference for novels about "one woman–one man" and their interest in the evolution of love. In fact, it is this preoccupation with the *gradual* removal of emotional barriers between two people who recognize their connection early in the story that sets the novels apart from other run-of-the-mill romances. Seven of the twenty marry hero and heroine within the first quarter of the book, while the rest establish an exclusive and intense, though less formal, relationship between them.[6] This structural device insures that the heroine and hero function as the single, dynamic center of the novels and facilitates a particularly intense identification between reader and heroine. Because her attention need never wander to take account of other characters' actions, the reader is permitted to live the heroine's relationship to the hero without distraction.

An examination of the actual portrayal of the principal characters in the ideal romances clearly reveals why this process of identification is so enjoyable for the reader. To begin with, the ideal heroine is differentiated from her more ordinary counterparts in other romance novels by unusual intelligence or by an extraordinarily fiery disposition. Occasionally, she even exhibits special abilities in an unusual occupation. Although the "spirited" heroine is a cliché in romantic fiction, these ideal women are distinguished by the particularly exaggerated quality of their early rebelliousness against parental strictures. The heroine of *Fires of Winter*, for instance, is first introduced to the reader as a young boy. Brenna affects Viking dress and style not simply because her father wanted her to be a boy, but also because she finds her woman's body "cumbersome" (p. 12) and all symbols of her inferior womanhood hateful. She deliberately hides her hair (p. 12) and refuses to do needlework because "she [cannot] abide any skill which [is] solely a woman's" (p. 21). Kathleen Woodiwiss's more typical heroine in *The Flame and the Flower* does not indulge in such egregiously antifeminine behavior, but her sensibility is, nonetheless, differentiated from other women's by the fact of her education and her "high-handed notions" (p. 10).

I do not want to suggest here that the romances most valued by the Smithton women deliberately challenge male and female stereotypes. Like all romances, these novels eventually recommend the usual sexual division of labor that dictates that women take charge of the domestic and purely personal spheres of human endeavor. These novels do, however, begin by expressing ambivalent feelings about female gender by associating the

heroine's personality or activities with traits and behavior usually identified with men. Although it is tempting to interpret this distaste for
women as evidence of female masochism and of a desire to see feminist
tendencies succumb to the power of love, it can be explained more fully by
connecting it with the heroine's and the reader's impulse toward individuation and autonomy, a step that must be taken, at least within patriarchy, *against* the mother, that is, *against women*. Before attempting an account of the ideal heroine's journey toward female selfhood as a chronicle
of her efforts to both reject and regain her mother, I think it best to
develop a more complete picture of the ideal heroine and the man she
"tames" and to summarize the manner in which they are coded by readers
at the beginning of the tale. We will return shortly, however, to this vision
of the romance as a quest for motherly nurturance.

Although the ideal heroine's aberrant personality is tempered and undercut by her extraordinary beauty, the fact of her initial rejection of
feminine ways is so essential to the plot that it is worth examining the
manner of her deviation in greater detail. Several writers establish their
heroine's refusal to be restricted by expectations about female gender behavior by assigning them unusual jobs. Elizabeth Peters, for example,
writes about Deanna Abbott's work as an anthropologist, while Florence
Stevenson preoccupies herself in the early pages of *Moonlight Variations*
with Lora's abilities as a virtuoso pianist. Noël Carter's Charlotte Hungerford is a writer "with a goodly quantity of successful novels to her
credit," a fact that makes her "independent financially" and endows her
with "a name . . . known in its own right," which means that "she [needs]
no man's title to give her place" (p. 21). True, she is a writer of romantic
novels on Regency England, but Carter makes it clear through Charlotte's
unladylike profanity (p. 15) and her penchant for argument with men that
she feels competitive with them and that they find her daunting. As her
nephew confesses, "she's too damned smart by half. . . . She makes a feller
feel a fool. They *look* at her and fall head over heels. They *talk* with her,
and it's like a cold bucket of ice water smack in the face" (p. 21). Just as
Charlotte refuses to be demure and *silent* in the presence of men, so do
Aislinn (*The Wolf and the Dove*), Julie (*Made for Each Other*), Brenna (*Fires
of Winter*), Nanny (*The Diplomatic Lover*), and Tessa (*The Proud Breed*)
exert their superiority by manipulating language.

Nearly all of the heroines in these female-sponsored fantasies, in fact,
explicitly refuse to be silenced by the male desire to control women
through the eradication of their individual voices. Susan Griffin has recently identified this desire as the central motivating theme in male pornography.[7] In order to make women into objects, Griffin tells us, male
pornographers give their female victims voices through which to express
their wills, only in order to silence those voices and to erase the will, a feat

that effectively denies their status as human subjects. The constant emphasis in these particular romances, then, on the heroine's stubborn insistence
that she be free to voice her will and desire is convincing evidence that
an impulse toward individuation and realization of an intentional self initially sets the romantic story in motion. Given this emphasis on her tom-
boyish defiance and her verbal facility, it is not hard to understand why
the Smithton readers describe their favorite heroines as "intelligent,"
"spunky," and "independent."

   If there is any doubt that the desire to separate from childhood attach-
ments by identifying with characteristically male behavior governs the
romance's early development, consider these events that take place within
the first fifty pages of two of the novels. As Tessa swims alone on her
sixteenth birthday in an isolated mountain spring, she is attacked by the
hero of *The Proud Breed.* Unlike many romantic heroines, she does not
succumb to his strength but stabs him and then *pushes* him to the ground.
In reply to his question about why she did not say "no" to his advances,
she observes that she had no way of knowing whether he was reasonable
and she wonders whether he would have done the same thing in her place.
When he admits he would have, he confirms their essential similarity
(p. 21).

   In the opening pages of *Fires of Winter*, a beautiful woman is raped by a
soldier. Because of the way these two characters are described, the reader
assumes she is witnessing the first battle between the heroine and the
hero. Her assumption is shattered, however, when a young boy appears,
"crosse[s] the room with purposeful strides, and raise[s] sword, then skillfully cut[s] into the stranger's behind" (p. 5). Before the reader can recover to sort things out, she is told that the boy is actually "the Lady
Brenna," the true heroine of the tale! As if this is not enough to establish
Brenna's deviation from the usual standards of femininity, the reader is
later treated to a picture of Brenna seated "in the center of her large bed
polishing her sword with the care given a prized possession, which indeed
her sword was" (p. 31) since it was a gift from her father on her tenth
birthday. Although I doubt very much that the Smithton readers know
how to read this psychoanalytically as a symbol of a desire for the power
associated with the penis, such skill is not necessary, for Lindsey translates
her symbolic language almost immediately. Not only does she write that
"Brenna cherished this sword more than any of her possessions . . . because it was a symbol of her father's pride in her achievements," but she
adds in the next paragraph that Brenna also worries about whether "her
female body [will] imprison her in her husband's land" (p. 31). In completing Brenna's thoughts, Lindsey makes it clear that at this stage in her
life the heroine sees no value in being a woman. She wonders: "Would she
ever be able to wield this sword again, to fight for what was her own as

any man would? Or would she be expected to act the wife in every way, never to use her skills again, to be a woman and do only what a woman should?" (p. 31).

The presence of another feature shared by ideal heroines seems to confirm their existence as symbolic representations of the immature female psyche. Although the women are unusually defiant in that they are capable of successfully opposing men, they are also characterized by childlike innocence and inexperience. Most of the heroines, in fact, are seventeen to twenty, yet only one of them has ever had any contact with a member of the opposite sex before her confrontation with the hero. Moreover, these heroines are completely unaware that they are capable of passionate sexual urges. Shanna Trahern, for example, has earned a reputation as "the ice queen, the unattainable prize," because of her refusal to reciprocate the advances of her many suitors (p. 21). Heather, of *The Flame and the Flower*, is so ignorant that she has no idea when she has been deposited in a brothel. Similarly, the heroine in *The Sea Treasure* informs the reader that she wants no man's attention "because a woman, at best, is a man's chattel, and if *she* has fires, she learns to dowse them" (p. 76).

The Smithton readers all approve of the romantic heroine's inexperience and code it as "true innocence." They believe that her lack of knowledge is entirely plausible not to mention desirable as well. They approve of her virginity, however, less on the basis of its status as an abstract moral principle than in accordance with their belief that a woman must protect herself from the many men who desire only her body and care little for her needs. According to these readers, female sexual response is something to be exchanged for love and used only in its service.

Despite a continuing refusal to acknowledge the significance and potential consequences inherent in her rapidly maturing body, the ideal romantic heroine is considered by everyone else, including the hero, to be an extraordinary example of full-blooming womanhood. Although not all romantic heroines are beautiful, those in the romances favored most by the Smithton women are characterized by an especially alluring appearance.[8] Invariably, they are unaware of their beauty and its effect on others. As a consequence, they are never vain, nor do they preen in an effort to attract a man. They always have "glorious tresses" and "sparkling" or "smoldering" eyes, inevitably "fringed by sooty lashes," that undermine their determination to remain detached from the opposite sex. In fact, it is her beauty that undoes the ideal heroine because it is always the cause of the hero's inability to master his desire for her once she is near him. When he forces his attentions upon her, she is inevitably "awakened" by his "probes," and overcome by her own bodily response which she cannot control. Female beauty is, therefore, inextricably linked with sexuality in the romance. It is a sign both to the hero and to the reader that the heroine is sensual and capable of carnal passion despite her immature repression of those urges.

The ideal heroine's thinly disguised sexuality and more explicitly developed rebelliousness do not threaten the reader, in large part because the fact of her true femininity is never left in doubt. No matter how much emphasis is placed on her initial desire to appear a man's equal, she is always portrayed as unusually compassionate, kind, and understanding. Typically, some minor disaster occurs in the early stages of the story that proves the perfect occasion for her to display her extraordinary capacity for empathetic nurturance and tender care. Alaina McGaren, for instance, the heroine of Woodiwiss's fourth book, *Ashes in the Wind*, spends almost the entire first half of the story (a good two hundred pages) disguised as a filthy, wisecracking boy. Not only does she save the hero's life but she works closely with him in a Civil War hospital where he is a doctor. When she works as an orderly, however, she demonstrates her female superiority by the proficiency of her cleaning skills and the particular compassion of her care for the wounded soldiers. Woodiwiss's description clearly establishes that Alaina is naturally feminine despite her disguise.

> Some soldiers struggled to retain some humor in this dismal place. With these Al exchanged light banter. Others were dismayed at their wounds and disappointed with the pain and effort of life. To these Alaina gave a challenge, a dare to live. To those who were deeply injured, she grudgingly gave pity and sympathy and an odd sort of bittersweet tenderness. She ran errands for those who couldn't go for themselves, sometimes purchasing a comb, a shaving brush, or a bottle of lilac water for a girl back home. . . . The dull gray silence of the wards had yielded to a youthful and oftentimes rebellious grin. The musty, cloying odor of molding debris became the pungent scent of lye soap and pine oil. The moans of pain were now more often hidden beneath the muffled chuckle of laughter or the low-voiced murmur of shared experiences. (p. 55)

This characteristic, early demonstration of the romantic heroine's ability to transmute the sick into the healthy reassures the reader that the heroine is, in reality, a "true" woman, one who possesses all the nurturing skills associated by patriarchal culture with the feminine character. At the same time, her success as a nurse foreshadows for the knowing reader her eventual success at transforming the hero's emotional indifference and sexual promiscuity into expressions of love, constant displays of affection, and the promise of marital fidelity. It is, in fact, the combination of her womanly sensuality and mothering capacities that will magically remake a man incapable of expressing emotions or of admitting dependence. As a result of her effort, he will be transformed into an ideal figure possessing both masculine power and prestige and the more "effeminate" ability to discern her needs and to attend to their fulfillment in a tender, solicitous way. Ironically, then, at the same time that the romantic fantasy proclaims a woman's power to re-create a man in a mold she has fashioned, it also covertly establishes her guilt or responsibility for those who remain unchanged. The romance blames not men's indifference, competitiveness, or ambition for their rigid indifference and their mistreatment of women but rather women's own insufficiency as perfect wife-mothers. While the romance creates its utopia by fantasizing about a new kind of male-female relationship where a man cares for a woman as she cares for him, it fails to explain convincingly exactly why and how each individual heroine is able to translate male reticence and cruelty into tenderness and devotion.

The typical romantic narrative need not provide a logical explanation for the personality transformation it observes so carefully, because it is prepared for by the hero's first introduction. The hero of the romantic fantasy is always characterized by spectacular masculinity. Indeed, it is insufficient for the author to remark in passing that the romantic hero has a muscular physique. The reader must be told, instead, that every aspect of his being, whether his body, his face, or his general demeanor, is informed by the purity of his maleness. Almost everything about him is hard, angular, and dark. It is, however, essential to add the qualifying "almost" here because, in descriptions of the ideal romantic hero, the terrorizing effect of his exemplary masculinity is always tempered by the presence of a small feature that introduces an important element of softness into the overall picture.

This anomalous, inexplicable aberration in his otherwise consistently harsh behavior and appearance is, of course, understood by the experienced reader, and occasionally by the heroine herself, as an indication that behind his protective exterior hides an affectionate and tender soul. Just as Dominic Pengallion's "fierce" demeanor is relieved by his occasional ability to be "generous, compassionate and full of humor" (*The Sea Treasure*, p. 11), so Hannibal Cheng's "romantically grim" visage is softened by "wide, melting Oriental eyes" (*Miss Hungerford's Handsome Hero*, pp. 37–38). Nicholas Raffer, who "gently" tries to determine whether the heroine has been injured in a car accident, has a "hard cut . . . jaw and sharply squared chin" that are nevertheless balanced by his "generous lips" which have a "sensual curve to them" (*Made for Each Other*, pp. 10, 19).

Few of these initial descriptions explore the reasons for the hero's warring tendencies in as much detail as Jude Deveraux provides in the following passage from *The Black Lyon*. However, all of them eventually reveal that the hero's wariness, like Ranulf's, can be traced to a previous hurt by another woman and to his justifiable distrust of all females. The reader is assured by this detail that the tenderness she thinks she detects behind the facade of his masculinity cannot help but reveal itself when he learns to trust and love a truly good woman:

> The Earl of Malvoisin's eyes reminded her of a dog she had seen once. The dog had been caught in a trap, his leg nearly cut in half, and the pain had made him almost mad. It had taken a long time for Lyonene to soothe the animal and gain its trust so that she could release the iron jaws of the trap, and all the while the dog had looked at her with just such an expression of wariness, pain and near-dead hope as did the man who stood before her now. . . . Her gaze fell on his lips, which were well-shaped but held too rigid. Lucy had been correct; he was a handsome man. She smiled, timidly at first and then with more warmth. She looked behind the lips that did not smile and saw a . . . yes, a sweetness there, the same gentleness that her mother had seen. (pp. 7–8)

The Smithton readers' favorite romances may stress the importance of such tenderness in men, but because they indicate that their reserved and cruel heroes are, in truth, compassionate and kind individuals from the start, they only pretend to explore creatively the way to ideal male-female relationships. The romantic heroine simply brings to the surface traits and propensities that are part of the hero's most basic nature. Consequently, the romance can say nothing about the more difficult problem of how to teach men to be gentle who have developed within a set of family relationships that systematically represses the boy's capacity to nurture and, then, in an act of overdetermination, reinforces that destruction by branding tenderness in a man a sign of weakness. The romance expresses women's dissatisfaction with the current asymmetry in male-female relationships but, at the same time, by virtue of its early presentation of the hero, represents the desired and necessary transformation as an already accomplished fact.

Still, these romances are able to convince their readers that a real transformation occurs because they repeatedly stress the hero's reserve, indifference, and even cruelty when he is first confronted by the heroine. The heroes in these ideal romances exhibit considerably less physical violence and brutality toward the heroines than do heroes in failed romances, but they are not above emotional blackmail and brusque indifference.[9] Although the reader never has to endure more than one or two short scenes where the hero actually hurts the heroine, his power to wound her emotionally by toying with her affections is demonstrated in vignette after vignette. The combination of this self-protective aggressiveness and the fleeting revelation of his underlying capacity for gentleness is responsible, then, for the Smithton readers' tendency to describe the ideal hero in paired terms. When asked in the interviews to provide an account of the perfect romantic hero, Dot and her customers replied with such phrases as "strong but gentle," "masculine but caring," "protective of her and tender," "a he-man but a lover-boy, too."

In addition to mentioning these features that they know are unusual if not improbable in combination, the Smithton readers volunteered the information that an ideal hero must be "a man among men," as one of Dot's customers explained. When asked to gloss her encomium, this woman added that he must be a "leader," able "to command respect from everyone around him." In fact, her observations accurately describe the social status shared by the heroes of these twenty romances. Not only are they wealthy, indeed, often aristocratic, but they are also active and successful participants in some major public endeavor. Whether it be in war (*The Wolf and the Dove, Fires of Winter, The Black Lyon, Ashes in the Wind*), the founding of some great commercial enterprise (*The Flame and the Flower, The Proud Breed, The Fulfillment, Shanna*), or in some social crusade (*The Sea Treasure, Made for Each Other*), these men prove the tenacity of their commitment to a transcendental public purpose by refusing to benefit personally from their success. While they are themselves morally pure, they also set an example so compelling that they are able to demand and receive the loyalty and commitment of other men as well. They are, of course, also extraordinarily competent and inevitably triumph over those who would attempt to deny their preeminence. In a fictional world that accords respect to men in general because of their strength, power, and ability to operate in the public realm, the romantic hero stands out as that world's most able representative and the essence of all that it values.

The Smithton readers are aware of the fact that even an ideal romantic hero has had sexual experiences before his encounters with the heroine. In fact, in these romances, the heroine's innocence is often contrasted explicitly with the hero's previous promiscuity, behavior that is made tolerable to both the heroine and the reader because it is always attributed to his lack of love for his sexual partners. His exclusive preoccupation with them as tools for achieving sexual release is never blamed on his callousness or lack of respect for women, but rather on his virility and his fear of emotional involvement with calculating women. This rationalization conveniently transforms his sexual promiscuity from an arrogant proclamation of his adherence to the double standard to a sign representing an absence, that is, the nonpresence of love. Perversely, it testifies, then, to his inescapable and intense need for the heroine. Once she can provide that love by persuading him to trust her, his promiscuous impulses are curbed. Sexual fidelity in the ideal romance is understood to be the natural partner of "true love."

Before summarizing these essential characteristics of the romantic heroine and hero, it should be pointed out that the meaning of their personalities is underscored for the reader by the presence of the secondary characters mentioned earlier. More specifically, the significance of heroine and hero as ideal feminine and masculine types is established by the existence of two abstract foils who embody those features of the female and male personalities that must be eradicated if women and men are to continue to love each other and fill one another's needs. The simple binary oppositions that are the basis for character differentiation in the romance are, therefore, a useful clue to the things women most fear as potential threats to heterosexual love and traditional marriage. Because their fears are embodied in the ideal romance in characters whose misbehavior is always explained away by their later destruction, the readers are encouraged to see those fears as unwarranted.

With its secondary characters, then, the ideal romance sketches a faint picture of male-female relationships characterized by suspicion and distrust in order to set off more effectively its later, finished portrait of the perfect union. In the act of substituting the one for the other by showing that the early hero/heroine relationship, although appearing as the former was, in reality, the latter, the romance ingeniously suggests to the reader that any evidence of worrisome traits and tendencies she finds in her own motives or those of her spouse can be reinterpreted in the most favorable light.

It can be seen from Table 4.1 that the heroine's sexual innocence, unselfconscious beauty, and desire for love are contrasted in the ideal romance with the female foil's self-interested pursuit of a comfortable social position. Because she views men as little more than tools for her own aggrandizement, the female foil is perfectly willing to manipulate them by flaunting her sexual availability. Incapable of caring for anyone other than herself, she makes demands upon the men she desires while promising nothing in return. This rival woman is the perfect incarnation of the calculating female whom the hero detests and thinks he sees hidden behind the heroine's beguiling facade. The heroine, of course, is never sure of the hero's true motives and often fears that he either loves the female foil or is taken in by her wiles.

Male rivals, on the other hand, are very shadowy figures in the ideal romance. While they do appear, they are described rather sparingly and almost never prove even momentarily attractive to the heroine. These foils are invariably of two types in the romances preferred by the Smithton women. Some, like Braeger Darvey in *Ashes in the Wind*, are sensitive, expressive, and overtly appreciative of the heroine's extraordinary qualities. Men like these are used to highlight the hero's surly reserve and his obstinate refusal to be persuaded that the heroine is not a femme fatale.

TABLE 4.1
Binary Oppositions in Character Portrayal at Beginning of the Romantic Narrative

Oppositional Pair	Heroine	Female Foil	Hero	Male Foil	Oppositional Pair	Villain
Virginal	+	−	−		Virginal	−
Experienced	−	+	+	Uncoded	Promiscuous	+
Desires love	+	−	−	+	Desires love	−
Desires wealth and position	−	+	+	−	Desires sexual pleasure	+
Unself-conscious	+	−	+	+	Unself-conscious	−
Vain	−	+	−	−	Vain	+
Beautiful	+	+	+	+	Handsome	−
Plain	−	−	−	−	Ugly	+
Nurturant	+	−	−	+	Tender	−
Demanding	−	+	+	−	Indifferent	+
Independent	+	−	+		Honest	−
Dependent	−	+	−	Uncoded	Corrupt	+
Intelligent	+		+	−	Courageous	−
Confused (gullible)	−	Uncoded	−	+	Cowardly	+
Fears men	+	−	+	−	Emotionally reserved	−
Desires men	−	+	−	+	Emotionally expressive	+

They are usually found lacking, however, because they are insufficiently aggressive, protective, and strong. The story suggests, in effect, that they are insufficiently masculine.

Ideal romances also employ another kind of foil, a true villain, who actually attempts to abduct the heroine from the arms of her hero. These figures are inevitably ugly, morally corrupt, and interested only in the heroine's sexual favors. They pose the constant threat of vicious rape and thus permit the author to differentiate the hero's "love-crazed" taking of the heroine from a truly malicious wish to use her for carnal pleasure. Although the heroine initially sees no difference between these individuals and the hero, their constant brutality and crude insinuations inform the reader that the hero is not cruel at all, only unskilled in the art of tender care for a woman. The presence of rival figures like Jacques Du Bonne in *Ashes in the Wind*, Thomas Hint in *The Flame and the Flower*, Louis in *The Proud Breed*, and Sir Morell in *The Black Lyon* is a constant reminder to the reader that a woman's sexuality contains the potential to do her great harm by virtue of its capacity to activate male lust and hatred of women. However, because the frequency and duration of the villains' attacks on the heroine are very carefully controlled by the authors of "ideal" romances, the suggestion that some men see women as sexual objects is made only fleetingly in order to teach the heroine the true worth of the hero. The fear is then banished effectively by the hero because he is finally portrayed as excited by the heroine's sexuality *and* respectful of her identity as an individual. His behavior informs the reader that what she most fears from men is really only a minor threat that can be eradicated permanently by the protective care of the man who truly loves her.

We will see in Chapter 5 that it is frequently this particular threat that is not controlled effectively in "failed" romances. In fact, villain figures run wild in these books. Moreover, they are not differentiated adequately from the hero. The happy union, then, at the romance's end is incapable of erasing the threat of violence and the fear it induces. It therefore fails to convince the reader that traditional sexual arrangements are benign.

Given the origination of this sample in actual reader selections from a large number of subgenres and publishing lines, it should not be surprising to note in turning from character to narrative that these ideal romances exhibit wide variation in superficial plot development. Nonetheless, when Vladimir Propp's method for determining the essential narrative structure of folktales is applied to these particular novels, it becomes clear that despite individual and isolated preoccupation with such things as reincarnation, adultery, amnesia, and mistaken identity, these stories are all built upon a shared narrative structure. Assuming first, as Will Wright does, that all narratives are composed of three essential stages—an initial situation, a final transformation of that situation, and an intermediary intervention that causes and explains the change—I then proceeded by trying to identify the common opening and conclusion of the romances in question. Once these had been isolated, I then looked for the most basic structure of embedded actions that could account coherently for the gradual transformation of the former into the latter. The result, a list of thirteen logically related functions, explains the heroine's transformation from an isolated, asexual, insecure adolescent who is unsure of her own identity, into a mature, sensual, and very married woman who has realized her full potential and identity as the partner of a man and as the implied mother of a child. The narrative structure of the ideal romance is summarized below:

1. The heroine's social identity is destroyed.
2. The heroine reacts antagonistically to an aristocratic male.
3. The aristocratic male responds ambiguously to the heroine.
4. The heroine interprets the hero's behavior as evidence of a purely sexual interest in her.
5. The heroine responds to the hero's behavior with anger or coldness.
6. The hero retaliates by punishing the heroine.
7. The heroine and hero are physically and/or emotionally separated.
8. The hero treats the heroine tenderly.
9. The heroine responds warmly to the hero's act of tenderness.
10. The heroine reinterprets the hero's ambiguous behavior as the product of previous hurt.
11. The hero proposes/openly declares his love for/demonstrates his unwavering commitment to the heroine with a supreme act of tenderness.
12. The heroine responds sexually and emotionally.
13. The heroine's identity is restored.

As the initial function indicates, the ideal romance begins with its heroine's removal from a familiar, comfortable realm usually associated with her childhood and family. Heather Simmons, for example, is taken away from her guardian by an evil uncle who intends to establish her in a whorehouse; Julie Dever is hurt in a car accident in an isolated mountain pass while away on vacation; Charlotte Hungerford leaves the privacy and protection of her writer's study to go to Brighton where her single status becomes the topic of disapproving gossip; Alaina McGaren is forced to flee her family's nearly destroyed plantation during the Civil War; and Deanna Abbott goes to a ranch in Arizona to escape her parents' efforts to mold her in their own image.[10] The details are different, but in each case the move terrifies the heroine because it strips her of her familiar supports and her sense of herself as someone with a particular place and a fixed identity. The mood of the romance's opening pages, then, is nearly always set by the heroine's emotional isolation and her profound sense of loss.

Keeping in mind what the Smithton women have said about their emotional state when they turn to romance reading, it seems possible that part of the attraction of the romance might be traced to the fact that this loss and the resulting emptiness it creates within the heroine continues and confirms a similar sense of depletion in the reader. The reader's sense of emptiness creates the initial desire for the romance's tale of a progressing relationship because the experience of being ignored by others is an emotional state both alien to women and difficult for them to bear. Because their family histories have created in them what Nancy Chodorow has identified as a "complex, relational self," romance readers need to avoid such feelings of emptiness by integrating important intimates into their psychic structures who will reciprocate their interest.[11] This profound need, which Chodorow maintains is rarely filled adequately by men because they have developed asymmetrically into individuals who do not define themselves in relation, is confirmed obligingly and addressed vicariously, then, by this story that relates another woman's successful journey from isolation and its threat of annihilation to connection and the promise of a mature, fulfilled female identity.

The complexities of Chodorow's theories are considerable and therefore cannot be reviewed in any depth here. Still, the remarkable similarity between her account of female personality development and the history of the ideal romantic heroine suggests that a broad outline of her argument's main points might be helpful in trying to explain the appeal of the romance. Essentially, Chodorow's thesis is that the characteristic sexual and familial division of labor in the patriarchal family, which accords mothering to women, results in an asymmetrical personality development in women and men that prompts them to reproduce this same division of labor. Her argument is grounded in object-relations theory and its primary insight that a child's social-relational experience from earliest infancy determines its later growth. This occurs because the child's early social relations with its primary caretaker(s) are internalized as its most basic model of itself as a self-in-relation. Thus the affective tone and residue of the intense mother-infant relationship in the patriarchal family continues to control the way the child encounters people and relies upon them to fulfill its adult needs. Chodorow maintains that the consequences of this relationship are different for male and female children when both relate most consistently to a female parent.

Early and exclusive mothering of a female child, for instance, tends to cement a daughter's identification with her mother, a state that later produces difficulties in the daughter's individuation. Chodorow explains that the early symbiotic union between mother and daughter is especially intense because the mother tends to experience her daughter as an extension of herself and because the father is rarely present continuously to act as a countering love-object. The lack of sexual difference, then, leads to a prolonged pre-oedipal state in the girl's development that tends to continue her dependency, ego-boundary confusion, and affective ambivalence about her mother. Because the daughter also experiences her mother as an extension of herself, she encounters considerable difficulties in recognizing herself as a separate person. The end result of this process, according to Chodorow, is an internalized portrait of the female self as a self-in-relation, which is later generalized as a view of the self as an extension or continuation of the world and others.

Chodorow argues further that the pre-oedipal mother-daughter bond is so strong that it even persists during the oedipal period when a girl turns her attention to her father. Differing, here, with Freud and his disciples, Chodorow maintains that the girl's turn is not motivated by a desire for the intrinsic properties of the penis but rather by a recognition of its value as a symbol of all that is not-mother. The oedipal move is partially initiated, then, by a daughter's desire to escape her intense symbiotic union with her mother. Her first real attempt at individuation is thus often expressed as identification with and desire for the father and all that is male. Chodorow adds, however, that the young girl also turns to her father because she "comes to realize that her common genital arrangement with her mother does not work to her advantage in forming a bond with her" (p. 125). More specifically, when she finds out that her mother prefers people like her father who have penises, she desires one for herself in order to secure her mother's love. Penis envy, identification with the father, and admiration of the male, therefore, are simultaneous expressions of a wish to assert her independence and of her love for and desire to win back the mother she has begun to relinquish.

Because the daughter's pre-oedipal ties to her mother persist throughout the oedipal period, her external and internal object worlds become triadic. This is to say that although her genital and erotic desires are focused on her father, she continues to maintain an intense emotional commitment to her mother and all that is female. The final result of this complex set of relationships for the girl, Chodorow maintains, is an "incomplete oedipal resolution." The girl becomes erotically heterosexual but at the same time carries an internal emotional triangle into adulthood, a triangle that is completed by her continuing need and desire for her mother. This finally produces in women a continuing wish to regress into infancy to reconstruct the lost intensity of the original mother-daughter bond.[12]

Although this is only a sketch of Chodorow's theory, it does enable us to provide a useful summary of her account of the typical female personality produced by the patriarchal family. Chodorow argues, first, that as a result of the difficulties of trying to separate from a parent of the same sex, girls tend to experience themselves as less differentiated than boys. They also feel themselves to be continuous with and related to the external object world and thus possess quite permeable ego-boundaries. As a result, they tend to experience an ongoing need for nurturance and attachment well into their adult lives. Their adult internal psychic world, moreover, is a complex relational constellation that continuously demands the balance and completion provided by other individuals. If this need is not adequately addressed by a relationship with an adult male, Chodorow reasons, a woman may turn to mothering as a way of establishing that necessary relationality. By identifying with the child she mothers, she imaginatively regresses to that state where all her needs were anticipated and satisfied without any exertion on her part.

Chodorow argues that women often resort to mothering as a source of vicarious nurturance precisely because men are emotionally constituted by female mothering in such a way that they find provision of this nurturance impossible. While there is no need to detail Chodorow's account of male development here, it is worth noting that the process tends to result in a negative definition of masculinity as all that is *not* female. This occurs in part because the pre-oedipal boy's attempt to separate from his mother is often bound up with gender-identity issues as a result of the fact that his mother could not help but sexualize their relationship. Because he thus becomes aware of his sexual difference from his mother, he often feels the need to suppress his feelings of dependence and his sense of having been merged with her in order to experience himself as fully differentiated from his mother. Later, in the oedipal period, when he must repress his oedipal attachment to her to avoid the competitive wrath of his father, he further denies his connection with anything womanly. Chodorow concludes that the final result of the boy's oedipal resolution is a personality structure defined by autonomy and independence, by a denial of rationality, and often by a corresponding devaluation of women.[13] The male endo-psychic world, moreover, "tends to be fixed and simpler" than that of the female, a fact that finally establishes the basic asymmetry in male and female personality development which explains a woman's desire and need to mother a child.

Although Chodorow emphasizes the effectiveness and success of mothering as an activity that compensates for the male inability to nurture, many women have also testified to the hidden costs of such a route to fulfillment. The activity of nurturing a child may indeed help to satisfy the female need for a self-in-relation and provide vicarious regression and affection, but it also makes tremendous demands on a woman to focus on the infant rather than on herself. Because she must at least delay and sometimes deny her own needs to provide her infant with all it requires, the very act of reinforcing her female identity and sense of self also draws on that self and may even seem to deplete it or negate it entirely. A woman is, therefore, likely to experience a sense of feeling empty of the self at the very time when she most desires to feel completed, petted, and fulfilled.

Within this context, the possibility that there may be a correlation between *some* romance reading and the social roles of wife and mother seems less than surprising. Given the nature of the female personality as a self-in-relation, the inability of men to function as completely adequate relational partners, and the reciprocal demands made upon women by the very children they rely on to satisfy their unmet needs, it is understandable that many women derive pleasure and encouragement from repetitive indulgence in romantic fantasies. On one level, then, the romance is an account of a woman's journey to female personhood *as that particular psychic configuration is constructed and realized within patriarchal culture*. It functions as a symbolic display and explanation of a process commonly experienced by many women. At the same time, because the ideal romance symbolically represents real female needs within the story and then depicts their successful satisfaction, it ratifies or confirms the inevitability and desirability of the entire institutional structure within which those needs are created and addressed.

In returning to the narrative structure of the romance, it should now be clear that the initial function dictating the heroine's loss of connections and identity is more deeply resonant in a psychoanalytic sense than it is overtly topical. When she is plucked from her earlier relationships and thrust out into a public world, the heroine's consequent terror and feeling of emptiness most likely evokes for the reader distant memories of her initial separation from her mother and her later ambivalent attempts to establish an individual identity. At the same time, it symbolically represents in a more general sense what it feels like for a woman to be alone without the necessary relation to another. As a consequence, the romance's opening exaggerates the very feeling of emptiness and desire that sent the reader to the book in the first place. The boyish independence of the typical heroine can be reinterpreted in this context as a symbolic representation of the initial step of a young girl's journey toward individuation and subsequent connection. The heroine, in effect, employs the usual method of individuating from the mother by turning to the next most proximate individual, her father. By identifying with him specifically or more generally with traits and achievements associated with men, the heroine simultaneously justifies her impulse to separate by degrading the feminine *and* accomplishes the actual rejection itself. She is free to embark finally on her quest for a new self and new connections. In rejecting her mother, the heroine immediately locates the reader's sense of loss and emptiness within a developmental pattern that holds out the promise of its later eradication in a future, perfect union with another.

Throughout the rest of the romantic narrative, then, two initially distinct stories are progressively intertwined. In fact, the heroine's search for her identity dovetails rather quickly with the tale of her developing relationship to the hero. Chodorow's theories are especially useful in explaining the psychological import of the stories' confluence. What the heroine successfully establishes by the end of the ideal narrative is the now-familiar female self, the self-in-relation. Because she manages this relation with a man who is not only masculine but redundantly so, the romance also manages to consider the possibilities and difficulties of establishing a connection with a man who is initially incapable of satisfying a woman. Thus the romance is concerned not simply with the fact of heterosexual marriage but with the perhaps more essential issues for women—how to realize a mature self and how to achieve emotional fulfillment in a culture in which such goals must be achieved in the company of an individual whose principal preoccupation is always *elsewhere* in the public world.

The problems posed for women by characteristically masculine behavior are highlighted early in the romantic narrative by function 2 and the frightened, antagonistic response of the heroine to the mere presence of an ambiguous man. Because the hero's hard physical exterior is complemented by his imperious, distant manner, the heroine automatically assumes that he finds her uninteresting or, in some cases, intends to harm her. Still, she is troubled by that contradictory evidence of his hidden, gentle nature and she therefore feels unsure of his motives. Because she cannot seem to avoid contact with him despite her dislike, the heroine's principal activity throughout the rest of the story consists of the mental process of trying to assign particular signifieds to his overt acts. In effect, what she is trying to do in discovering the significance of his behavior by uncovering his motives is to understand what the fact of male presence and attention means for her, a woman.

It should be clear by now that romance authors raise this issue of the import of male motives for sound material and psychological reasons. In a culture that circumscribes female work within the domestic sphere by denying women full entry into the public realm, any woman who cannot attach herself to a member of the culture who is permitted to work runs the risk of poverty, if not outright annihilation.[14] At the same time, because men are parented within the culture solely by women, they tend to individuate and define themselves in explicit opposition to anything female. If this does not always result in misogyny or in its expression by violence against women, it does end at least in the repression of traits and emotional tendencies typically identified with them. Therefore, even men who are not brutal tend to relate to women on a relatively superficial emotional level just as they define them principally as sexual creatures because their physiological characteristics are the most obvious mark of their difference from men. Given the fact that a woman and any future children she might have are economically dependent on such men, it becomes absolutely essential that she learn to distinguish those who want her sexually from that special individual who is willing to pledge commitment and care in return for her sexual favor.

Male reserve and indifference also become issues in the romance because, if left untempered, they can hinder a woman from satisfying her most basic needs for relationality and emotional nurturance. Because women move out of their oedipal conflict with a triangular psychic structure intact, not only do they need to connect themselves with a member of the opposite sex, but they also continue to require an intense emotional bond with someone who is reciprocally nurturant and protective in a maternal way. The homophobic nature of the culture effectively denies them the opportunity to receive this from the hands of someone who resembles the woman responsible for their memory of it. Therefore, because direct regression through an intense relationship with an individual resembling her mother is denied a woman (as it is not denied to a man), she must learn to suppress the need entirely, to satisfy it through her relationship with a man, or to seek its fulfillment in other activities. Although the ideal romance initially admits the difficulty of relying on men for gentleness and affective intensity, thus confirming the reader's own likely experience, it also reassures her that such satisfaction is possible because men really do know how to attend to a woman's needs.

This peculiar double perspective on male behavior is achieved by a narrative structure that allows the reader greater knowledge of the hero than the heroine herself possesses. Because she is given access to his true feelings and intentions by an omniscient narration that reveals something about his past that justifies his present behavior, the reader can reinterpret the action in functions 4, 5, and 6. For example, where the heroine believes the hero's behavior is merely ambiguous (function 3), the reader knows that his unreadable actions are the product of emotional turmoil prompted by his feelings for the heroine. Similarly, when the hero appears to punish the heroine (function 6), the reader can tell herself that such punishment is the result of hurt and disappointment at the heroine's supposed infidelity or lack of interest in him. It is, then, a sign of his love for her, not of his distaste. The double perspective on the hero's behavior thus allows the reader to have it both ways. She can identify with the heroine's point of view and therefore with her anger and fear. The act of reading, in that case, provides her with an imaginative space to express her reservations and negative feelings about men. On the other hand, she can rely on the greater knowledge accorded to her by the narration and enjoy the reassurance it provides that, in fact, men do not threaten women or function as obstacles to their fulfillment. In the safe realm of the imaginary, then, the romance reader is allowed to indulge in the expression of very real fears that she is permitted to control simultaneously by overruling them with the voice of her greater knowledge.

The importance of this dual perspective is made especially clear by the ideal romance's peculiar treatment of rape. Although rape does not figure in all twenty of the books in this sample, when it does, it occurs as function 6 in the narrative. Remember that in the discussion of the Smithton group's taste in romantic fiction in Chapter 3, it was noted that while they do not like stories that dwell on violent rapes, Dot and her customers will tolerate and rationalize rape if it occurs under certain circumstances. The portrayal of violence in general and rape in particular in their favorite romances bears out their claim. When rape is included, authors of ideal romances always make a clear distinction between men who rape as an act of aggression against women and those who, like their heroes, do so because they misinterpret a woman's actions or find her irresistible. *The Proud Breed*, for instance, includes a violent rape of the heroine by a squatter, but the incident is integrated into the narrative for two larger purposes. On the one hand, it permits the author to "educate" her readers about the real consequences of rape: Tessa does not secretly love it but is physically and emotionally scarred by the experience. Indeed, she thinks of it as "[t]he final threat, not just an invasion of the land, but of herself, her body, and her soul" (p. 373). De Blasis uses the rape to extend her characterization of Tessa's husband as an extraordinary individual. Gavin does not indulge in the familiar practice of blaming his wife for what has been done to her nor does he find her less desirable after she has been "used" by another man. Instead, he responds to her overwhelming need for tenderness by comforting her and by making no sexual demands until she indicates that she is ready.

In a now-famous essay that first appeared in *MS* magazine in 1976, Molly Haskell suggested that female fantasies about violence and rape are exploration fantasies born out of anxiety and fear rather than wish-fulfillment fantasies originating in sexual desire.[15] Rape, she argued, is not their "end point and goal" but their "beginning and given."[16] A woman who fantasizes about rape often does so, Haskell maintained, because she knows violence against women is prevalent in her culture and because she fears it deeply. By imagining it occurring to her, she makes projections about how she would react or whether she would survive. In effect, through her imagination she controls an occurrence that is widespread in her culture which she can neither predict nor prevent. Although not all rape fantasies serve this function, as Haskell herself noted, it seems very clear that De Blasis's presentation in *The Proud Breed* projects a utopian conclusion to an event that she and her readers have good reason to fear. Nonetheless, while her portrayal may be applauded for its willingness to admit that rape is intrinsically horrible and should be blamed on men, as well as for its suggestion that some women are capable of repulsing the violence directed at them, its optimistic conclusion runs the risk of undercutting her original intent because it perpetuates, albeit inadvertently, the illusion that rape is not really a serious threat to female integrity.

If this tendency to minimize a serious problem out of a profound need to believe that it can be controlled characterizes De Blasis's relatively honest description of rape, it is even more characteristic of the other, typical violations that occur in *The Flame and the Flower*, *The Black Lyon*, and *Ashes in the Wind*. In each, the rape comes about in large part because the hero believes the heroine is a prostitute or at least sexually promiscuous. In the course of violating her, the hero always discovers that the heroine is a virgin and responds to her in a way he has "never responded to a woman before." His subsequent remorse and acknowledgment that the heroine is somehow different seem to excuse and justify his behavior to the narrator and to the Smithton readers, although, I should add, not before provoking in them a good deal of indignation and anger about his "stupidity" and "pig-headedness."[17] Like the heroine herself, the Smithton readers are outraged by the hero's behavior. The narrative's double perspective gives them an additional advantage, however, because it informs them that the hero would never have mistreated the heroine if he had known she was a truly good woman.

In questioning Dot and her customers about their angry response to romantic rape, it became clear that they did not blame the hero for violating a woman but rather for lacking the perception to see that the heroine was not a prostitute. They seem to accept the axiom common in their sexist and patriarchal culture that all women must control their sexuality if they do not wish to be raped. The Smithton readers believe that if a woman fails to disguise her sensuality properly, she will run the risk of exciting the uncontrollable male "sex-drive," which will then demand to be released. Although Dot and her customers claim they do not believe in the double standard, they continue to hold women responsible for applying the brakes to sexual passion just as they persist in "understanding" men who take advantage of "loose women." Their anger is directed not at men's lack of respect for female integrity but at their inability to discriminate between innocent women and bad.

It might also be said about rapes in the ideal romance that because the hero initiates the sexual contact that the heroine later enjoys, it is ultimately he who is held responsible for activating her sexuality. She is free, then, to enjoy the pleasures of her sexual nature without having to accept the blame and guilt for it usually assigned to women by men. Rape in the ideal romance thus helps to perpetuate the distinction between "those who do and those who don't," just as it continues to justify and make possible the repression of female sexuality. This is especially ironic because, as we shall see shortly, subsequent developments in the ideal romantic narrative attempt to demonstrate that once awakened by a man, a woman can respond passionately to him unhampered by her previous repression. Female sexuality, in fact, is not banned in the ideal romance. It is, however, always circumscribed by the novel's assumption that patriarchy, heterosexuality, and male personality are givens that are absolutely beyond challenge. The narrative action demonstrates that in order to secure the nurturance and security that they need for themselves, women must confine their sexual desire to the marriage bed and avoid threatening men with a too-active or demanding sexuality.

This is made especially clear by the ideal heroine's typical response to her rape by the hero. Although she usually experiences twinges of pleasure after the initial shock of penetration, no heroine in the twenty books in the sample responds completely to the initial violation. More often than not, she is both bewildered by her reaction and appalled that she cannot control her body as successfully as she can control her mind. She continues to hate the hero for his mistreatment of her although it is quite clear to the reader that what the heroine takes to be hatred is, in fact, disappointment that the man she has fallen in love with has not treated her as the precious beloved she would like to be. It is only after the hero demonstrates in a moment of crisis or unusual spontaneity that he can be gentle with her that the ideal heroine feels free enough to respond and eventually to enjoy herself.

Woodiwiss's treatment of this issue in *The Flame and the Flower* is worth looking at here because it shows how the typical ideal romance ignores the fact that a rape has occurred by stressing the hero's remorse and by demonstrating his potential to make adequate reparation in the future. Of the actual rape, Woodiwiss writes:

> A half gasp, half shriek escaped her and a burning pain seemed to spread through her loins. Brandon started back in astonishment and stared down at her. She lay limp against the pillows, rolling her head back and forth upon them. He touched her cheek tenderly and murmured something low and inaudible, but she had her eyes closed and wouldn't look at him. He moved against her gently, kissing her hair and brow and caressing her body with his hands. She lay unrespon-

sive, yet his long starved passions grew and soon he thrust deeply within her, no longer able to contain himself. It seemed with each movement now she would split asunder and tears came to her eyes.

The storm at its end, a long quiet moment slipped past as he relaxed against her, once more gentle. But when he finally withdrew, she turned to the wall and lay softly sobbing with the corner of the blanket pulled over her head and her now used body left bare to his gaze. (p. 34)

Brandon slowly regenerates himself in the reader's eyes first and then in the heroine's by treating her with increasing tenderness. Although he continues to believe Heather is an opportunist and she herself remains angry with him over the rape (function 7), their emotional separation does not stop him from surprising her with especially thoughtful gifts (function 8). For example, he manages to get a bathtub for her on board their ship and has long underwear made to keep her warm on the winter voyage. Both presents prompt Heather to wonder whether Brandon is as cold as he seems. She further doubts his detachment when she recovers from a long delirium and fever to discover that he has nursed her himself without the assistance of others.

Woodiwiss continues to increase the frequency of tender incidents like these, demonstrating ever more insistently *to the reader* that her hero does cherish the heroine despite his stubborn pride and that he is supremely capable of caring for her in an unusually nurturant way. Although Heather continues to accord more importance to his lingering reticence and refusal to acknowledge his love verbally, his gentle behavior gradually crumbles her defenses until she wants to respond passionately to his sexual advances. Just when she is about to admit that she wants him, however, a small insensitivity on his part prompts an angry meditation that indicates very clearly what she expects to get from her husband: "What thinks he that he may come in here while the house is overflowing with his friends and among them that blond bitch [his former fiancée] and command me to spread my thighs for him? Does he think there need not be words spoken of love nor soft caresses to soothe my body? Am I truly then to him a possession and not a wife, a whore who's met his fancy?" (p. 349). Clearly, she wants to be petted and fussed over as intensely and repetitively as a child might be by its mother. She also wishes to receive constant verbal assurances of love that will obviate the need to interpret the covert meanings of her husband's typically distant behavior. In thus giving form to her desires, she and all of the other heroines in these ideal romances openly deny what several analysts have said of romantic heroines and of the women who identify with them, which is that they masochistically enjoy being brutalized, terrorized, and hurt by men.[18] What all of the

heroines want is tenderness and nurturance. Because their stories are utopian fantasies, they receive both; in accepting them, they finally respond
freely to a man and learn that they are mature women with sexual desires
and tastes that can lead to very personal pleasure.

Parris Afton Bonds's description of Julie's first "perfect" coupling with
Nick in *Made for Each Other* is typical of those in the other nineteen ideal
romances that stress the hero's tenderness and the heroine's subsequent
assistance and participation in the sexual act. It is significant that this
occurs immediately after Nick has given Julie an especially meaningful
Christmas gift:

> With deliberate leisureliness, she unbuttoned Nick's shirt. Nick's
> brows raised questioningly, as though to ask her if she understood
> the implications of what she was doing.
>
> Her hand reached for the snap of his slacks, her fingers deftly
> loosening the catch. Still, Nick did not move. His eyes scorched her
> face. Julie's fingers halted at the zipper, and she stood on tiptoe, her
> hands splaying against his chest for balance, and kissed the carved
> lines of his lips before playfully teasing them with her tongue. . . .
>
> The realization slowly dawned on Julie that no longer was she the
> seducer. Nick had swiftly turned the tables, and it was she who lay
> trembling, waiting for him to make her complete. He came to her
> then, gently, tenderly, patiently. And when it was over, she buried her
> head in the hollow of his shoulder, so he would not see the ecstasy,
> the love, that she felt surely must shine in her eyes. (pp. 159–60)

Despite her initiation of sexual contact, Julie is transformed in the
course of this passage into a passive, expectant, trembling creature who
feels incomplete without the attentions of the hero. While one might say
that she simply has adopted the typical stance prescribed for women in
patriarchal culture, it should also be noted that she has become infantile in
the sense that she is all passive, incomplete desire, yearning for the life-
giving nurturance of a tender and gentle but all-powerful individual. A
description like this quite obviously expresses a desire for a heterosexual
partner but, at the same time, it also seems to mask a covert and unconscious wish to regress to the state of infancy in order to experience again,
but this time completely and without the slight withholding born of
homophobia, that primary love the infant received at the breast and hands
of her mother. The very particular manner in which the crucial love scene
is described in the ideal romance suggests that the heroine's often expressed desire to be the hero's formally recognized wife in fact camou-
flages an equally insistent wish to be his child.[19]

Elisabeth Barr's *The Sea Treasure* is especially interesting to consider in
this context because she converts what are usually only covert hints into

the explicit theme of her book. Her heroine, Leonora, is more than physically cut off from her family and earlier identity. The victim of a shipwreck, she suffers from severe amnesia. When she is rescued by the hero, she possesses only two distant memories—one of a loving woman, the other of a terrifying man. Because she fears all men as a consequence, she refuses to respond to Dominic who falls in love with her almost immediately. Barr's subsequent treatment of his efforts to prove his love makes the regressive impulse at the heart of the romance unusually explicit. Consider this passage detailing the way he comforts her after a nightmare:

> He went across to her, and held the shaking body close to his, stroking her hair. . . .
> He lay on the coverlet, putting his arm around her and cradling her head against his shoulders. Leonora sighed once, deeply, and her lids fluttered over her eyes. In a little while she slept. . . .
> In the fireplace, the dying coals fell with a soft crash, making Leonora start and tremble in her sleep, until he soothed her with the touch of his fingers on her cheek, and she slept again. (pp. 86–87)

Barr here embodies an ideal hero's love for his heroine in the image of a mother who stays with her child through a storm to soothe away its fears. In fact, she later writes that Leonora recalls that night with "a clear picture of [a] man, one who had stayed with her through the long night, holding her as carefully as though she had been a sick child. *That* memory warmed her, put soft color in her cheeks" (p. 89). This romantic heroine is not excited by brutality but sensuously aroused by the promise of being nurtured as a child is by its mother. Barr's descriptions make it unusually clear that the fantasy that generates the romance originates in the oedipal desire to love and be loved by an individual of the opposite sex *and* in the continuing pre-oedipal wish that is part of a woman's inner-object configuration, the wish to regain the love of the mother and all that it implies—erotic pleasure, symbiotic completion, and identity confirmation.

Barr renders this most obvious in the final pages of *The Sea Treasure* when she has Leonora explicitly connect her love for her mother with her newfound love for Dominic. At the moment when she confronts sure death, Leonora thinks of "her mother, who had loved her so selflessly, and whom she had loved deeply in return." The sentence continues, however, with a "but" that indicates that a new love has replaced that primordial one. Barr continues, "but the realization of her great love for Dominic Pengallion was a new and frightening thing" and adds later that now Leonora "realized how much she loved the man who had brought her from death to life" (p. 191).

In finally rescuing Leonora from danger, Dominic once again tenderly carries her against his chest, calls her his "Sea Treasure," and insists, despite her returning memory, that she will always be Leonora (a name he gave her) to him. But even as he demands that she relinquish her old identity, he also restores it to her by reuniting her with her real mother. It is only then, when she has regained her mother both actually and symbolically, that Leonora finally declares her love for Dominic. He is the ideal male partner who is capable of fulfilling both object roles in this woman's triangular inner-object configuration. His spectacular masculinity underscores his status as her heterosexual lover and confirms the completeness of her rejection of her childlike self. At the same time, his extraordinary tenderness and capacity for gentle nurturance means she does not have to give up the physical part of her mother's attentions because his "soft" sexual attention allows her to return to the passive state of infancy where all of her needs were satisfied and her fears were erased at her mother's breast. The symbolic recovery of primary love and the total security and identity confirmation it implies finally enable her to embrace her new identity as a mature woman.

Thus the romance originates in the female push toward individuation and actualization of the self, but because it is written by women who have been engendered within a patriarchal family characterized by exclusively female "mothering," that drive is embodied within the language and forms created and prescribed by patriarchy. Consequently, to achieve *female* selfhood in the romance, which is an expression of patriarchal culture, is to realize an identity in relation not merely to one but to two important others. The romance does deny the worth of complete autonomy. In doing so, however, it is not obliterating the female self completely. Rather, it is constructing a particular kind of female self, the self-in-relation demanded by patriarchal parenting arrangements.

It is obvious, then, why the romance must also concern itself with the nature of masculinity and its implications for women. The stories are written from a perspective that is well aware of the difficulties posed by male autonomy and reticence and, as a result, they are exercises in the imaginative transformation of masculinity to conform with female standards. This is precisely what occurs when the emotional standoff between hero and heroine is partially broken in the ideal romance by the hero's act of tenderness (function 8). What makes this so interesting, however, is not the fact that it occurs. This is, after all, a woman's fantasy and, as such, it fulfills desires and satisfies wishes that are basic to her psychological construction. Function 8 of the ideal romance is intriguing precisely because it is *not structurally explained* by the narrative *at the time that it occurs*. No action on the part of the hero or, for that matter, on the part of any other character can be said to cause or explain the magic transformation of his cruelty and indifference into tender care. The abrupt transformation simply takes place.

Although the hero's punishment of the heroine results in his separation from her, the separation is never connected explicitly *at this point in the story* with his ensuing act of kindness. Because the hero does not indicate overtly either in his thoughts or in conversation that this separation causes him to recognize his dependence upon the heroine, function 7 is not presented as the effective agent in the transformation of function 6 into function 8. The separation simply occurs and then the hero demonstrates miraculously that he can be tender with the heroine. Of course, the fact that this transformation has been prepared for surreptitiously by earlier descriptions of the hero, which contain a clue to the underlying softness hiding behind his impassive facade, makes the shift palatable to the reader. But in relying on the reader's greater knowledge, the romance author avoids having the hero openly declare his dependence on a woman. He continues to be seen as a supreme example of unchallenged, autonomous masculinity. Later in the text when hero and heroine are finally united, he confesses that it was the prospect of losing her that frightened him and prompted his decision to woo her with tenderness. In falling back on this kind of retroactive interpretation, however, the romance avoids considering the problem of the contradiction between admission of dependency and relationality and the usual definition of masculinity as total autonomy. The hero is permitted simply to graft tenderness onto his unaltered male character. The addition of the one, the romance implies, need not transform the other. Consequently, the genre fails to show that if the emotional repression and independence that characterize men are actually to be reversed, the entire notion of what it is to be male will have to be changed.

The romance inadvertently tells its reader, then, that she will receive the kind of care she desires only if she can find a man who is *already* tender and nurturant. This hole in the romance's explanatory logic is precisely the point at which a potential argument for change is transformed into a representation and recommendation of the status quo. The reader is not shown how to find a nurturant man nor how to hold a distant one responsible for altering his lack of emotional availability. Neither is she encouraged to believe that male indifference and independence really can be altered. What she is encouraged to do is to latch on to whatever expressions of thoughtfulness he might display, no matter how few, and to consider them, rather than his more obvious and frequent disinterest, as evidence of his true character. In learning *how to read* a man properly, the romance tells its reader, she will reinforce his better instincts, break down his reserve, and lead him to respond to her as she wishes. Once she has set the process in motion by responding warmly to his rare demonstrations of affection (function 9), she will further see that his previous impassivity was the result of a former hurt (function 10). If she can recognize that, she will understand, as the romantic heroine always does, that her man really loves her and that he is dependent on her even if neither of them wishes to admit it openly.

The romantic narrative demonstrates that a woman must learn to trust her man and to believe that he loves her deeply even in the face of massive evidence to the contrary. The fantasy's conclusion suggests that when she manages such trust, he will reciprocate with declarations of his commitment to her (function 11). That commitment, the romance further insists, which also implies his need for her, is the condition for her free and uninhibited response (function 12). Once she responds to his passion with her own, she will feel as the heroine does, both emotionally complete and sexually satisfied. In short, she will have established successfully an external connection with a man whose behavior she now knows how to read correctly. The romance's conclusion promises her that if she learns to read male behavior successfully, she will find that her needs for fatherly protection, motherly care, and passionate adult love will be satisfied perfectly. The explanatory structure of this argument is represented in Table 4.2.

Clifford Geertz has observed that in attending a cockfight, the young Balinese receives from this essential art form of his culture "a kind of sentimental education."[20] "What he learns there," Geertz writes, "is what his culture's ethos and his private sensibility . . . look like when spelled out externally in a collective text."[21] The experience of reading the romance is little different for Dot and her customers. In effect, they are instructed about the nature of patriarchy and its meaning for them as women, that is, as individuals who do not possess power in a society dominated by men. Not only does the romantic drama evoke the material consequences of refusal to mold oneself in the image of femininity prescribed by the culture but it also displays the remarkable benefits of conformity.

Equally significant, however, the romance also provides a symbolic portrait of the womanly sensibility that is created and required by patriarchal marriage and its sexual division of labor. By showing that the heroine finds someone who is intensely and exclusively interested in her and in her needs, the romance confirms the validity of the reader's desire for tender nurture and legitimizes her pre-oedipal wish to recover the primary love of her initial caretaker. Simultaneously, by witnessing her connection with an autonomous and powerful male, it also confirms her longing to be protected, provided for, and sexually desired. The romance legitimizes her own heterosexuality and decision to marry by providing the heroine with a spectacularly masculine partner and a perfect marriage. In thus symbolically reproducing the triangular object configuration that characterizes female personality development through the heroine's relationships, the romance underscores and shores up the very psychological structure that guarantees women's continuing commitment to marriage and motherhood. It manages to do so, finally, because it also includes a set of very

TABLE 4.2
The Narrative Logic of the Romance

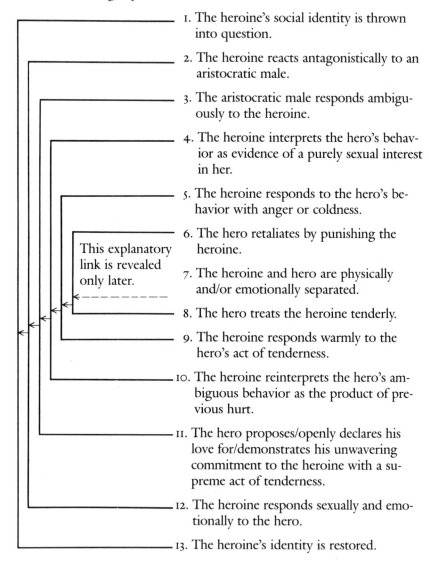

1. The heroine's social identity is thrown into question.

2. The heroine reacts antagonistically to an aristocratic male.

3. The aristocratic male responds ambiguously to the heroine.

4. The heroine interprets the hero's behavior as evidence of a purely sexual interest in her.

5. The heroine responds to the hero's behavior with anger or coldness.

6. The hero retaliates by punishing the heroine.

This explanatory link is revealed only later.

7. The heroine and hero are physically and/or emotionally separated.

8. The hero treats the heroine tenderly.

9. The heroine responds warmly to the hero's act of tenderness.

10. The heroine reinterprets the hero's ambiguous behavior as the product of previous hurt.

11. The hero proposes/openly declares his love for/demonstrates his unwavering commitment to the heroine with a supreme act of tenderness.

12. The heroine responds sexually and emotionally to the hero.

13. The heroine's identity is restored.

usable instructions which guarantee that *she* will not reject her current partner or hold out for the precise combination of tenderness and power that the heroine discovers in the hero. Because the romance provides its reader with the strategy and ability to reinterpret her own relationship, it insures patriarchal culture against the possibility that she might demand to have both her need for nurturance and adult heterosexual love met by a single individual.

The romance thematizes the activity of interpretation and reinterpretation for a very good reason, then. In suggesting that the cruelty and indifference that the hero exhibits toward the heroine in the early part of the novel are really of no consequence because they *actually* originated in love and affection, the romance effectively asserts that there are other signs for these two emotions than the traditional ones of physical caresses, oral professions of commitment, and thoughtful care. When the heroine retroactively reinterprets the hero's offensive behavior as equivalent expressions of his basic feeling for her, the reader is encouraged to engage in the same rereading process in order to understand properly what she is offered daily in her own relationship. The romance perpetuates the illusion that, like water into wine, brusque indifference can be transformed into unwavering devotion. Its value derives from its offer of a set of procedures that will accomplish the transformation. In learning how to read male behavior from the romance, a woman insulates herself from the need to demand that such behavior change. As Geertz has said of quartets, still lifes, and cockfights, the romance is not merely the analogical representation of a preexisting sensibility but a positive agent in its creation and perpetuation.[22]

As a coda to the argument presented in this chapter that some romance fiction is as much about recovering motherly nurturance and affection as it is about the need to be found desirable by men, I would like to point out that romances vary considerably in the explicitness with which they acknowledge and represent this persistent desire to merge with a wholly attentive, gentle other. Kathleen Woodiwiss, for instance, places heavy emphasis on the nurturing abilities of her heroes but does not concern herself overtly with the heroine/mother relationship. Elisabeth Barr, on the other hand, parallels her love story with another tale about the heroine's efforts to recover her lost identity and her real mother. Despite such internal variation within the genre, however, all popular romantic fiction originates in the failure of patriarchal culture to satisfy its female members. Consequently, the romance functions always as a utopian wish-fulfillment fantasy through which women try to imagine themselves as they often are not in day-to-day existence, that is, as happy and content. Some writers are simply more successful than others at refusing the language of desire and satisfaction offered to them by their culture. A few have managed to retain a semblance of a more independent voice in order to say that it is not hardness, indifference, and emotional cruelty that women want but an exclusive and intense emotional relationship with a tender, life-giving individual. This longing, born of relational poverty, is implicit in all romantic fiction; only occasionally does it manage to forge for itself a language of forms capable of giving it fuller expression. This has occurred, however, in one of the novels in the sample selected for this chapter. I would like to close, then, by looking at *Green Lady* by Leigh Ellis to show what can happen when the desire that inhabits all romances refuses to be contained completely within patriarchal forms.

Green Lady (1981) was written by the mother-and-daughter team of Anne and Louisa Rudeen. Educated at the University of Kansas (Anne) and at Yale (Louisa), they are much more conscious of literary history and generic conventions than most typical authors of romances. Their literary consciousness in part explains their ability to see that the romance is an alterable set of generic conventions rather than a natural and immutable organic form. Although their book has been published by Avon as a romance complete with the standard cover and blurbs, in fact it takes important liberties with the genre's conventions. The novel employs many standard characters and events, but its plot structure does not conform to the usual pattern. Its deviations are significant because, in altering the romantic plot, the Rudeens have made more explicit the romance's usually submerged concern with the mother-daughter relationship. I should add that Dot awarded the book five stars, reviewed it enthusiastically as a "unique" offering, and featured a short biography of the authors in her May 1981 newsletter. She also urged her customers to read it and reported that the many who did agreed that it was a very good book.

Green Lady opens conventionally enough with the heroine's entrance into a London disco. It differs almost immediately from the typical romance, however, because Dorinda Westerly is accompanied by her actress-mother whom she very obviously admires (p. 11). It soon becomes clear that the story will focus on both women. As soon as they enter the nightclub, Dorinda and Emma encounter a man they knew long ago in Newport. In conversing with Emma, this friend makes it immediately clear to the reader that all three witnessed a murder some years ago. When Emma and Bill agree to meet the next day, it is obvious that the mystery will also figure centrally in the narrative.

The second chapter returns to the usual concerns of the romance as it describes the first encounter of the two women with the men who become their suitors. While waiting for her mother to audition for a play, Dorinda is transfixed by another waiting actor, Paul Innowell, who is typically handsome and sexually attractive. She thinks to herself, in fact, that "[n]ever in her life had she felt so powerful an urge just to pounce on a strange man and start kissing him" (p. 24). She does not have to wait long, for on the next page, after asking her permission, he kisses her passionately. As in most romances, it is obvious to the reader that they have fallen in love instantly. Her encounter with Paul is paralleled by her mother's introduction to Trevor York. His "adventurous" appearance immediately distinguishes him from her former husband who was "more an ardent fan than a dashing lover" (p. 23).

Despite the complication provided by the mystery, the love plots remain central to the novel for several chapters. Dorinda's involvement in particular deepens rapidly; when she and Paul make love after their first date, it becomes even clearer that *Green Lady* is different from other ideal romances. The one feature it shares with the others is its emphasis on the hero's tenderness in sex and on the feeling of complete union the heroine achieves with him. Nonetheless, when the following description, which evokes the climactic passage usually found on the final pages of a four-hundred page historical, appears on page 43, the reader cannot help but wonder what kind of misunderstanding could possibly separate them. At this early stage in the novel, the heroine achieves the kind of oceanic merging with a nurturant, heterosexual lover that is the final goal of every other romance:

> [H]e bent over her and started to kiss her, beginning at her throat and working downward, evoking delicious sensations that again quickly became so intense that she held onto his shoulders with both hands and felt pleasure spiraling through her body until even her perception of herself was swept away and she felt boundless and pulsing, helpless to stop the tide of feeling that swept over her and left her only after an ecstatic moment that went on unendurably, past all boundaries shattering in its impact. (p. 43)

What is even more astonishing than their early lovemaking is that nothing occurs to distance the lovers from each other. Their mutual attachment continues to grow because they are both open and honest. As a result, there is no need for the usual romantic skill of reinterpretation. The relationship between Dorinda and Paul simply develops as an ideal romantic passion. The fact that there are still 150 pages to be read suggests, even if only implicitly, that this idyllic union is still somehow incomplete.

In the meantime, Emma's connection with Trevor York stalls because she soon becomes convinced that the Mafia is murdering all witnesses to the killing in Newport. She is terrified because she knows Dorinda was known to have been in the club at the time. When she feels certain her daughter is being stalked, she formulates a plan to protect her; Emma proposes to fake her own death in order to guard her daughter surreptitiously.

There is no need to recount the rather complicated story that ensues, but one incident is crucial here. When Emma's death is successfully staged on the island of Ibiza, Dorinda returns to England with Paul while looking everywhere for her mother who promised her she would never be far from her though she would be disguised. At one point, Dorinda goes to a nightclub thinking she might draw her mother into the open. When she sees a familiar-looking woman, she is convinced she has found her mother. Dorinda approaches her and offers her a drink. Taken aback, the woman agrees, telling her she looks like "a little girl who's lost her mother" (p. 116). Of course, Dorinda takes this as a sign that the woman is indeed Emma. She accepts an invitation to go to her apartment thinking that then they will be reunited. Later, exasperated that her mother does not reveal her identity, she exclaims, "Mother, honestly, what is this?" She is shocked when the woman kisses her and tells her that she is not old enough to be her mother, but "will be, if that's what you'd like" (p. 120). Realizing that the woman is a lesbian, Dorinda runs out thinking to herself, "The countess hadn't anything to do with Mother!" (p. 120).

It should be clear by now that *Green Lady* is preoccupied explicitly with the search for the lost mother. Although I think it unfair to attribute deliberate intent to the writers here, it is obvious that this scene has been included as a kind of red herring. Subliminally aware that longing for reunion with the mother overrides taboos on homosexuality, the authors have included the scene to demonstrate otherwise, to assert, in effect, that mother has nothing to do with lesbianism! Having assured themselves of that, the Rudeens are free to imagine otherwise unimaginable possibilities.

The first half of the book ends at this point with Dorinda's vow to return to America. The second half chronicles her efforts to find out the truth about the Mafia killing in the hope that she will learn enough to tell the police. In the course of the narrative she gets involved with an attractive but cruel man whose brutal sexual attentions she merely endures. She eventually stumbles across the real killer, of course, tries to bait him, and is wounded seriously for her efforts. When she passes out only a few pages from the end of the book, the unsuspecting reader is left almost totally at sea. Then, in a surprising third section, the reader learns that the Dorinda of Part 2 was, in fact, Emma. In order to protect her daughter, she decided to *become* her daughter. She had plastic surgery to change her facial features and then set out to draw the murderers out into the open before they found her real daughter.

The final scene of the novel takes place in Emma's hospital room. Now mirror images of each other, mother and daughter are reunited. Emma's delirious memories are interspersed with the crooning of a nurse who calls her "baby" and tries to get her to eat. Then, suddenly, she hears a voice call, "Mother." Her subsequent thoughts are especially revealing. Although she recalls that she is a mother, what she really wants is to *have* a mother: "It was the voice of a young girl; almost her own voice. Had she spoken? But she would never call, 'Mother.' The idea of having a mother—she had been a mother, but she had never really *had* a mother, not since so long ago when she had been ordered to leave home" (p. 206). Again, I hesitate to attribute conscious intent here, but the passage is a remarkable illustration of Chodorow's argument that behind a woman's desire to mother a child hides her own wish to be mothered. Emma's longing to be taken care of is granted, but not before she establishes with her daughter the fact that they are safe. As she regains consciousness, Emma tries to recall what she has done to protect her daughter: "The man who had frightened her for so long was gone," she wondered, "[w]asn't he?" (p. 207). When Dorinda responds that he is dead, she adds, "We're safe. You did what you wanted to do—you saved us both."

In a book written, marketed, and read as a romance, it is indeed curious that mother and daughter are restored to each other *only* when the male threat has been eradicated. Not only has Emma killed the man who wanted to take her daughter from her, but Paul is not permitted to witness their reunion. Free of all male presence, then, mother and daughter reverse roles as Dorinda reassures Emma that she will be fine by tenderly pressing her mother's hand to her cheek. When Emma protests that she will have to have the plastic surgery reversed, Dorinda answers that although Trevor might prefer it *she* likes Emma's face the way it is. In this utopian female fantasy, male wishes are ultimately ignored. Mother and daughter, who are now actually one person, lose themselves in each other's gaze. The final two lines of *Green Lady* describe the real merging, which is the deepest desire of the ideal romantic heroine who usually must rest content with a symbolic satisfaction of that desire through union with a nurturant hero. Here, mother and daughter merge into each other without the disruptive, intermediary presence of a man: "Emma's dark eyes widened as she gazed into her daughter's. Together, they laughed" (p. 207).

Although *Green Lady* is obviously different from most other romances, it need be considered aberrant only if one assumes, as so many students of the genre have, that the romance originates in female masochism, in the desire to obliterate the self, or in the wish to be taken brutally by a man. Investigation of romances highly valued by their readers reveals, however, that the fairy-tale union of the hero and heroine is in reality the symbolic fulfillment of a woman's desire to realize her most basic female self *in relation* with another. What she desires in this imaginary relationship is both the autonomy and sense of difference guaranteed by connection with someone experienced as "other" and the erasure of boundaries and loss of singular consciousness achieved through union with an individual indistinguishable from the self. Romances vary in the emphasis they place on the one, usually achieved through the spectacularly masculine hero, or the other, granted by his nurturant, essentially "effeminate" attention. *Green Lady* differs only in that it finds the perfect union with this nurturant male still unsatisfying. The desire to recover the life-giving care of the primary caretaker is so strong here that it can be fulfilled only through a literal recovery of the lost mother. What the ideal romance usually grants the heroine covertly in the person of a strong but tender man is here given Dorinda overtly in an unmediated union with her mother who is, in fact, indistinguishable from her. *Green Lady* closes with the reestablishment of that original, blissful symbiotic union between mother and child that is the goal of all romances despite their apparent preoccupation with heterosexual love and marriage.

The Failed Romance
Too Close to the Problems of Patriarchy

In turning now to failed romances, those that the Smithton women have found lacking in various ways, it is worth recalling that despite its emphasis on the positive pleasures supplied by the reading of "ideal" romances, Chapter 4 also suggests that those stories might inadvertently activate unconscious fears and resentment about current patriarchal arrangements. In doing so, it was proposed, the romance's fantasy ending might defuse or recontain emotions that could prove troublesome in the realm of ordinary life. To put it differently, it seems possible, in view of its narrative organization, that before the ideal romance induces pleasure in the reader by providing her with vicarious nurturance and by reassuring her that standard female development does indeed lead to emotional rewards, it may first evoke equally powerful feelings of anger and fear directed at the fictional hero and thus more generally at men. The story may subsequently disarm those feelings by explaining satisfactorily why the hero had to act precisely in that way.[1]

The hypothesis that romance reading might actually elicit and then deflect protest about the character of patriarchal social relations is based on the discovery that the activity of reinterpretation is essential to the achievement of a final rapprochement between heroine and hero. This activity may be essential to the genre because its creators and readers need strategies for coping with male emotional reserve, independence, and even cruelty. Nevertheless, the initial stages of the process also may be valuable because they provide women with an opportunity to express proscribed emotions and to acknowledge repressed fears in the free realm of the imaginary. When told of the hero's early indifference, insensitivity, or brusque dismissal of the heroine, it seems possible that the reader might indulge more freely in feelings of outrage and self-righteous anger that she would otherwise censor if they had been prompted by related occurrences in her own life.

In calling attention to this claim that good romances may operate as a kind of cultural release valve, I do not intend to minimize the difficulty of proving its accuracy. Because ideal romances preoccupy themselves with the reinterpretation of a hero's only mildly disturbing behavior, it is difficult to see how his minor transgressions could call forth strong feelings in the reader. However, when the ideal romances are compared with those deemed disappointing or "disgusting" by Dot and her women, and both are correlated with their comments about how they feel when they read bad romances, it becomes evident that one of the measures of an ideal book's success is its ability to deal convincingly with female fears and reservations by permitting them to surface briefly during a reading process that then explicitly lays them to rest by explaining them away. This is made clear by contrast because the failed romances exhibit heroes with similar attitudes and behaviors toward women that are alike supposedly transformed into devotion by the time the story ends. However, these novels, which clearly aspire to the ideal fantasy conclusion, also differ from those earning higher rankings in that they greatly exaggerate the extent of the hero's independence, taciturnity, cruelty, and violence.

It seems entirely plausible, then, that these particular stories of a man's transformation from enemy into lover might be less convincing and enjoyable than the ideal version of the transformation because, unlike that version, they do not so effectively set to rest the anger and fear his early behaviors evoke in the reader. Instead of quashing the reader's suspicion that such is the inevitable character of the male personality, this reading experience might exacerbate that concern. Consequently, it might also suggest that her preferred ideal can be mandated artificially only through the contrivances of a literary plot.

This entire methodological procedure of using the failed romance to highlight the complex way in which the ideal romance manages women's covert fears was first suggested to me by several crucial conversations I had with the Smithton women about the experience of reading "bad" romances. These discussions stood out in my mind because they focused not on the aesthetic qualities of bad stories nor on the uninspired nature of overly repetitive plots, but rather on the intense emotions that the process of reading a bad book evoked in the women themselves. For example, in explaining that she likes romances to be "light and escapist," Susan defined those terms further by noting that such fare differs from her own life and by describing how she thinks all readers feel when a story does *not* exhibit this requisite distance. To her initial response, she added: "We want something that's light because we're trying to get away from our problems. And that's why we read books. And we don't like to read books and have those kinds of problems because then we're not escaping. We're right into that kind of problem again. It's no enjoyment. I just don't enjoy books like that. And I like it when I lay down in the afternoon—light reading—easy reading—a little humor. And just don't make me mad when I get off the divan!"

This last, uttered as a vehement threat, seemed to be directed at writers who had made her angry in the past. When I asked specifically whether some romances had annoyed her, she said yes and cited the "I-hate-you-type" books where the hero and heroine are "at each other's throats" for almost the entire tale. Although it would be unfair to conclude from this simple statement that extreme contentiousness is a problem Susan must deal with in her own relationship, it is at least clear that romantic escape is ruined for her when it treads too closely to situations, problems, and emotions that she understands to be part of her daily life. Romances like these portray behavior and events she does not approve of or want to experience in the time she has set aside for her own pampering and enjoyment.

Like Susan, Maureen also remarked explicitly that bad romances make her feel unhappy or angry. In discussing the identification process whereby she actually lives through the reading experience as the heroine, she observed, "I am whatever is going on in the story." She added immediately that this "is why I resent characters in books that are absolutely too naive to be believable, because that way I feel the reader is—the writer is putting me down." "So I will be offended," she continued, adding finally, "That's why I avoid these books that are so depressing. All these terrible things that happen to the heroine are happening to me—and I hold these emotions over."

Maureen, like all of the Smithton readers, turns to romances because they provide her with the opportunity to experience pleasure and happiness. Her search for this emotional state is, in fact, the goal that directs the entire process, as it is for her sister readers. Consequently, neither she nor the Smithton women want to endure even vicariously situations or treatment they consider intolerable or depressing because they call forth emotions similar to those occasioned by their own problems. It seems possible, then, that an examination of books given an unfavorable evaluation by Dot and her customers might lead us to those behaviors typically legitimated by the ideology of masculinity that these women nonetheless find distasteful and even fear. Their negative evaluation of romances portraying such behavior could be seen, then, as a form of safe protest against certain kinds of patriarchal treatment of women—protest because the negative evaluation is prompted by a refusal to subject the self even vicariously to such treatment, safe because the refusal is not made in the sphere of real social relations where it might lead to the severance of a connection that, though not ideal, at least promises the economic protection of patriarchal support.

This chapter focuses, therefore, on twenty books actually identified as less than ideal by Dot and her customers. Instead of investigating only those deemed totally beyond the pale, however, I have decided to examine a range of romances in an effort to identify the precise way in which the ideal version of the form fades gradually into the good, the mediocre, and the unambiguously awful. I devised this procedure in the hope that it might provide a more detailed picture of the kind of male-female interactions considered ideal, acceptable but not especially moving, and openly intolerable by these readers.

In an effort to make these discriminations, I have included in this sample a variety of books ranging from those deemed offensive and unreadable through those awarded one, two, and three stars by Dot herself. I have also included the one book the women could recall having read recently that was sold under the romance-category title but that was, in fact, not a romance. This was *Bitter Eden* (1979) by Sharon Salvato. Within the sample of twenty books, then, there are ten considered not worth reading by the Smithton women. Six of these were included on the basis of Dot's classification of them as worthy of the "garbage dump." The titles include *The Second Sunrise* (1981) by Francesca Greer (Frankie-Lee Janas), *Desire's Legacy* (1981) by Elizabeth Bright, *Savannah* (1981) by Helen Jean Burn, *Alyx* (1977) by Lolah Burford, *Passion's Blazing Triumph* (1980) by Melissa Hepburne, and *Purity's Passion* (1977) by Janette Seymour. Another four titles were added on the basis of the unanimous disapproval of their author by the sixteen women I interviewed at length. All of these women mentioned Rosemary Rogers's books as perfect examples of bad romances. Although most confessed that they liked her first novel, *Sweet Savage Love* (1974), all asserted that beginning with *Dark Fires* (1975), her work had become progressively offensive and pornographic. To test their observation, I have included the above two novels with the later *Wicked Loving Lies* (1976) and *The Insiders* (1979).

These ten clearly unacceptable books are joined in the sample by nine considered readable by Dot herself but not among the very best of any month's offerings. It is important to observe here that Dot's monthly rankings are not based on an absolute scale of ideal types but are the product of an effort to evaluate the available books *relative to each other*. Five- and four-star books, then, are those she believes to be worth the expenditure of a particular month's book allowance. Three-, two-, and one-star ratings are provided to assist readers with more money to discriminate among the less pleasing but still adequate stories. Considered barely tolerable here and worthy of one star are *A Second Chance at Love* (1981) by Margaret Ripy and *Winter Dreams* (1981) by Barbara Trent. The two-star entries, or those Dot evaluated as "moderately good" books, were *The Wanton Fires* (1979) by Meriol Trevor, *Bride of the Baja* (1980) by Jocelyn Wilde (John Toombs), and *Jasmine Splendor* (1981) by Margo Bode. The three-star books, those thought to be "good" but not "better" or "best," are *High Fashion* (1981) by Victoria Kelrich, *Captive Splendors* (1980) by Fern Michaels (Roberta Anderson and Mary Kuczir), *Adora* (1980) by Bertrice Small, and *The Court of the Flowering Peach* (1981) by Janette Radcliffe (Janet Louise Roberts).

Proceeding as with ideal romances, I first attempted to isolate the essential narrative structures of these weaker books. This proved surprisingly difficult because identification of the principal characters could not be easily accomplished. The heroine was generally recognizable, although in two cases (*High Fashion* and *Desire's Legacy*) her particular narrative role was divided between two different women, each of whom became romantically involved during the novel. Identification of the "hero," however, proved especially troublesome. Although I found it difficult to get the Smithton women to define the term "hero," their most common definition, "the man who the writer gets you to like and want the heroine to have," worked in the case of the ideal romances because they were so manifestly *about* the heroine's ever-deepening relationship with a single man. The definition was virtually worthless, however, with respect to these failed romances because all involved their heroines with more than one man and most portrayed both men in the heroine's life as interesting and desirable. Similarly, I found I could not necessarily identify secondary characters as rival figures or as villains because in many cases the relationship between these figures and one or the other of the two principals was viewed neither with alarm nor with outright disapproval.

This difficulty with character identification was both the symptom and the product of a plot structure that deviates substantially from the spare, tightly organized narrative core generating ideal romances. In fact, the most obvious difference between the failed romances and those considered ideal by the Smithton women is that the former do not focus on the developing relationship between a woman whose point of view dominates the story and a man who alternately pursues her and resists the attraction she has for him. The failed romances, indeed, consistently fail to satisfy the Smithton readers' primary stipulation that the romantic fantasy focus only on "one woman–one man." These are not stories where narrative tension increases gradually and inexorably as the heroine and hero spend more time together, grow emotionally dependent on each other, and yet still resist giving total consent to their impending union. Rather, they are characterized by a rising and falling action that seems to parallel the couple's alternating connections and separation. Where the ideal romance appears to be about the *inevitability* of the deepening of "true love" into an intense conjugal commitment, failed romances take as their principal subject the myriad problems and difficulties that must be overcome if mere sexual attraction is not to deteriorate into violence, indifference, or abandonment.

Before exploring the many ways in which failed romances deviate from the core fantasy by focusing mistakenly on these impediments to the ideal relationship, I would like to look first at *Bitter Eden* in an effort to clarify the distinction between a bad romance and a love story that is *not* a romance according to Dot and her customers. Here the impediments to love become so powerful that they destroy the essential structure of the genre.

Bitter Eden, a 672-page novel, was published by Dell in 1979. Marketed as a romance, the book was publicized in the usual manner, linked with the author's previous bestseller in the genre, and described as the story of Peter Berean and Callie Dawson. The cover blurb proclaimed, "He taught her what it means to live—she taught him what it means to love." In fact, the story does not conform to the expectations such copy establishes in the reader, for it details a more complicated plot that includes long passages about Peter's political interests as well as a love triangle. Although Peter does love Callie, he is committed to agricultural reform, a cause that often takes him away from her. Indeed, when he is jailed and then deported, Callie is supported emotionally by Peter's gentle brother, Stephen, whom she gradually grows to love.

In any typical romance with this sort of early development, the point of view would normally shift at this point and the younger brother would develop as the "true" hero. Reader identification with Stephen would be insured by viewing Callie from his point of view while Peter slipped into the background. This fails to occur, however, in *Bitter Eden*. In fact, Callie is occasionally left behind completely as large chunks of narrative are devoted to Peter's torture at the hands of an "unjust" judicial system. Salvato's interest in exposing injustice becomes so strong in the last quarter of the book that it not only intrudes further on the initial love story but finally derails it. When Peter is executed for his crimes, Callie is grief-stricken but supported by Stephen, which seems to imply that they will wed in the future. Although the story technically ends, then, with the free and unfettered union of two lovers, the last words of the novel cast a final, definitive pall over what might otherwise have been a kind of happy ending. Salvato writes: "Then Peter prayed. Silently, lips firmly closed, but unafraid, at long last within himself at peace. The wormwood cup was emptied" (p. 672).

What is especially striking about this peculiar conclusion is that Callie's feelings for Stephen have been portrayed as less intense and passionate than those she had felt for Peter. Although the reader is told that she loves Stephen deeply because he is kind, generous, and tender, it is also clear that this relationship is a quieter, more even version of the magnetic attraction that existed between Peter and Callie. The story seems to suggest, then, that worldly concerns make the permanent maintenance of such an intense relationship impractical and even undesirable. *Bitter Eden* implies instead that what is truly possible is a life filled with a measure of sorrow and pain that can be mitigated by a supportive but unspectacular love between two mature individuals. It seems logical to conclude, finally, that the Smithton women excluded this novel from the category of romance because it ends not by closing with a vision of the promises of marriage but with a demonstration of the need to accept distraction, sorrow, and imperfection as inevitable components of adult human existence.

In comparing *Bitter Eden* with the nineteen other books in this sample, it quickly becomes evident that a story will earn the categorical title of romance from the Smithton women if it supplies the requisite ending to a male-female relationship. This is made especially clear by Helen Jean Burn's *Savannah*, a novel that Dot relegated to the "garbage dump." The book is interesting because, like *Bitter Eden*, it focuses on the hero's political commitments that take him away from the heroine. Burn, however, unites hero and heroine definitively at the end of the book, but their many separations and problems, together with detailed reports of physical violence and brutality, insured *Savannah*'s low rating. Yet it was obviously the ending itself that guaranteed its inclusion in the romance category. Although *Savannah*'s ending is complete with the requisite projection of a blissful future, that conclusion was apparently not strong enough to banish the fears and anger provoked by the earlier sequences of separation and violence. The happy ending, then, is a necessary but not sufficient feature for distinguishing between good romances and bad. Although it will guarantee a love story its designation as a romance by the Smithton women, this ending alone will not lead to the kind of reading experience necessary for its further recognition as an ideal, even good, example of the genre.

Indeed, all nine of the titles in the sample relegated to the garbage dump include the happy ending. The Smithton readers, nonetheless, find those endings unconvincing and even ludicrous because the portrait of the heroine-hero relationship is so far from the ideal they hold dear that they cannot imagine how the heroine could shrug off her earlier experiences. When the novels themselves are examined, it becomes clear that the women's skepticism is, in reality, a function of the rudimentary nature of the plot that ostensibly ties individual incidents together. Although these novels are plotted in the sense that they attempt to explain why characters behave the way they do and provide reasons for the resolution of events, those logical explanations appear far-fetched, preposterous, and contrived because they consistently fail to account for behavior and events that the women themselves believe would necessarily result in a different outcome. The narrative is so badly managed in some of these stories that one is tempted to conclude that the plot is nothing more than a pretense designed to justify what is really a highly repetitive series of graphically described sexual encounters.

While all of these novels emphasize the sex act to the exclusion of everything else, none is more contemptuous of the conventions of storytelling than Lolah Burford's *Alyx*. Indeed, it is almost impossible to understand how or why this particular piece of writing was published. Not only is the tale itself preposterous and inadequately detailed, but it is disclosed in ungrammatical, often incomprehensible prose. The first paragraph of the book is as good an example as any of its near-incompetent storytelling and obsession with the simple mechanics of the sexual act:

> The door to the breeding hut was closed, but the men beside him pushed it open, and pushed him inside. . . . He took off his breeches, a courtesy left him now, since he had proved tractable, to do for himself, dropping them by the door where they could be easily found again, the darkness all about him, thick and silent and warm. He gave no thought to what he had come for, although his body anticipated the brief comfort, moving by habit across the small room in the dark to the bed that was the only furniture or object of any kind in it. He reached down and pulled the spread aside to slip in beside the woman who would be waiting, willing as himself or quiescent, her features never known to him, only the unchanging soft warmth of breast and belly, and passages made free to him, and the bittersweet smell of unwashed sweat that was no longer unpleasant to him. For a moment only his hand touched flesh. The spread was pulled away; and the stillness was broken by sudden movement, a gasping sharp intake of breath, the sound of the cloth on the dirt floor on which bare feet made no sound, and then silence again. (pp. 1–2)

In commenting on this passage, one of Dot's customers observed accurately that "you can't figure out what the situation is." Unfortunately, the reader's ignorance is dispelled only a short time later when it is made clear that the book is about white slavers. who force their human property to breed. The next two paragraphs, in fact, detail this unidentified man's unsuccessful attempt to copulate with a woman who turns out to be a child. The characters later prove to be the hero and the heroine. Of the sixteen Smithton women I interviewed in depth, six had purchased *Alyx*. None of them finished the novel, and four had deliberately discarded it. This is easily explicable given the novel's endless chronicle of sex act after sex act, each of which is described in too-explicit, unromantic detail.

Although *Alyx* is not the worst offender among the garbage-dump romances, it, like all of the others, employs a sexual slang more commonly associated with male pornography. The Smithton women, however, object to more than just the "gutter" language. While they find both the clinical terms and sexual profanity disturbing, what they object to most in these books is the degradation, violence, and brutality that the heroine is forced to endure before the hero is transformed into her lover. Of Rosemary Rogers's *The Insiders*, Dot herself observed that it is filled with "sicky stuff." She added, "It's really pornography, you know." In a separate conversation about bad romances, another reader also mentioned *The Insiders* with disdain. Although she began reading romances when a friend gave her *Sweet Savage Love* while she was convalescing in a hospital, she explained that she now refuses to read any of Rogers's new books because "they are modern day and filled with filth. They are really nothing more than sex books."

The Smithton readers unanimously dislike Rogers's novels. Indeed, when *The Insiders* is compared with romances like *The Wolf and the Dove*, *The Sea Treasure*, or *Miss Hungerford's Handsome Hero*, it is hard to dispute their claim that Rogers is writing only to titillate and that her books "are a man's type of book" because of the way sex is portrayed. Although *The Insiders* concludes with a happy ending, which suggests very briefly that the hero has realized that he loves the heroine and will treat her well in the future, the rest of the book is devoted to the depiction of sadistic and brutal sexual encounters. Nor is Rogers content with the description of simple heterosexual intercourse. She includes scenes between lesbian lovers, describes her heroine, Eve, masturbating with a vibrator before a mirror, discusses anal intercourse in several scenes, describes the hero's brutal treatment of a fifteen-year-old girl, and finally details at great length a gang rape of her heroine in which the hero participates. In all of these passages, Rogers is careful to use language in such a way that the scenes are visually displayed for the reader. The language, in fact, seems to function principally as a voyeuristic tool, enabling the reader to witness the brutal violation and degradation of women. Although many passages could be cited here to illustrate Rogers's preoccupation with men's power to inflict pain on women, one will suffice:

She heard Jerry Harmon's voice.

"We watched you through the two-way mirror for a while, after you disappeared in here. Whatsa matter, Brant baby, you getting selfish?"

"Yeah, you usually call us in sooner. You're slipping as a host—you used to be better about sharing, didn't he, Mel?". . . .

"Too bad, Eve. But maybe you prefer it this way."

His voice was soft, meant only for her—his words cruel. He pulled the spread from her suddenly nerveless fingers and moved back, shrugging carelessly, letting those others crowd closer in, their eyes leering, their words beating against her ears. . . .

"If it's going to be a gang-bang, then I want in on it, too—women's lib and all that!"

A woman's wet mouth grazed Eve's; she turned her head away, but not quickly enough. The woman laughed. . . .

"Damn you, Brant Newcomb, damn you, damn you!" She sobbed until some other man, kneeling over her head, pushed his penis into her mouth, gagging her, making her retch.

Their hands and mouth [sic] and stiff, thrusting cocks were everywhere on her body—hurting her, invading her, ravaging her, while she shuddered and cringed and made choked, terrified animal noises in her throat. . . .

Suddenly she felt him [Brant] drive himself deep inside her—deeper than any of the others had gone. She felt him battering up against the opening to her womb, and the pain was so great that she screamed, over and over again, until she fainted—with her screams still echoing in her ears. (pp. 159–63)[2]

It is important to keep in mind here that Dot's romance readers do not, as Ann Douglas has claimed, enjoy the titillation of seeing themselves as some men would like to see them.[3] Indeed, the Smithton readers' vehement refusal to be subjected to this kind of degradation, even when it is experienced vicariously and later explained away, suggests that we must be careful not to assume that the publication of such books implies that all romance readers are actually reading them. We must not only recall that accurate sales figures are virtually impossible to unearth but also realize that sales figures alone tell us very little about the actual incidence of reading. In a literary system that contains only a few critical services like Dot's, most romance buyers are forced to choose their books on the basis of covers, blurbs, and familiarity with an author. When a book like *Purity's Passion* sports a highly romantic, dreamy portrait of a man kissing a woman chastely on her forehead and says only on the back cover that "her innocence could last no longer. . . . Her bold desires could burn forever. . . . Her woman's heart would love but once," the prospective reader has no way of knowing that the book contains repeated rapes of a heroine who enjoys the sexual stimulation despite her lack of consent. The reader's purchase of that book, then, may indicate nothing more than that the cover artist captured pictorially the tender essence of the ideal romantic fantasy that the story itself neither understands nor contains. It is essential to realize, therefore, that the act of book purchase does not necessarily entail reader approval of the book's content, although it *may* suggest reader belief in its potential to satisfy.

Despite its near obsession with violence against women, *The Insiders* is interesting precisely because it tries to use the same explanatory pattern employed in ideal romances to account for the final union between heroine and hero. Although similar in content, however, this explanation differs substantially from the others because the transformation of the hero's behavior upon which it depends is too sudden, has not been anticipated by earlier plotting, and thus appears artificial and contrived, not to mention unconvincing. The reader is told, in fact, *only four pages after the hero's final anal rape of the heroine* (to whom he is now married) that he suddenly realizes he loves her. Although the penultimate chapter closes with his bitter vow to leave her, Eve later discovers him lying on the floor in the nursery with his son held on his chest. When she asks, "What in hell are you doing back here?," he responds only that "I found I missed you both. So I turned around and came back" (p. 309).

This is followed by a highly condensed, two-page version of the narrative structure of the last half of a typical ideal romance. Once Brant acknowledges that he misses Eve, acts tenderly with her son, and admits it is hard to learn how to communicate "when you're used to holding things in," she finally feels safe enough to admit that she loves him. When she responds with words of love that sound "rusty and hesitant," she feels his "arms tighten around her body as if he meant to hold her close forever" (p. 310). Brant, however, never quite manages to express his feelings openly. He replies to her admission of love only with the comment, "I guess that's what I was trying to tell you awhile back, Eve. But some words aren't easy for me to say" (p. 310). Unlike the more demanding ideal heroine who would insist that this love be declared, Eve absolves Brant of the need to be openly expressive. When she responds, "Don't say them, then. You don't have to. Show me" (p. 310), the book concludes with a passage that insists that despite Brant's still intact masculine reserve, Eve, too, has found a man who will make her feel loved and cared for in the future. "And he did—renewing his lease on her, she thought crazily, all the time he was making such tender, beautiful love to her. Renewing it for the next hundred years, maybe. Which was the way she wanted it" (p. 310).

Brant Newcomb and the heroes of the other garbage-dump romances, then, like their ideal counterparts, are stereotypically masculine. Not only are they ruggedly handsome in a Byronic manner, but they are also emotionally reserved, controlled, independent, aggressive, and scornful of feminine weakness. They differ chiefly from heroes in ideal romances by the unrelieved nature of their masculinity. Whereas both the physical and emotional hardness of the ideal hero were mitigated slightly by his possession of a somewhat feminine physical feature that testified early on to the real warmth and tenderness of his hidden personality, the exterior of heroes like Newcomb is only the surface manifestation of a cold and unchanging emotional demeanor.

Despite this discrepancy in the extent to which they insist on the purity of their heroes' masculinity, however, good and bad romances alike suggest by their conclusions that such behavior is not threatening to women. Masculine behavior is benign because it does not prohibit the establishment of a relationship that can provide a woman with the relationality she needs. In good romances, that overly aggressive masculine behavior is exposed as a false or defensive facade that, when removed, as it inevitably is, reveals the true male personality to be kind and tender. In bad romances, the hero's masculine behavior is never transformed totally. As a consequence, it continues to be presented to the reader as a natural and inevitable fact of social relations. Nonetheless, these stories still demonstrate that the occurrence of such behavior does not necessarily imply lack of love. They suggest, in fact, that male aggression, independence, and reserve are the causes of sexual attraction, which, in these romances, is taken to be the first step toward the love that is the heroine's goal.

Given this essential similarity in structure, it seems clear that romances are, in fact, exercises in extrapolation. They are experiments in the sense that they explore the meaning and consequences of behavior accepted by contemporary society as characteristically masculine. Despite the varying intensity of the masculine behavior that is portrayed, all romances "discover" that it need *not* be seen as contradictory to female fulfillment. Regardless of the extremity of the misogyny exhibited by their heroes, then, romances all suggest in the end that when properly interpreted, masculinity implies only good things for women. It is the sign of sexual difference and thus a fundamental condition for the love, marriage, and attention women seek.

When romances are understood as the experimental projection of the consequences of masculine behavior and patriarchal control, it seems possible that certain writers do not depict extreme violence out of a masochistic desire to experience it vicariously. Rather, their preoccupation with misogyny may be the mark of a desperate need to know that exaggerated masculinity is not life-threatening to women. They may also want to know that this trait need not be deplored actively because such a response would undoubtedly prompt its even more vicious expression and jeopardize the all-important protection that is its positive consequence. Behavior like Brant Newcomb's may be incorporated into the romantic fantasy, therefore, not because certain writers and readers enjoy it but because they cannot imagine it away. To them, such behavior may seem so natural, permanent, and unassailable that they hunger even more for a fantasy that will contradict their suspicions and convince them that it can lead to female contentment and happiness.

However, this sort of fantasy could very well backfire for readers seeking a similar promise about much less extreme versions of masculine reserve and power. If these women need not, indeed would not, tolerate this kind of exaggerated behavior in their own lives, vicarious witnessing of it might prompt such strong reactions of fear and anger that they could not be explained away merely by a happy ending. Such a story would fan the readers' fears by pursuing too realistically the logical implications of a gender definition that celebrates power, self-sufficient individuality, and aggressive competitiveness. The reader would close her book in anger rather than in hope and contentment.

Given what the Smithton women have revealed about their responses to "bad" romances, it seems likely that this is precisely what is occurring when they read books like *The Insiders*, *Alyx*, or *The Second Sunrise*. Instead of indulging in a fantasy that allows them to suppress their fear of abandonment and rape, they immerse themselves in a story that immoderately emphasizes those fears and permits them to get out of hand. For these readers, the happy ending is not only powerless to recontain those fears, but it is also an offensive justification of extreme behavior.

All romances grapple with at least one fear prompted by current sexual arrangements. The fear of the consequences of masculinity is usually dealt with by evoking male power and aggression and then by demonstrating that if not illusions they are at least benign. However, another fear figures in the romantic narrative whose presence is once again highlighted by the failed romance's inability to control it. This fear of an awakened female sexuality and of its impact on men is usually dealt with in the ideal romance by confining the expression of female desire within the limits of a permanent, loving relationship.[4] Such stories thus suggest that womanly desire is acceptable to men, but they also perpetuate the usual connection between sex and love. The failed romances sever that link by depicting heroines who enjoy casual sex with several partners. Nevertheless, in spite of their ostensible celebration of a liberated female sexuality, such books actually violate, humiliate, and punish it through the hero's extraordinary violence. Thus, Rosemary Rogers's single heroines who enjoy sex are also brutally mortified throughout her novels. Her literary violence against women, then, may be a sign both of her despair at the persistence of male power and of her guilt at her efforts to subvert that power by positing sexual equality in women. By humiliating her female characters, she may in fact be chastizing that part of herself that desires to challenge the current balance of power in sexual arrangements.

It is worth noting again that Dot and her customers do not like Rogers's books or others like them. They are neither so cynical about men nor so uneasy about womanly sexuality, perhaps because they do not long for or approve of such a radical alteration in female sexual behavior in the first place. Their distaste for books like Rogers's may be the mark of their desire for the liberation only of female sexual *response* within the confines of a relationship that still does not challenge the man's right to initiate connection or the basic structure of patriarchal marriage. Although the authors of ideal romances treat female sexuality with approval, they do not imply, as do Rogers, Francesca Greer, or Melissa Hepburne, that there is nothing wrong with casual sexual liaisons or with a woman who actively seeks sexual pleasure. They endorse the open expression of sexual desire *only* if it is understood as the sign or symptom of a previously existing love.

Where the garbage-dump romances begin with sexual attraction and suggest that love may develop subsequently as the consequence of an erotic interaction, the ideal romances work hard to maintain that love of one individual for the unique personality of another must and does precede its embodiment in sexual expression. It is true, of course, that an ideal hero is characteristically attracted to the heroine early in the story. However, because the sexual nature of this attraction is masked by the narrative's insistence that it is simply the heroine's beauty that draws the hero to her, the ideal romance persists in maintaining on an overt level that loving commitment is the proper condition for complete sexual fulfillment. This explanatory principle is reinforced later by the process of reinterpretation that permits both the heroine and the reader to reread any early sexual initiatives on the part of the hero as the unmistakable consequences of his love for her. The Smithton group's favorite romances, then, continue to advance the ideology of romantic love, insisting thereby that marriage between a man and a woman is not an economic or social necessity or a purely sexual affiliation but an emotional bond freely forged.

It becomes evident that whereas a happy ending to a courtship is the minimal feature necessary to a book's identification as a romance, a narrative logic that convincingly attributes that marriage to the mutual appreciation of the partners is essential to the further judgment that the book is worth reading. Although the garbage-dump romances appear to attempt this endorsement of romantic love, the endorsement rings false because the narrative has not only emphasized the hero's extraordinary cruelty but has also stressed the purely sexual nature of the attraction exerted by the heroine upon the hero. As a consequence, the heroine's formal attachment to him at the end seems more a capitulation or a surrender to uncontrollable sexuality than a triumph effected by her ability to transform him into an emotionally expressive individual. Although we will see shortly that two- and three-star romances differ from the ideal romances in other respects, they at least share their ability to set womanly intelligence and individuality above sexual attractiveness as the cause or determinant of male attention.

These less satisfying romances also differ from their more successful counterparts by a surprisingly different internal narrative structure. They begin and end in the same way and likewise employ similar reasoning to account for the resolution. The interim paths taken by their principal characters, however, deviate so substantially that the lesser stories carry implications about heterosexual relationships and marriage that are somewhat different from those postulated by ideal romances.

This variation occurs because the stories consistently violate the most basic preference and rule articulated by the Smithton women, the stipulation that a romance focus only on "one woman–one man." Although these books all end with the happy union of the hero and heroine, none of them chronicles the uninterrupted, inexorable deepening of this relationship alone. Where the ideal romance binds the heroine and hero together early in the tale, maintains their close physical proximity throughout, and finds the impediments to their final union in their own individual failings, these less satisfying romances provide different kinds of interactions. They introduce their principal characters to each other only to separate them once again, chronicle one or the other partner's confusion about another satisfying relationship during this separation, and thus blame the inability to achieve the ideal romantic relationship not on the individuals involved but on external impediments that must be removed. These romances cannot suggest as successfully, then, that a less-than-ideal relationship might be transformed into a perfect union by partners who are willing to change their behavior.

Because they do not focus on the ameliorable internal problems of an already established relationship but on problems that must be dealt with even before such a relationship can be established, these romances do not address as effectively the particular situation of the married reader. Although these stories might be evaluated more favorably by single women still worried about their chances of finding the right life partner or of winning one in competition with other women, it is not hard to understand why they are deemed less than compelling by women already in relationships that they would like to believe they can perfect. Dot's comment that "I don't want her to do her thing and he his and then they get together" makes sense because such a story could not provide information about how to transform those aspects of an already established relationship that inhibit emotional intensity and thwart the provision of nurturance and tender care.

The weak romances, then, involve the principal characters not only with each other but with other individuals as well. Whereas in the ideal romance character foils remain truly peripheral and thus are used only for the diacritical purpose of contrast, in these less valuable versions of the genre the foils actually figure in the developing story. Yet these stories do not utilize their narrative foils in identical ways, and, therefore, do not expand the narrative core uniformly. Indeed, the romances in this sample show much wider variation in plot structure than do the ideal romances that resemble each other so remarkably. As a consequence of this varying use of secondary characters and of differing explanations about why they fail as permanent partners, these romances evoke many different fears about male-female relationships and disagree, finally, about the nature of a satisfying marriage and the proper route to its establishment.

There is no point to examining all of the failed romances in this sample in order to develop a list of the Smithton group's fears about male-female relationships. Because the sample itself is not exhaustive, analysis cannot provide a comprehensive list of the behaviors and situations legitimated by patriarchy that distress Dot and her customers. I would, however, like to look briefly at two representative romances to show precisely how they also manage to elicit different fears they cannot control and thus fail to live up to the Smithton standard. Because two-star romances seem to differ from three-star books in a consistent and coherent way, I have selected Janette Radcliffe's *The Court of the Flowering Peach*, a three-star romance, and Meriol Trevor's two-star book, *The Wanton Fires*.

In general, it might be said that a romance is apparently weakened for Dot and her customers by *any* narrative digression that detracts from or retards the development of an increasingly intense emotional connection between a single pair of ideal lovers. However, it also seems to be the case that delays or digressions are more tolerable if they do not prevent the author from devoting at least some attention to an "ideal" relationship even if it does not survive the eventual outcome of the story. Although three-star romances vary in the way they employ character foils and triangle relationships, all manage to trace the development of such an ideal connection at some time in the story. Two-star romances, interestingly enough, do not. Thus the same halting narrative progression characterizing both two- and three-star books is evaluated less favorably in the former by Dot and her customers. I suspect that the two-star books are less successful because they cannot supply even the temporary experience of vicarious nurturance and enjoyment that the three-star books provide. Whereas both two- and three-star romances alike fail to supply the reading experience desired most by the Smithton women, the three-star romances at least continue to hold out the possibility that an ideal man, capable of loving a woman as she wants to be loved, can, in fact, be found.

In *The Court of the Flowering Peach*, for example, such a relationship is established and maintained between pages 103 and 368. This relationship between Katie Llewellyn and the extraordinary Chinese Prince Chen Yee is only temporary, however, for it is preceded and supplanted by Katie's relationship to her husband, Rupert, who is neither as dashing as the Prince nor deeply in love with Katie herself. In fact, Rupert only marries Katie because his first love had married his brother. Nonetheless, Katie eventually returns to Rupert even though she knows that, unlike the Prince, "[h]e [will] not write poetry to her, and it embarrasses him to speak of love out of the marriage bed, in daylight" (p. 423). She returns to him, the reader is told, because "he was solid and English and dependable and had a strong sense of duty" (p. 423). Obviously such an ending suggests that ideal relationships like those in Kathleen Woodiwiss's books are impractical and ephemeral. To understand, then, why a story culminating in such a suggestion still warrants a "good" rating, it will be necessary to look more closely at Radcliffe's narrative structure and the fears it can only partially allay.

Part of the problem with the book rests with its opening pages and its early descriptions of Rupert's feelings for Katie. Not only does he marry her on the rebound, but on their wedding night he thinks of her as a "frightened pale girl" (p. 52), "a drab sparrow" (p. 54), and feels "no rising desire for this pale child" (p. 52). Later, when he rapes Katie in an angry fit, Radcliffe emphasizes the pain and humiliation it causes her heroine. This incident only underscores Rupert's insensitivity (which had already been established earlier by a passage describing his mechanical lovemaking) to a wife he does not love and whose pleasure he never considers. Such a passage undoubtedly activates discomfort and worry in readers who would rather be told that a woman *can* be the principal object of a man's attention:

> If only he could truthfully say that he loved her. But for nights in Canton he had lain awake in the heat and thought bitterly of his lost love, Selina. One could not change one's heart so readily, he knew now. He should never have let his father persuade him to marry a woman he did not love. When one has loved so much, another woman could not completely fulfill a man's needs. Yet Selina was lost to him, Katie was his wife, he wanted a son one day—He turned again to Katie, and more feverishly he pressed his kisses on her. . . .

He enjoyed it so, the release of his need into his wife, the relief of
the movements, the pleasure he had on her soft body. He rolled off,
finally, and gasped with receding delight. She lay still, then pushed
down the hem of her nightdress. He fell asleep as she got up to open
one of the shutters slightly. . . . Dear Katie, she was so thoughtful.
(pp. 143–44)

Given Rupert's insensitive use of his wife's body, it is not surprising
that Katie is overwhelmed by the Prince's attentions. Not only does the
Prince believe her beautiful, but he appreciates her unique intellectual and
artistic abilities. "You are different," he assures her. "You have a mind to
comprehend, a heart to understand, an artistic hand to paint eloquently"
(p. 187). Radcliffe further underscores Chen Yee's superiority to Rupert
with Katie's comparative recognition that her husband "did not hang on
her words . . . did not speak with her for hours on end . . . did not watch
her paint with such intensity . . . did not write poems to her!" (p. 190).
Thus when Rupert leaves Katie in China and she is delivered to the Prince
by a jealous woman, the reader cannot help but see this as a positive
development that will eventually result in a permanent, perfect marriage.

Indeed, such a denouement appears inevitable given Radcliffe's description of the intensity of the Prince's love, Katie's developing response, and
the passion of their lovemaking. The following are only excerpts from a
long, explicit passage whose detail and tenor are repeated several times in
the next hundred pages:

"Softness, sweetness, fragrance, gentleness," he murmured against
her breasts. "The body of a girl, the heart of a lioness, the spirit of a
winged bird, the fragrance of a flower." He caught her lips delicately
in his, savored them, sucked at them, until her mouth answered his
lips, and her tongue timidly touched his large tongue. . . . [H]is . . .
hand moved up and down her side, then held a breast in careful
fingers, teasing the nipple with his thumb, moving it, brushing
against it with a soft touch. . . .

Then he moved above her, and into her still-quivering body he
gently pushed his own instrument. She moaned with the strong,
heady delight of it; she came again in ecstasy at the power of his body
pushing against hers. In and out, slowly, so slowly, in and out, again,
again—She came again and cried out. . . .

She had never dreamed of such power in a man, not even in
Rupert's arms. Rupert had made love to her, let her go, and slept.
This man could not sleep; he desired more and more. (pp. 265–66)[5]

The principal difference between this description and those provided by
the writers of ideal romances is that the event occurs not at the end of a

narrative between two people about to live happily ever after but between a man and a woman who are unmarried and who remain that way. Although Katie bears the Prince's child, their cultural differences ultimately lead to their separation. She eventually returns to England and a now-transformed Rupert but continues to remember her year of bliss with the Prince, wondering, "To be so adored, so loved—for one year. Was it enough to last a lifetime?" (p. 370).

Radcliffe appears to be suggesting that an ideal relationship in which the woman is valued as a mature individual *and* tenderly nurtured as a dependent child is only a temporary fantasy that can never be established permanently in the real world. The conclusion of the story bears out the suggestion, for in reestablishing her relationship with her husband, Katie repudiates the role of beloved child and accepts Rupert's now-mature appreciation of her as an accomplished, adult individual (p. 394). Although Katie appears to be pleased by his attentions and satisfied by their now-passionate lovemaking, their relationship still seems to be different from her first, magical connection with Chen Yee. That difference, oddly enough, is emphasized in the final elegiac passage of the novel. Radcliffe ends the story of Katie and Rupert not with a vision of their future but with a nostalgic, backward glance at the lost idyll. The unmistakable tone of sadness and longing cannot help but convey to the reader Katie's apparent knowledge that this wondrous experience can never be repeated:

> Sometimes it seemed like a dream, now in London, in her new matronly state, expecting her second child. Rupert loved her, cherished her, and her love was returned in full measure. His parents loved her as their own daughter. Society welcomed her and her husband, and their business prospered also.
>
> Yet—yet when Katie went to the warehouse and sniffed the sharp tang of spices and sandalwood, or when she looked at the miniature of her son in the privacy of her room, or when she fondled a bit of green jade—
>
> Sometimes a dreamy look came into her eyes, and she drifted away from the stately London home, and for a little time, a few minutes only, he [*sic*] lived again the days and nights in the enchanting Court of the Flowering Peach. (pp. 460–61)

Given this ending and the preferences of the Smithton women, it is not hard to understand why this novel received less than their highest rating. Although it undoubtedly provides its readers with the pleasurable experience they desire by enabling identification with Katie during her perfect romance with the Prince, its elegiac ending also asserts too candidly that such a romance is nothing more than a temporary dream. Instead of masking the reader's experience as the fleeting product of an imaginary fairy tale by maintaining the illusion of reality to the very end, *The Court of the Flowering Peach* calls attention to the fantastic character of Katie's relationship and thus to the nature of the entire romantic fantasy by noting once again the difference between the dream and the reality. Radcliffe's story seems to suggest in the end that while the ideal romantic relationship is possible, it is not hardy enough to withstand the practical demands and vicissitudes of real existence. Better to rest content with a less dashing lover and more adult marriage, she seems to counsel her readers, than to long forever for an ideal that is attainable only temporarily and through the imagination.

I think it likely that *The Court of the Flowering Peach* failed to win its last two stars because it does not successfully allay all of the fears activated by its narrative action. By involving Katie in two relationships—one marked "real," "less intense," and "mature," the other marked "dreamlike," "exotic," and "perfect"—the story unfortunately tells its readers that the feelings they turn to romance reading for are indeed possible only through such an imaginary experience. Radcliffe implies that they cannot be found in actual adult relationships that necessarily provide other advantages such as security. Therefore, her narrative only confirms her Smithton readers' unwanted knowledge and fear that the relationships in romances are little like those they participate in in daily life.[6] Those relationships, like the more "real" one between Rupert and Katie, are probably characterized by occasional outbursts of anger, indifference, or, even possibly, cruelty. Radcliffe's refusal to maintain the illusion that an ideal relationship is a plausible and extended possibility in the real world is finally the cause of her book's failure to provide the perfect romance-reading experience for the Smithton readers.

Although this failure to insist on the essential reality of the ideal romantic relationship is the cause of the novel's less than perfect rating, it can also be demonstrated that it is Radcliffe's inclusion of at least a temporary version of this ideal that garners the novel its third star by comparing it with the two-star *Wanton Fires*. Like *The Court of the Flowering Peach*, this novel suggests that not all men are dashing princes. Indeed, Sir Miles Dynham, who eventually marries Georgie, the heroine, is presented to the reader as bumbling and inept, though a well-meaning young man. Although Georgie "likes" him, his "gentle affectionate" kisses do "not disturb her at all, one way or the other" (p. 32). She is aroused, however, by Miles's friend Adrian, who is introduced as if he were the typically dark, charismatic hero: "He was taller than Miles, graceful and energetic, with thick waving brown hair and fine dark grey eyes, brilliant and teasing, glancing from under a fringe of black lashes a woman might envy. Yet his features were entirely masculine in cast and his face weather-browned; he had a straight nose and a generous, smiling mouth" (p. 46).

Georgie, of course, immediately falls in love with Adrian. She is later embarrassed, however, when Adrian refuses her attentions and turns to other women. When Miles confesses that he knows Georgie does not love him, Georgie suddenly begins to see him in a new light. Indeed, she is impressed for the first time by his generosity, kindness, and maturity. She even thinks him "distinguished" and "certainly decisive" (p. 77).

Although the rest of the novel preoccupies itself with many events peripheral to the central romance, a narrative structure it shares with all the other "failed" romances, it does manage to chronicle Miles's gradual transformation in Georgie's eyes. This does not come about, however, because Miles himself changes, but because Georgie matures, gives up her girlish fantasies, and begins to appreciate Miles's quality as a steady, dependable friend and protector. A rhetoric of reinterpretation thus characterizes this novel as it does the ideal romances, although the movement here is reversed. Where the ideal heroine learns that the independent and antagonistic man to whom she is attracted does indeed love and cherish her, Georgie grows to understand that the rather unexciting person who first courted her is actually lovable. The logic of the story suggests that a merely mediocre suitor can become a loving and satisfying marriage partner even though he might not be as spectacularly masculine as the typical romantic hero. Although the ending of the novel stresses the happiness of their final union, which Trevor characterizes as "wholehearted and deep-rooted, not a mere passing attraction" dominated by "the youthful greed for love" (p. 195), it cannot override the feeling created in the reader by passages such as the following, which show that Miles is as imperfect as any lover in the real world:

> But the months spent in London under his [Miles's] uncle's eye had made him more accustomed to such formal dress and as his figure, though on the thin side, was not unpleasantly so, he did not look awkward as Georgie had feared, watching anxiously for his entrance into the drawing room. Although he would never be noticed when either Edmund or Adrian was of the company, she thought he was acquiring a mild distinction of his own and that his spectacles made him look scholarly rather than foolish. (p. 182)

Instead of providing the reader with the opportunity to participate vicariously in an ideal romantic courtship and to hope that her present, real relationship might be transformed into a mirror image of this ideal, *The Wanton Fires* appears to recommend that the reader remain content with what she very likely already has. With the story of Miles and Georgie, Meriol Trevor also suggests that sexual passion is not always earth-shattering or even necessary to a strong and stable relationship. What is important, she argues, is compatibility, generosity, and dependability, all qualities that insure a woman's continued protection by a man. Although the emotional gratification such a relationship provides will not always be intense, magical, or overpowering, it will be consistent, warm, and satisfying. Her vision of Miles and Georgie on their wedding day is as good an indication as any of the scaled-down, essentially practical, and domestic nature of the romantic fantasy she provides: "Because it was at Brentland, Miles was not nervous and awkward at his wedding, but still looked as if he could hardly believe he had actually won his shyly smiling little bride, looking more like a cottage rose than ever in her white dress and satin bonnet, while Georgie herself promised to love, honour and obey him with a feeling of great thankfulness" (p. 217). Small wonder, then, that the Smithton women, who seem to be searching for emotional intensity in their fantasy lives, found this novel drab, dull, and unworthy of enthusiastic recommendation. It comes much too close to suggesting explicitly that the romantic dream is an illusion and that women ought to lower their expectations and rest content with lesser men.

Although I have examined only a few bad romances in this chapter and thus have not been able to describe all the possible ways in which such books can fail to live up to the Smithton standard, it does seem clear from even this cursory examination that failure is somehow wrapped up with the inability to provide the reader with the right kind of vicarious emotion. As a result, these romances do not supply a reading experience that replenishes and restores the female reader. Garbage-dump romances, for instance, fail because they ask the reader to identify with a heroine who is hurt, humiliated, and brutalized. At the same time, they evoke fear and worry about female sexuality and hint that a woman's sexual desire might, in fact, prove threatening to men. Two-star romances ask the reader to identify with a heroine who learns to adjust to scaled-down desires and comes to accept the fact that ordinary men are not like romantic heroes. Although better than garbage-dump romances because they do not require the reader to experience being punished, these books ask the reader to endure the embarrassment of confessing with the heroine that her desires are unrealistic and far-fetched.

It is understandable, then, why three-star romances are more acceptable to Dot and her readers. After all, they do provide a brief interlude during which the reader is petted, cared for, and loved in the person of the heroine. However, because the experience itself does not last and is, in fact, shown to be impractical, the stories also fail because they cannot tell the women what they want to hear. They fail to demonstrate that a long-term ideal relationship is possible and that it can provide all the nurturance, care, and love that women need. As a result, they do not permit the reader to escape completely from the real world into a fantasy realm where she can enjoy the pretense of being the center of someone else's attention.

Additional evidence is probably unnecessary at this point to underscore the finding that the longing for a feeling of self-worth and the attentive care of another has generated the entire Smithton system for evaluating romantic fiction. Nevertheless, it might prove useful to look very briefly at two more failed romances precisely because they fail in such interesting ways. Though very different, *Bride of the Baja* and *High Fashion* each fail, as do so many others, because they do not trigger the essential emotions in the reader.

In one of our early conversations about romances, Dot mentioned that her customers can always tell the difference between a story authored by a man and one written by a woman. Skeptical at first, I asked her about the mark of their difference. She replied that a man's story always gives the hero's point of view more extensively than that of the heroine. Even though her customers insisted separately that they too can always ferret out romances written by men under female pseudonyms—indeed Laurie remarked that a man "always clips the woman short"—I still wondered whether this was, in fact, possible. In reading one of the two-star books in the sample, I discovered to my surprise that it was, for after finishing half of Jocelyn Wilde's *Bride of the Baja*, particularly its descriptions of sexual contact between the heroine and various male characters, I realized that the crucial passages about emotional satisfaction were not centered on the heroine's experience at all but expressed the male fantasy of what it would feel like to find a totally uninhibited female. In looking at the copyright page, which I had not checked earlier, I discovered that Jocelyn Wilde is, in reality, John Toombs.

Like all of the other failed romances, *Bride of the Baja* does not follow the one man–one woman rule. In fact, the intensely sexual heroine of the story becomes involved with three different men, all of whom are portrayed favorably by the author. This treatment is so evenhanded that it is nearly impossible to identify the real "hero" until the final pages of the story. Indeed the book does not really define its narrative problem as the ideal romance does, that is, as the question of how a woman is to find a man who will appreciate her for herself alone and not for her sexual being. Rather, this story preoccupies itself with the issue of how a woman can gradually shed ingrained cultural inhibitions and come to recognize her inherently physical and sexual nature.

This preoccupation is made especially clear by the narrative structure of the story and by its treatment of sex scenes that are told from a male point of view and always depict a woman's generous offering of herself to that individual. Surprisingly enough, *Bride of the Baja* fails to keep the heroine at the center of the romance. Indeed, a forty-page section of the book focuses on the exploits of Jordan Quinn, who eventually turns out to be the hero. What is especially peculiar about this section of the book, however, is that this character has not yet even met the heroine. As a result, the reader is asked to give up her identification with Alitha and view events from the point of view of a man. This proves especially strange in a love scene between Jordan and his fiancée, Margarita. Not only is the woman unknown to the reader, thus hindering identification, but the passage itself gives no information about her thoughts and feelings and therefore asks the reader to identify with Jordan:

> "I'll do whatever you want, Margarita. Do you want to wait?"
>
> She didn't answer. Instead she reached up and unbuttoned her dress and let it fall to the deck; unfastened her petticoats and stepped out of them; lifted the chemise over her head and threw it to one side. She stood naked before him.
>
> The ship pitched gently and she let herself fall into his arms. With one hand around her bare waist, Jordan began to fumble with the buttons of his shirt with the other.
>
> "Let me," she said. . . .
>
> When he was naked, she lay on the bunk and opened her arms to him. He let her enfold him, trying to enter her gently, yet still she gasped with pain so he waited, moving slowly above her, their love-making matching the rhythm of the sea. He felt her cling to him, arch to him as she kissed him, and he sensed that her pain had lessened, replaced by a pounding surge of pleasure until she trembled in his arms. When at last they slept, she lay with her arms and legs wrapped tightly around him. (pp. 78–79)

Although this passage emphasizes the hero's tenderness with Margarita, apparently demonstrating Toombs's intuitive understanding of the nature of the ideal romantic fantasy, it cannot function for the reader as a parallel passage might in an ideal romance because it tells her nothing about the woman's feelings. Even if she approved of such behavior, the emotionally needy reader could not experience vicarious satisfaction unless she were willing to shift her identification entirely and share in Jordan's pleasure. The fact that the book received only two stars from Dot and was not considered memorable by any of the other readers seems to indicate that such a process proved impossible. Their rejection makes sense given what they have said about their reasons for reading romances. No matter how tender the scene, no description of lovemaking that fails to concern itself with a heroine's sense of emotional fulfillment can offer the reader the imaginary experience of feeling cared for and attended to by another. On the contrary, a passage like the one quoted above simply asks the reader to assume her real-life role (assuming she is married) and to offer love and affection to a man, albeit in freely sexual terms.

Bride of the Baja fails in the end not because the heroine does not win the tender, perfect hero at the story's conclusion (she does), but because its manner of narrative construction asks the reader to identify herself first with a man and then with Alitha, who is always shown giving herself to men rather than receiving from them. Although the book ends properly in the sense that it rewards the heroine with a hero who truly appreciates her as a person and excites her sexually, it does not permit the reader to enjoy vicariously the fruits of her triumph. Indeed, Alitha and Jordan never make love in the novel and spend no more than a few hours (and pages) together before their final union. Such a narrative structure fails to provide the reader with the opportunity to imagine herself so valuable an individual that she is actively pursued, gently caressed, and passionately loved by a man who also promises safety and protection. *Bride of the Baja* includes all of the necessary features of the ideal romance, but because its narrative construction does not enable the reader to indulge in the desired feelings as she reads, it fails to live up to the Smithton standard.

Victoria Kelrich's novel, the three-and-a-half star *High Fashion*, apparently comes closer to the Smithton ideal. The book itself is much more explicit about promiscuous sex and violence than most ideal romances. However, when *High Fashion* is examined closely, it becomes clear that these ordinarily objectionable features must have been overridden for Dot because Kelrich offers the reader an opportunity to identify with a woman who succeeds spectacularly in business even though she does not marry the romantic hero she also wins. While it is not identical to an ideal romance, then, this book does at least enable a woman to experience vicariously feelings of strength, power, and achievement.

High Fashion differs from most other romances because it alternately follows the fortunes of two heroines as they make their way through the world of New York couture. Although Sugar Dawson and Elisabeth Vail both figure centrally in portions of the narrative, the book eventually becomes Elisabeth's story. Sugar's tale is really one of decline because it traces the course of her imprisonment within an unhappy marriage and focuses on her moral corruption brought about by extreme competitiveness. Elisabeth, on the other hand, flowers in the course of the story into a self-confident and successful woman.

This can be demonstrated easily by recounting an incident that occurs early in *High Fashion*. Although Elisabeth arrives in New York lacking self-confidence, she is strong enough to oppose her professors at the Design Institute. Her iconoclasm brings her to the attention of one of the institute's most respected teachers, and they immediately establish a sexual relationship. Although she loves Carlo, Elisabeth also suffers at his hands because he sometimes goes an "entire week without a private word, a glance, a surreptitious caress" (pp. 64–65) and because he insists that she not lean upon him. As she begins to succeed at school and become more independent, their relationship becomes more equal and is characterized by a mutual give and take in their sexual life. Surprisingly enough, at the end of a long description of one of these sexual encounters, the reader is told that when Elisabeth awoke, "she had no need to cling to him nor to beg another five minutes' tenderness; her work was waiting for her, and she was anxious to begin" (p. 73). This is not the world of the typical romance where the love and attention of an extraordinary man are all that a woman needs or wants. Although love and sex are important to Elisabeth, they are no longer the goals of her existence. She enjoys her work and intends to set about building a career for herself.

This is precisely what she does. Although Elisabeth is aided at strategic points by more powerful men, she does exhibit real talent. By avoiding sexual entanglements, she devotes all her attention to her work, gambles several times, and makes a success of her small design firm. She eventually "makes it big" just as she meets a man whom she loves and who loves her in return. Peter Brent, who does not appear until page 321, is the typical romantic hero. Dark, magnetic, and successful, he is also spontaneous, gentle, and thoughtful. Nonetheless, Elisabeth delays their involvement until she can combat Sugar's calculated attempts to steal her designs and to destroy her success.

Once her preeminence is reestablished, Elisabeth returns to Peter. Although the reader is permitted to witness their temporary reunion and passionate lovemaking, their mutual declaration of love is *not* accompanied by Elisabeth's abandonment of her public, work-associated persona. Indeed, her vision of her future, which closes the book, seems clearly designed by Kelrich as a "feminist" ending to a romantic novel. The passage is worth quoting in full just because it is so different from the typical passionate embrace and suggestion that hero and heroine will live happily ever after.

> She placed the call to Dherain [where Peter lived], debating if she should nap while waiting or if she should begin organizing her time for the coming year. A few months in New York, then time in Los Angeles to experiment and make notes and dream ideas for other forms of dress, for other tomorrows.
>
> And then there would be Peter again, and Dherain. She wondered how long it would last. Peter spoke in terms of a lifetime, of the year cut into segments of duty and work and pleasure. *I love him*, she thought. *That will last, even if our lives pull us apart. No*, she amended, forcing herself to be honest, knowing that only the truth would enable her to live each moment as fully as she could. *It will last as long as*

it lasts. If it's for a lifetime, wonderful. If it's for a while, that's wonderful, too. There are no guarantees. There's only the trying.

Elisabeth pulled out a sketch pad and wrote "Components" at the top of the page. She looked at the name, wondering if she was about to diagram her life or a new dress line. Then, nodding to herself, kicking off her shoes, she got down to work. (p. 378) [emphasis in original]

Kelrich's highly unusual ending did not escape Dot's notice. In fact, she commented explicitly about it in her May 1981 review of the book. Her brief remark, "ending was left too much in the air," implies, however, that she did not understand Kelrich's suggestion that it will be Elisabeth's work that directs her life in the future, even though she intends to try to integrate it with a personal life. Dot's observation reveals that her eye is still trained on the idea of romance as the proper route to feelings of fulfillment, happiness, and success. She believes the book is ambiguous because she feels this aspect of the story was not fully resolved as, indeed, it was not. And yet, given all that she and the other women have said about the necessity of the happy ending, it is striking that this book still earned three and a half stars.

Although Dot's review comments are very short, they point to the feature of the story that seems to override all of its other failings, that is, to the character of Elisabeth Vail. This was her comment in full: "This story stood a better chance had Ms. Kelrich written the story on Elizabeth [*sic*] Vail and kept Sugar Dawson as a minor character. As it was, the story line was split and not always for the best. Still, her descriptive narrative was well done. Ending was left too much in the air."[7] Elisabeth Vail, it seems, proved an interesting character to read about despite the fact that the story does not chronicle the usual vacillations in the establishment of a relationship between her and an ideal hero. She does find Peter, of course, but this event is only one among many in her life, as even she admits. Her story is nevertheless characterized by advances and setbacks as she moves upward in the fashion world. In the process, she increasingly draws the attention of others to her, receives admiration and praise, and grows ever more confident. It seems possible that this rather different chronicle of a woman's triumph may still have evoked the same kind of desired feelings in Dot and some of the other Smithton readers usually called forth by the ideal hero's appreciation of the heroine.

It seems clear, therefore, that while the romantic relationship is generally important to the ideal romance, it is so *because* it satisfies the heroine and the reader who identifies with her. This seems to suggest further that what is perhaps crucial to the ideal reading experience is the woman's success and the particular feelings of worth, power, and satisfaction it engenders in her as well as in the reader who vicariously shares her life. *High Fashion* appears to offer the reader all of these things. What it does not offer is the equally essential vicarious experience of being nurtured and cared for by a man who reduces the strength of his commitment to the outside world in order to admit his dependence on a woman and his recognition of the value of loving her. Lacking this, the story cannot replenish as successfully the emotional energy and strength of the emotionally needy reader. Hence, its failure to achieve the highest rating in the remarkably coherent Smithton system.

That system, it is worth repeating one last time, originates in the extraliterary desires and needs of the Smithton women. Thus the emotion generated within the reader by her identification with the heroine is the crucial determining factor in distinguishing between good romances and bad. If the events of the heroine's story provoke too intense feelings such as anger at men, fear of rape and violence, worry about female sexuality, or worry about the need to live with an unexciting man, that romance will be discarded as a failure or judged to be very poor. If, on the other hand, those events call forth feelings of excitement, satisfaction, contentment, self-confidence, pride, and power, it matters less what events are used or how they are marshaled. In the end, what counts most is the reader's sense that for a short time she has become other and been elsewhere. She must close that book reassured that men and marriage really do mean good things for women. She must also turn back to her daily round of duties, emotionally reconstituted and replenished, feeling confident of her worth and convinced of her ability and power to deal with the problems she knows she must confront. When a writer can supply a story that will permit the reader several hours of vicarious experience living as a woman who flourishes because she receives the attention, devotion, and approval of an extraordinary man, that writer will have written an ideal romance in the judgment of Dorothy Evans and the Smithton readers.

The Smithton group's reliance on this evaluation system enables the women to insure that a media institution, which in fact operates to benefit others financially, also benefits them emotionally. As a result, they at least partially reclaim the patriarchal form of the romance for their own use. By selecting only those stories that will reinforce their feelings of self-worth and supply the replenishment they need, they counter the force of a system that functions generally by making enormous demands upon women for which it refuses to pay. This is not to say, however, that the Smithton readers' romance constitutes a fundamental, material challenge to patriarchy. Such an assertion must await a more extensive assessment of the *effects* of prolonged romance reading upon these and other women. Yet it will be worthwhile to look at one final factor in romance reading in this ongoing effort to reveal the complexity of the connection between this literary form and the lives of real women. What I propose to examine in the final chapter, then, is the narrative discourse of the genre and its possible ideological impact on women who read romance after romance, day in and day out.

Language and Narrative Discourse
The Ideology of Female Identity

When the Smithton women insist that romantic fiction is fantasy and their reading activity simple escape, they seem to state the obvious. Indeed their assertion appears only to corroborate the familiar assumption in popular-culture study that because it is stereotypical, repetitive, and unrealistic, popular literature must be more closely related to fairy stories and myths than to "serious" considerations of pertinent human problems.[1] The Smithton readers' added assertion that they do not expect their own lives to resemble the lives of romantic heroines suggests further that they do not apply the principles of organization of the fantasy world to their own nor do they learn how to get more from their own relationships through romance reading. And yet, the group's equally insistent emphasis on the romance's capacity to instruct them about history and geography suggests that they also believe that the universe of the romantic fantasy is somehow congruent, if not continuous, with the one they inhabit. One has to wonder, then, how much of the romance's conservative ideology about the nature of womanhood is inadvertently "learned" during the reading process and generalized as normal, natural, female development in the real world.

It would be easy enough to dismiss the Smithton readers' conflicting beliefs about the realism of the romantic fantasy by attributing them to a lack of literary sophistication. Such a move, however, would once again deny the worth of the readers' understanding of their own experience and thus ignore a very useful form of evidence in the effort to reconstruct the complexity of their use of romantic fiction. It seems advisable, then, to treat their contradictory beliefs as evidence, at least, of an ambivalent attitude toward the reality of the story. The women may in fact believe the stories are only fantasies on one level at the very same time that they take other aspects of them to be real and therefore apply information learned about the fictional world to the events and occurrences of theirs. If they do so utilize some fictional propositions, it may well be the case that the readers also unconsciously take others having to do with the nature of the heroine's fate as generally applicable to the lives of real women. In that case, no matter what the women intend their act of reading to say about their roles as wives and mothers, the ideological force of the reading experience could, finally, be a conservative one. In reading about a woman who manages to find her identity through the care of a nurturant protector and sexual partner, the Smithton readers might well be teaching themselves to believe in the worth of such a route to fulfillment and encouraging the hope that such a route might yet open up for them as it once did for the heroine.

In an effort to assess the nature of the connection between the world of the romance and the world inhabited by the Smithton reader, I would now like to look more closely at the language and the narrative discourse of these stories and the kinds of activities and responses they elicit from their readers. Although it is true that romance reading evokes a process of identification whereby the reader responds to events lived through by the heroine, this is not the only level at which the reader reacts. The act of romance reading must first involve any reader in a complex process of world construction through which the reader actively attributes sense to the words on a page. In doing so, that reader adopts the text's language as her own and appears to gesture toward a world she in fact creates. Because the process must necessarily draw more or less on the language she uses to refer to the real world, the fictional world created in reading bears an important relationship to the world the reader ordinarily inhabits. The activities of reading and world construction, then, carry meaning for the reader on a purely formal level in the sense that they repeat and reinforce or alter and criticize the nature of the world as the reader knows it.

In discussing the character of this text-reader interaction in the reading process, Terry Eagleton has observed that texts "do" things to the people who read them.[2] "What they bring about," he adds, "is not something that happens after we have finished reading them, like joining a picket line or being kinder to one's children, but is effected (if at all) by and in the reading."[3] This occurs, he maintains, because literary signs do not simply denote things in some objectively given and immediately present world but because they represent language. In doing so, they refer to an imaginary *act* of speaking or writing about an equally imaginary world that is itself brought into being and conceptually organized in the very act of commenting about it.[4] It might be said, then, that the language of the literary text imitates not the world but an ideological speech act that takes a world as its object. A literary text can be said to operate on the reader in the sense that she must treat it as a set of instructions directing her to adopt the position of an imaginary speaker or writer who uses words as if there were indeed just such a universe already "out there" about which she might tell this story.

Traditional popular-culture criticism has assumed that the world "out there" is a fantasy world bearing little resemblance and no applicability to the reader's own. Kay Mussell, for instance, has asserted categorically that "popular fiction is not *realistic*, is not intended to be by its authors, and is not desired to be by its readers."[5] Romance writers and readers, however, seem to disagree. Phyllis Whitney advises prospective writers that if they cannot afford a research trip to an exotic locale, they can just as easily rely on library books or locations they are familiar with in their own lives.[6] Careful descriptions of real places, she observes, can be transposed automatically into the settings for a story. Whitney assumes, as do the Smithton readers, that the romantic universe is identical to the universe inhabited by real women. Thus the question of the romance's mimesis is a good deal more complex for the women who write and read these books than it might first appear to a critic accustomed to Henry James or William Dean Howells.

It is certainly true that, when prompted, the Smithton readers are perfectly willing to admit that the romantic stories themselves are implausible because the characters are "better" than real people and because events resolve themselves unambiguously. Nevertheless, they also believe implicitly in the accuracy of the fiction's rendering of the material world. Indeed, it is precisely because their faith in this verbal transcription of the "real" is so complete that they are able to file away verbal assertions about historical customs and geographical locales as "facts" and "knowledge" about this world and its history. Their faith in the realism of the contemporary romance is, in actuality, a function of the peculiar way the language is organized by the author and then actively construed by them as readers.

Because the authors represent acts of designation that are familiar in form and substance to those ordinarily employed by the Smithton women, the texts appear to the readers to be about their own world. In adopting the romance's signifying intention, then, the Smithton women simply duplicate in imaginative experience a relationship to the world that they live daily. To understand just why this occurs and how it might later affect the reader's attitude toward behavioral propositions about the romantic action itself, it will be necessary to trace the interaction between textual properties and reading strategies.

Any cursory glance at a popular romance reveals that the form uses few linguistic techniques capable of thwarting a reader's efforts to "discover" immediately the sense of the story's words. The contemporary romance's prose is dominated by cliché, simple vocabulary, standard syntax, and the most common techniques associated with the nineteenth-century realist novel. Quick reader comprehension is therefore made possible by the resolute familiarity of the romance's language. Although it is true that readers never discover meanings "in" or behind the words they find on the page but actively attribute significations to the verbal structure from their own linguistic repertoire, it is nonetheless clear that Dot and her women read the romantic text *as if* such simple discovery of meaning was possible. In fact, the above-mentioned linguistic techniques all maintain the illusion that language is a transparent window opening out onto an already exist-tent world because the readers themselves treat these linguistic features in a particular way. Their crucial interpretive strategy is itself governed by a set of assumptions about language and meaning that the women take entirely for granted.

Dot displays these assumptions herself in her newsletter when she praises "well-written" romances. Of Kim Hansen's *Rebecca McGregor*, for instance, she once observed, "a very well written book set in Australia."[7] Dot did not intend to use this term, however, as a literary critic might, to single out the writer's unusual abilities at description or at finding unique ways to reorder perception. Rather, she employed it to refer to Hansen's ingenious plot. Dot is not interested in the skill with which the author uses language because she is looking first for variety in the things to which that language refers. In explaining specifically why she awarded five stars to *Rebecca McGregor*, she made it clear that she believes that success in writing has nothing to do with elegant phrasing or the quality of percep-tion but is a function of the uniqueness of the characters and events intended by the most familiar of linguistic signs. This helps to explain why, when asked to comment on what establishes the book as a well-written one, Dot did not mention Hansen's literary style but launched enthusiastically into a summary of her plot: "To be quite frank, the cover was just not that enticing. Ah, it was almost drab. It was the story's line—this was in Australia. It starts from the man's point of view and he comes over from England to make his fortune because . . . he's been accused of theft in a job; he was working in a bank. And he was engaged. And when he was accused of theft, the engagement was broken off and he left." Dot seems to judge writing solely on the basis of the efficiency with which it gets its job done, that is, tells the story. Dot treats language, then, in utilitarian fashion as a tool for accomplishing some purpose.[8] In sum, it "says" things.

If this representative comment about a well-written romance is an accurate indication of her reading behavior, Dot seldom attends consciously to the material presence of an author's words as she reads. In fact, during the entire time we talked about romances, on only three occasions did she remember and direct my attention to an author's felicitous phrasing. For Dot, words are not entities that can be manipulated to mean in new ways, nor are they things requiring conscious attention or interpretation on the part of the reader. Because words have meanings, in the sense that they contain or possess them, she understands them to refer definitively to actions, places, and events completely separate from the words that merely describe them. Moreover, Dot's readers are even less likely than she to comment on the language of a romance. They think of the terms "good" and "bad" as evaluations applicable only to the quality of the story a particular novel tells. No matter how often I asked readers to clarify the difference between a well-written book and a poorly written one, I always received an answer dealing with the exceptional nature of a plot or the likeable personality of the heroine or the hero.

Dot and her readers all come to the romantic text, then, with the understanding that its language is there to describe, in simple and unambiguous terms, events that for all intents and purposes were "completed" just before the fictional narrator described them. They assume that, as in the real world, fictional events are distinct from the words and verbal statements that can be used to designate them. In addition, these women also believe that the author herself provided the meaning of the story for her readers by expressing it in words. They believe that meaning is *in* the words only waiting to be found. Reading is not a self-conscious, productive process in which they collaborate with the author, but an act of discovery during which they glean from her information about people, places, and events not themselves *in* the book. The women assume that the information about these events was placed in the book by the author when she selected certain words in favor of others. Because they believe words are *themselves already meaningful* before they are read, Dot and her friends accept without question the accuracy of all statements about a character's personality or the implications of an event.

It should, however, be pointed out here that what the women really do when they read is to link or associate linguistic signifiers with meanings they understand or take to be their necessary significations. They rely on standard cultural codes correlating signifiers and signifieds that they accept as definitive. It has simply never occurred to them that those codes might be historically or culturally relative. Thus the romantic heroine becomes *their* version of an "independent" and "intelligent" woman. Neither Dot nor her women doubt the capacity of language to describe and designate external reality adequately. When they encounter familiar words, epithets, and modes of designation in a book, they automatically attribute to these signs the sense they have always had for them previously, assuming all the while that this sense is natural, immutable, and unproblematic. Because Dot and her friends believe that words always say what they mean (how could they do otherwise if indeed they contain their meanings?), they never question those words and thus do not become conscious of what they themselves attribute to them as inert verbal signifiers. Although they actively construct the heroine and the significances of her story, they are not aware of this at all. They assume instead that this is the way she and her world "really" are.

It might be said accurately, then, that Dot and her customers carry over to the activity of reading the very same principles and procedures of the empiricist epistemology that guides their activities in the world they believe to be "real." They view objective reality as a thing distinct and fundamentally different from language, which is itself nothing more than a system of names for that which truly exists. When these women encounter these same names in fiction, they deal with them as they would had the words been uttered in their presence by a speaker using them to indicate and describe the world at which both were together present. They treat that language, therefore, as if it simply designated a world entirely congruent or continuous with their own. Because they are not aware that this simulacrum is itself constructed by the language, just as they are not aware that the world they inhabit is in part a creation of the codes used to articulate it, they freely assimilate the fictional world to their own, assuming, in effect, that all imaginary worlds "naturally" resemble the world with which they are so familiar.

Despite the importance of these assumptions and the reading behavior they prompt with respect to the final construction of textual meaning, it should be pointed out again that these interpretive strategies are not alone responsible for the creation of the fictional world that so closely resembles the one inhabited by the reader. Because romance authors share the same assumptions about language and meaning, they write texts designed to be read in this straightforward manner. The characteristic verbal structure of the contemporary romance thus conveniently lends itself to this kind of interpretation by refusing to present the reader with anything capable of disorienting her or of forcing her to attend differently to the substance and organization of signs that cannot be taken so easily as simple, referential gestures.

Perhaps the most striking linguistic feature of the contemporary romance is its constant use of an exceedingly simple syntax that yet manages to mark itself as "literary." This syntactic simplicity effectively insures that individual signs can be understood immediately by even an inexperienced reader. The efficacy of the language's referential function is therefore never called into question. However, even though romances rely heavily on simple subject-verb constructions, most also exhibit a marked tendency to lapse into the passive voice. When they do so, they often seem to be straining after an identifiably "literary" effect because they combine it with subordinate clause constructions, elaborate similes, and rhetorical flourishes.[9]

In opening a book, for example, whose very first sentence explains that "Somewhere in the world, time no doubt whistled by on taut and widespread wings, but here in the English countryside it plodded slowly, painfully, as if it trod the rutted road that stretched across the moors on blistered feet,"[10] the reader cannot help but know immediately that she has been transported out of her daily world into an imaginary realm existing only between the pages of a book. The verbal structure obviously does not repeat the simple patterns of daily speech. Yet the sentences immediately following this opening contradict or, better yet, *balance* that effect by focusing attention on the spatial and temporal particularity of the moment. The author's insistently referential discourse deliberately emphasizes the historical specificity of the scene, which was first introduced, even before that "literary" opening cited above, as "June 23, 1799": "The hot sweltering air was motionless; dust hung above the road, still reminding the restless of a coach that had passed several hours before. A small farm squatted dismally beneath the humid haze that lay over the marsh. The thatched cottage stood between spindly yews and, with shutters open and door ajar, it seemed to stare as if aghast at some off-color jest."[11]

This peculiar blend of a deliberately referential language with the signs of "the literary" serves the dual purpose of signaling "escape" while suggesting to the reader that the imaginary world is congruent with her own and, therefore, dominated by events that might well occur in a life such as hers. This hybrid opening is characteristic of romantic fiction. Unlike the fairy tale that calls attention to its fantastic shape with the opening, "Once upon a time," which establishes a mythic space incalculably distant from the real world, the popular romance simultaneously collapses the distance between its fantasy world and the real *and* slyly admits their disjunction. It thus demonstrates that the story is realistic even though it is also a literary fiction.[12] The discourse of each book ingeniously informs the reader that its story will provide the escape into the imaginary realm she so desires even as it instructs her about strange and unknown facts concerning the history of her own. The opening paragraphs, then, conveniently proclaim the book's ability to fulfill the two essential functions of romance reading and establish a conflicted or ambivalent feeling about the essential reality of the about-to-be-told tale.

Despite its willingness to acknowledge stylistically that its tale is a fantasy, the popular romance also goes on to exhibit a marked attention to the material details of the world in which that fantasy is set. The effect is so overpowering that the technique may well persuade the reader that the tale need not be considered a fantasy at all. The romance's consequent equivocation about its status as myth or realism could conceivably be the mark of its authors' and readers' deep-seated unwillingness to admit that the perfect union concluding the story is unattainable in life. If so, it is possible that while learning about the material world through romance reading, the Smithton women also actively extrapolate information gained about relationships and apply that information to their own lives.

Although the romance's mimetic effect can be traced to several linguistic devices, one of the most crucial is the genre's careful attention to the style, color, and detail of women's fashions. Extended descriptions of apparel figure repeatedly in all variations of the form, but they are especially prominent in gothics and long historicals. However, even the shorter Harlequins and Silhouettes make use of pared-down descriptions that still manage to evoke the aura of the female world. While relatively short, the following is a characteristic fashion vignette:

> Outwardly, she must look much as they did. She had worn a simple white silk brocade of her own design, and with it the set of diamonds and sapphires on the silver filigree chain which she had completed recently. In her small ears were sapphire studs, and on one finger an immense sapphire ring. The white and silver set off her dark curly hair and luminous gray eyes. Leah, her abigail, had set her hair in a high pile with long curls to her neck. Some stray tendrils drifted about her ears, and she brushed them back nervously.[13]

The clothes described in these passages almost never figure significantly in the developing action. Instead, the plot is momentarily, often awkwardly, delayed as the narrator accidentally notices seemingly superfluous details for the reader. The details, however, are not really superfluous at all. They are part of an essential shorthand that establishes that, like ordinary readers, fictional heroines are "naturally" preoccupied with fashion. Romantic authors draw unconsciously on cultural conventions and stereotypes that stipulate that women can always be characterized by their universal interest in clothes. However, at the same time that the fictional characterizations depend on these previously known codes, they also tacitly legitimate them through simple repetition, thereby justifying the readers' own likely preoccupation with these indispensable features of the feminine universe. The final effect of endless attention to "pink-striped shirt waists," "sandy-tweed jackets," "long-sleeved dresses," "emerald-green wrappers,"[14] may be the celebration of the reader's world of housewifery, dominated as it often is by shopping trips, homemade wardrobes, and reliance on magazines like *Family Circle* and *Good Housekeeping* for tips about replicating *Vogue* couture on a tight budget.

A similar sort of descriptive detail also characterizes the mention of domestic architecture and home furnishings in romantic fiction. If the novels are set in the historical past, the narrator's eye lingers lovingly over the objects and accoutrements of preelectrical living. If the story's setting is contemporary, brand-name appliances, popular furniture styles, and trendy accessories such as "lush" green plants, macramé wall hangings, and silk flowers typically populate the heroine's apartment. Both kinds of descriptions assert tacitly that the imaginary world of the novel is as real as the reader's world because it is filled with the same, solid, teeming profusion of commodities. The emphatic massing of detail in the following, characteristic passage reveals little about character or mood. It seems to exist only to call attention to itself as a descriptive litany:

> The large den was paneled with rich walnut wood. Sunlight filtered through the sheer curtains over the windowed door opening onto the rooftop of the penthouse apartment. The walls gleamed with a natural luster. Few books lined the shelves which ran floor to ceiling in one corner of the room. The volumes it contained were devoted to weapons and hunting and were worn from frequent handling. Mostly the shelves held souvenirs and photographs of a hunter posed beside his kill. A mounted wolverine prowled an upper shelf while a lacquered coiled rattler threatened the unwary from its shelf nearer the floor.[15]

This deceptively casual but absolutely necessary description of the domestic environment is a variation of a literary practice that Umberto Eco has aptly named "the technique of the aimless glance."[16] In analyzing the discourse of Ian Fleming's James Bond novels, Eco has noted that Fleming suspends his narration in favor of a "minute and leisurely concentration" on "descriptions of articles, landscapes, and events apparently inessential to the course of the story."[17] Not only are the descriptions characterized by "high technical skill which makes us see what he is describing," Eco writes, "but they are inevitably focused on the obvious and the usual rather than on the exotic or unfamiliar." In attempting to explain this extreme preoccupation with "the already-known," Eco suggests that "Fleming takes time to convey the familiar with photographic accuracy because it is with the familiar that he can solicit our capacity for identification." He continues that "our credulity is solicited, blandished, directed to the region of possible and desirable things. Here the narration is realistic, the attention to detail intense." Eco concludes, finally, that Fleming's minute descriptions function as a "literary evocation" of the familiar world inhabited by the reader.[18]

Romantic fiction also employs the technique of the aimless glance. The genre's characteristic attention to the incidental features of fashion and domestic interiors clearly serves to duplicate the homey environment that serves as the stage for female action in the "real" world. However, it is not true, as it is with the thriller, that such leisurely concentration is never devoted to the exotic, the faraway, or the unknown; nor is it true that such descriptions fail to operate as encyclopedias for their readers. In fact, romantic authors often squander lavish amounts of space on the descriptions of foreign environments and historical customs that are very likely not already known except in the most skeletal way by the reader. Furthermore, as has been pointed out before, the readers themselves "frame" or type these descriptive passages as valuable "information" and "instructional" material that can be stored as "knowledge" for use at a later date. It seems likely that romance readers find it easy to dub these simple descriptive assertions about the past or places they have never seen as "fact" because those other descriptions of a familiar domestic environment are so evocative of the world they inhabit. The success with which the ordinary is typically mimed in the romance thus seems to confer factual status on all of its other verbal assertions as well. Thus when the romance reader encounters a sentence that takes the form of syntactic assertion, even if she has never seen the place it refers to or the object or custom it describes, she simply assumes that what it claims is true; she accepts it as fact.

Again, one is prompted to wonder whether the same process of "infection" is operating with respect to the romantic story.[19] If romance readers believe assertions made about subjects they know nothing about, perhaps they also believe in the possibility of a romantic relationship they have never experienced. Before speculating on whether this is the case, however, I would like to look a little longer at some of the romance's other linguistic techniques that also foreground language's referential function and thus stress the centrality of *story* to the romance-reading experience.

Quick reader comprehension and visualization are further guaranteed in the romance by repetitive use of the same, limited vocabulary. Romantic authors endlessly repeat descriptive phrases both within a single novel and from book to book as well. For instance, despite important differences, the Regency, the gothic, the historical, and the contemporary all characterize their romantic heroes as "passionate," "hard," "mocking," "indifferent," "moody," "masculine," "magnetic," "fierce," "ruthless," and "overbearing." Marked redundancy and intertextual repetition are characteristic of romantic fiction. Such a recurring vocabulary inevitably creates stock descriptions and formulaic characterizations that reconfirm reader expectations over and over again.[20] The redundancy of the discourse permits the reader to get by with a minimal amount of interpretive work after her initial encounter with the romantic form. Each subsequent appearance of the first stock adjective can invoke the entire characterization and trigger the reader's usual emotional response as a result of its prior formulaic linkage with an entire set of descriptions and reactions in earlier acts of reading. There is little need for that reader to attend to the nuances of any particular novel in order to understand the nature of the story. Her energy is reserved, therefore, for the more desirable activity of affective reaction rather than prematurely spent on the merely intermediary task of interpretation.[21]

Romances further obviate the need for self-conscious interpretation by almost never assuming that their readers are capable of inferring meaning, drawing conclusions, or supplying "frames." Typically, after describing a verbal response that any reader can infer is prompted by anger, the writer confides redundantly, "she was angry." Repetition is the rule, not the exception, governing these novels. Even in passages obviously intended to evoke a mood, romance writers cannot resist the temptation to assist the reader in her interpretive efforts. For instance, the gothic writer, Phyllis Whitney, manages to suggest a mood in the first three sentences of the following passage, only to close off speculation about its exact character with her last assertion: "The room was so still that a bit of charred wood falling in the grate made an explosive sound and Mignonette's purr was like a kettle boiling. Booth shrugged and sat down, dropping again into the shadows. Letty's crochet needle paused in mid-air. Hortense clasped her fingers tightly together in her lap. Tension crackled in the room."[22]

It is important to point out here that these practices are not cited as evidence of the lamentable quality of writing in popular romantic fiction. Indeed, this writing can be judged harshly only if one agrees with Henry James that all fiction ought to demonstrate with subtlety rather than tell overtly.[23] Romance readers, of course, do not; for them, redundancy and overzealous assertion perform important and particular functions. Together, these functions combat ambiguity, imply that all events are definitively comprehensible, and reassure the reader that whatever minimal inferences she might construct, they will be adequate and accurate. In short, these techniques cancel the anxiety and contingency prompted by the fact that reading is a temporally open-ended act, just as they guarantee that even the laziest and most unimaginative reader will know not only what is occurring but what it means as well.

By masking the interpretive character of the act of reading, the redundant and simple language of the romantic novel minimizes the labor the reader contributes to the production of the story. This particular linguistic practice then insures that reading will be marked not as "work" but as "pleasure" by the women who indulge in it so frequently. They seem to be at least partially aware of this, for in discussing the novels of Jane Austen, several of the women admitted that although they liked her heroines and found her stories intriguing, they could read her only if they were not tired, if they were alone, or if they were willing to pay particular attention to her verbal structures. "Her sentences are so confusing," Joy lamented, "that I really have to work at it to understand what she's saying. I can't read her and do something else at the same time. It's hard work."

In fact, all of the linguistic practices discussed thus far mask the reader's active collaboration in the production of textual meaning. The simple syntax, elementary realism, repetitive vocabulary, and authorial interpretation characteristic of romantic fiction together create a verbal structure that can be "decoded" easily and quickly on the basis of previously mastered cultural codes and conventions. Because the prose is so familiar, individual words or signs appear to make their meanings immediately available to any reader operating according to certain procedures and assumptions. Consequently established as the passive recipient of previously selected meanings by these features, the reader is never forced to recognize that it is indeed she who actively supplies the significance of the words she encounters.

Moreover, this kind of language use enables the reader to maintain her illusory view of herself as the simple recipient of the story because it limits the actual labor she must perform to that of simple memory.[24] In order to make sense of its individual signs, more complex sentences, or even of its entire fictional events, the reader need only recall what such units usually mean in ordinary daily discourse. Because words are rarely employed in unfamiliar ways, because syntax is almost never deformed for "poetic" or shock effect, because events themselves are always interpreted redundantly in conventional ways by a trustworthy narrator, the reader is never required to forge new interpretive conventions or to construct consciously a theory about character motivation. Neither is she encouraged to view the fictive analogues of real human activity in a new or unusual light. Reading the romantic novel is an event that is dominated by the typical reader's unconscious but nonetheless active recall of learned cultural conventions, but because the reader herself does not recognize those conventions, she continues to view that event as a simple matter of receiving that which is already fully there *in* the text.

If the reading habits of the Smithton women are any indication, the language of the romantic novel can be said to function as an instrument for the transfer of meaning, which writers and readers seem to believe preexists both the decision to communicate and the activity of reception. Words, phrases, and sentences do not themselves become the object of attention but exist as a channel or conduit through which the reader gains access to the truly important, the meanings that constitute the romantic story of the lovers. Romance writers and readers alike understand the purpose of the text to be the romantic tale itself, just as they conceive the activities of writing and reading as a *storytelling* cycle. From the perspective of its participants, then, romance reading might be characterized as the reception of a completed tale offered to a reader by a writer who not only "speaks" the same language but similarly understands the conventions of romantic storytelling and the significance of romance as an archetypal event in a woman's life. This form of interaction between two parties who are established as equals creates the illusion of a spontaneous, unmediated communication between individuals capable of telling and receiving a story about themselves whose meaning is not only unambiguous but *already known* by both parties because they have "heard" it before.

Popular romances, as they are habitually read and understood by the Smithton readers, it seems, resemble the myths of oral cultures in the sense that they exist to relate a story already familiar to the people who choose to read them. Although romances are technically novels because each purports to tell a "new" story of unfamiliar characters and as-yet uncompleted events, in fact, they all *retell* a single tale whose final outcome their readers always already know. The peculiar, but nonetheless crucial, fact that these novels are consumed repetitively by the same readers guarantees that the first recurrence of a familiar phrase, stock description, or stereotypical event in a novel still partially unread will inform the reader that the fate of these "new" lovers is as immutable and irreversible as the already completed and fixed destiny of any mythical deity. As Umberto Eco has observed with respect to myths, the accounts "greatly favored by antiquity [were] almost always the story of something which had already happened and of which the public was aware. One could recount for the *n*th time the story of Roland the Paladin, but the public already knew what happened to the hero."[25] Therefore, the act of retelling that same myth functioned as the ritual reaffirmation of fundamental cultural beliefs and collective aspirations.[26]

If this phenomenon of repetitive reading is accorded the importance it deserves, it becomes clear that romantic novels function for their reader, on one level at least, as the ritualistic repetition of a single, immutable cultural myth. However, one must also recognize that the Smithton women do not simply reencounter the story of a single heroine-hero pair because the romantic myth is itself disguised in the form of the realistic novel. In fact, the women believe the books they buy *are* novels, which is to say, stories about unknown and distinct characters whose fates are not yet determined but whose individual development can be observed in the working out of a narrative. Not surprisingly, then, when asked specifically to describe the "typical romantic heroine," all of Dot's readers insist that the task is impossible because the heroines "are all different." The Smithton women also refuse to admit that the books they read have a standard plot, although as noted in Chapter 3, they will go so far as to categorize them as "romances" because all are stories about a "man and woman meeting, the obstacles to their love, and their final happy ending." The women even claim that they most value unpredictable plots because they create the excitement and tension associated with not knowing what will happen.

In comparing myths with the literature of the modern world, Eco has observed further that "the 'civilization' . . . [of the latter] offers a story in which the reader's main interest is transferred to the unpredictable nature of *what will happen* and, therefore, to the plot invention which now holds our attention. The event has not happened *before* the story; it happens *while* it is being told and usually even the author does not know what will take place."[27] Romances seem to function as novels do, then, because in beginning a new one, the reader appears to accompany just-met acquaintances on a journey whose final destination is unknown at the moment of embarkation. Thus the act of reading a romance that is constructed like a novel is fraught with the excitement of open-ended potential and simultaneously marked by the threat of the unknown. The conventions of the novelistic discourse itself seem to be at odds with the reassuring redundancy of the prose just as they apparently contradict, even if they cannot fully undermine, the security provided by the reader's prior acquaintance with the romance as a fixed myth embodied in other nearly identical "novels."

The romance-reading experience, in short, appears to provide both the psychological benefits of oral myth-telling and those associated with the reading of a novel. This dual functionality was illustrated graphically by Ann when she remarked that before she began to rely on Dot's advice about romances, she always read the first and last pages of every book before she decided to purchase it. She read the beginning, she explained, to make sure the "story got off to a fast start" and to see if she could predict what its resolution was likely to be. If she could not, she assumed the book would be exciting. She read the ending, she added, to see that the author had not "pulled any dirty tricks" by ending the lovers' tale unhappily. Ann explained that she simply did not want "to get involved with the characters" if she was destined to feel sad when events did not turn out as they should. She sees no contradiction in desiring an unpredictable plot and wanting to know how it ends before she reads it through.

While her behavior and reasoning may sound idiosyncratic, they are not. Despite the fact that seventeen of the forty-two Smithton women said they "never" read the endings of romances before they begin the whole book, twelve responded that they "sometimes" engage in this behavior, five maintained that they do it "often," and eight replied that they "always" read the endings first. In all, twenty-five (60 percent) of this group of readers find it at least occasionally necessary to counteract the novel's power to threaten them with the contingency of the unknown.

Although this widespread need to learn of the ending first could be interpreted as evidence that the text's stock descriptions and clichés do not identify individual books as a retelling of the basic romantic myth, this seems inadequate, finally, as an explanation. The very same women who need reassurance about particular endings also become angry when they discover that a book they thought was a romance on the basis of its cover and narrative opening turns out to be something else. In this instance, the conventions seem to operate as claimed by establishing certain expectations that the story will proceed and end in the prescribed manner. If the romance's stereotyped, formulaic conventions operate as signals to at least some of the readers that the book in question is another adequate retelling of the romantic myth, it becomes necessary to ask why so many of the others still need to reassure themselves about the nature of each particular ending. The Smithton women themselves have provided no further explicit information about why they want to read stories pretending to witness as yet uncompleted and unique events and also simultaneously desire to know beforehand that those very same events have indeed concluded and that the outcome is properly and reassuringly fixed. By turning once again to the texts themselves, perhaps accurate inferences can be made about the likely effect particular textual features have on the reader. Of special relevance here are the popular romance's delineation of character and its typical narrative structure.

As most major commentators on the novel have observed, one of its principal characteristics is its pretense that it chronicles the life of a unique individual whose very particularity resembles that of all the other discrete individuals thought to comprise the social universe.[28] Unlike the mythic or allegorical character who embodies a limited set of laws understood to be the symbolic summary of his or her already completed destiny, the novelistic character is intended to appear as a complex, human figure whose often contradictory traits and motives are a function of the need to deal expediently with an entirely contingent and particular reality that is itself not only incomplete but unpredictable as well. In the words of Eco once again, "the character of a novel wants . . . to be a man [*sic*] like anyone else, and what could befall him is as unforeseeable as what may happen to us."[29] Every version of the form is "novel," then, precisely because it eschews "traditional" plot and "typed" characters in favor of a detailed rendering of the responses made by a singular, apparently "real" individual to the unique conjuncture of events and characters encountered solely by him or her. As Ian Watt has demonstrated, this is accomplished stylistically by lavishing space and attention on personality and consciousness as well as on the particularism of individual circumstance.[30] Characters in the novel are distinguished, finally, by a unique and persistent identity as well as by the unfamiliarity of their situations.

Given their experience with novelistic renderings of character and contingent event as specific and precise as those of George Eliot, Henry James, or William Faulkner, it is not surprising to note that most literary critics who even bother to mention popular literature dismiss the characters that inhabit its forms as formulaic, stereotypic, and reminiscent of morality plays or myth. Popular authors are routinely accused of simplifying complex moral problems because they embody them in a conflict between characters who are simplistically good and purely evil. Although the virginal heroines and mysteriously masculine heroes populating romances understandably appear to be mere abstract types to those accustomed to Isabel Archer and Gilbert Osmond, they are not perceived as such by women who read nothing but romances. Not only do the Smithton readers assert that all romantic heroines are different, but they can demonstrate quite adequately that, in fact, they are distinguished clearly in their minds by the peculiarity of their circumstances and by the specificity of their responses to events.

Very often during the group interviews, for example, one of the Smithton readers would recall a favorite title that several others could not remember having read. Those who had read the book immediately tried to refresh the memories of their sister readers by briefly summarizing the plot. These plot summaries proved especially intriguing because they inevitably began "that was the one where she . . ."; the speaker always finished with the heroine's response to one of the hero's comments or actions. Although the women almost never remembered the names of principal characters, they could recite in surprising detail not only what had happened to them but also how they had managed to cope with particularly troublesome situations. Dot's tendency to evaluate the "believability" of characters and events, then, is wholly in keeping with her customers' demands that character motivation be realistic and convincing. When she recommends Roberta Gellis's *Siren Song* (1981) because "the characters are wonderfully human with a full range of emotions, desires, and thoughts,"[31] she is indicating to her readers that this book, despite its adherence to the requirements of the fantasy or myth, will be satisfying because its characters will make that fantasy appear "real" and, therefore, possible. It is not surprising that the Smithton women reserve their greatest scorn for novels with heroines whom they consider either too meek or too aggressive to be believable. As Maureen remarked, "We know how men react to that kind of behavior. No real woman would ever think of trying to get away with that. She'd get hurt."

In claiming here that Dot and the other women accept romantic characters as "real" because they are convinced by the narrative's display of their individual particularity, it may seem to be contradicting data cited in a previous chapter suggesting that many readers do not believe characters in romances resemble those people they have met in their own lives. Indeed, twenty-two (52 percent) of the Smithton women did claim that the characters in romances "are not at all similar" to "the people [they] meet in real life," although twenty (48 percent) still maintained that the fictional characters are either "somewhat similar" (eighteen; 43 percent) or "very similar" (two; 5 percent) to people met in real life. I wondered enough about the apparent contradiction to question the women about the opposition between their constant references to "believable" characters and their answers to the questionnaires. They very readily explained that they had taken the question literally to mean that they ought to compare the fictional characters to actual people they meet or know. They did not understand the query as an abstract question about categorical similarities between novelistic figures and real human "types"; hence, the high proportion of apparently negative answers about the realism of fictional characters. In fact, those answers indicate only that romantic characters are often not like people the women already know or are likely to meet. It seems worth quoting one of the relevant exchanges at some length here, for it demonstrates clearly that although the women acknowledge that the romantic hero and heroine are idealized figures, they want very much to be convinced that such individuals are plausible if not really possible:

> Interviewer: One of the answers I got on the questionnaires back from everybody—if you remember, there were questions like, "Is the heroine like you or is the hero like men you've known in your life?" Nearly everybody said "not at all like" or "only slightly like." . . . I was talking to Maureen today and she's writing a book, and she was talking about making the characters real, like ordinary people with regular emotions and that seems like it conflicts somehow.
>
> Dot: It would. I'm sure it does. But it's kind of like going to a movie and seeing all these characteristics in a hero that you would like. Well, for that time, that is a real man; that is a real person and embodiment. And I guess the actors go to a great deal of trouble—at least they say they do anyway—to get into the character, as it were. As it is written, in making this a really believable character. When I

	say this [the hero] is not my husband, it's not my husband! I wasn't kidding. There's no way that these heroes emulate my husband at all. And I don't know that I could live with the hero in here.
Susan:	Maybe you could say it's a dream person that you *wish* . . .
Dot:	Yes!
Susan:	was real. You know, everybody has in their mind a certain type of person. And you know no person could possibly have all the good qualities you would like to have in your husband. Maybe you would say in your mind, this is a perfect character. This would be my hero-type.
Sally:	There is no such person.
Dot:	You know, I often tell my children, "In life there's what you want and there's what you get—no—there's what you dream about, there's what you really want—and then there's what is laid out there for ya!"
Interviewer:	Okay, I think I understand better. So they're motivated like normal, real people. . . .
Dot:	Right, right.
Interviewer:	But they're not specifically like real people you've known.
Dot:	Right.
All:	Yes.

Fictional characterization, it would seem, is successful for these women because it manages to convince them that even though they know the characters are more perfect than they or their husbands can ever hope to be, they are yet entirely persuasive and believable as possible human individuals. The women can thus believe in them *and* in the verity of the happy ending that concludes the story.

This implicit faith in the reality of the romantic novel's world may explain the need to know from the beginning how a particular story will be resolved. The Smithton women trust the mimesis to such a degree that they truly seem to believe in the ominous contingency of the heroine's situation. Even though most of them have read hundreds of other romances before, they are so completely taken in by each book's claim to its status as a novel that they are not at all willing to trust those purely discursive markers that otherwise identify the tale as a romance and establish the expectation that it "ought" to end in a certain way. In effect, the Smithton women want to participate in the ritualistic reaffirmation of a fixed myth, but they also want to be convinced that it is not merely a twice-told fairy tale but the fortuitous working out of one more individual woman's problems.

The peculiar narrative structure of the popular romantic novel also seems to satisfy this desire to believe that what they know is myth or fantasy is also possible because it happens in an obviously "real" world, in a plausible manner, to quite believable people. The very plausibility of those events is in no small way a function of the popular romance's typically novelistic rendering of time.[32] Unlike earlier literary traditions that relied on "timeless stories to mirror the unchanging moral verities,"[33] the novel insists, in its portrayal of chronological causality, that the historical past is the condition of the present. Its preoccupation with the development of its characters through time is the logical consequence, then, of this characteristically "modern" view.

Although the story told by all romances can be considered a myth because every book is dominated by the same set of events resolved in an identical way, each individual romance nonetheless insists in its very first paragraph on the temporal specificity of the tale it is about to relate. Romances do not begin by placing their characters in the timeless, mythical space of the fairy tale. Rather, they are remarkably consistent about relying on one of two specific techniques to inform the reader that fictional time operates as time does in the real world. One of these techniques insists that the novel's time is merely the historical antecedent of the reader's time. Historical novels employing this technique begin, as do *The Flame and the Flower*, *The Proud Breed*, and *The Sea Treasure*, by making specific reference to the historical date on which the story begins. This strategy tacitly avers that the heroine, who also typically appears in the first paragraph, was a real figure who inhabited the reader's world at an earlier moment in its single, continuing history. It should also be noted, however, that while such dating places these stories in the past and suggests that the events have already been completed and resolved, the narratives progress *as if* those events are occurring concurrently with the account of them. This practice preserves the illusion of threat and contingency that accompanies any story whose outcome is unknown.

Historical novels that do not rely on this technique of specific dating still manage to fabricate a parallel universe by pretending that both the narrator and the reader are about to witness a story already in the process of unfolding. This is accomplished by opening the tale in medias res as the heroine or hero performs some action while simultaneously contemplating another event that at least preceded it. By referring strategically to the past and the present moment in the same paragraph, the text suggests that the heroine, like the reader who is opening the book, is a product of her past and awaits the unfolding of her future. She is established, therefore, as a historical being who exists in time and in the "real" world. Such deliberate use of the conventions of the realistic novel thus denies that the romance is only a timeless fairy tale existing solely within the reader's imagination or between the pages of a book. In fact, these explicit references to time and to the familiar objects of the real world help to dissolve the very materiality of the book itself by conjuring for the reader people who are as real as she and events that may not have happened to her but, given their plausible "ordinariness," certainly still could.

The romance's depiction of familiar temporality, like its "realistic" character portrayal and its simple miming of a world filled with domestic commodities, acts to undermine the reader's knowledge that she is indeed reading another romance and therefore has already heard *this* story before. Given their assumptions about language, their interpretive strategies, and their trust of assertion, it should not seem surprising, then, that some of the Smithton women are so convinced by these discursive practices that they actually feel the need to reassure themselves that the ominous future threatened in the opening pages will not materialize in so disastrous a form. By reading the ending first, they confirm for themselves the story's formulaic and, therefore, mythic status, a status that is established for other readers by the characteristic, clichéd markers of the romantic myth. These less trusting readers simply have to work a little harder to reassure themselves at the outset that the tale really is completed. Having done so, when they read the book through, they can give themselves over even more completely to the act of experiencing that real, open-ended future that its realistic discourse projects. By assenting to the reality of that future, they can then believe fully in the reality of the happy ending when it finally does appear.

Another narrative technique employed by the romance suggests that the typical reading experience is oddly conflicted in the sense that the reader holds an ambivalent attitude toward the reality status of the story. This technique suggests that readers both believe in the threat of the unknown as it opens out before them and demand continual reassurance that the events they suspect will happen, in fact, will finally occur. Like most narratives, the romance proceeds by setting up an initial situation whose very instability raises multiple possibilities of future resolution. The reader is invited to project these possible endings through suggestions made by a narrator or by the heroine herself. These potential endings are then kept consistently before the reader by the seemingly endless repetition of threats to the heroine's virginity or life. While this initial situation continues as an unresolved problem, however, secondary narrative puzzles are presented and subsequently solved within a very short amount of reading time. The reader is asked by the text to supply a narrative projection that is then confirmed almost immediately by actual events or corroborated by a character in the story.[34]

Consider, as an example, the romance's treatment of foreshadowing, which typically reduces to a minimum the space between the initial hint of ominous happenings and the actual event that inevitably confirms the reader's hypothesis. In most cases, competing possibilities are allowed to open up only for a few paragraphs. Soon after the initial warning to the reader, the dreaded event occurs, only to be interpreted immediately by the narrator or by one of the witnesses. In Phyllis Whitney's early gothic, *Thunder Heights*, the reader is asked to focus on the mysterious "accidental" death of the heroine's mother. The heroine naturally refuses to believe that her mother was thrown from her horse on a mountain path. Midway through the narrative, she stumbles upon a riding crop in a ravine below the bluff that others claim was the scene of her mother's fall. Initially, because she cannot imagine whom the crop belongs to, the reader is prompted to provide the very obvious answer. Lest she guess wrong, however, Whitney closes off potentially infinite speculations, narrowing them down to only one: "She realized suddenly that the sorry object she held in her hand was a woman's riding crop. To whom had it belonged, and how had it been lost in so odd a place? At any rate, she would carry her find home, clean it up and polish the silver. Then if it didn't look too bad perhaps she could carry it when she went riding. Undoubtedly, someone at the house would know to whom it had belonged. Her mother, perhaps?"[35]

If this is not definitive enough, Whitney provides further corroboration only eight pages later when the heroine's Aunt Letty identifies the crop as her sister's. Her redundant elaboration serves a triple purpose. It reassures the reader that she has indeed projected the proper "solution" to a minor narrative problem. It contributes simultaneously to the essential mystery at the heart of this characteristic plot by adding to the suspense about the actual circumstances surrounding the death of the heroine's mother. Finally, this manner of narrative disclosure also suggests tacitly to the reader that just as she "knew" the answer to this problem so does she know the answer to those crucial, still unanswered questions about the hero's love for the heroine and her ability to realize her individual identity.

This internal narrative structure contributes to the reader's ability to maintain a kind of dual consciousness about the status of the story she is reading. On the one hand, the repetitive posing of new, unsolved narrative problems permits the text to continue the illusion that it is revealing events only *as they occur*. In thus successfully managing the reader's activity so that she will feel constantly in the dark about what will happen next, the device insists on the book's status as a novel about new characters in a new situation, the resolution of which cannot be foreseen. At the same time, by constantly confirming the projections she cannot help but make, the narrative structure reassures the reader not only that she is making sense of the story properly but also that at each stage along the way she always already knows the answers. The narrative structure tacitly hints, then, that even though it appears to be a novel, it is, in actuality, just another version of the mythic story whose ending the reader already knows.

The romance's peculiar narrative strategy seems to encourage the reader in her desire to have it both ways. She can read the story as a realistic novel about what might plausibly occur in an individual woman's life without having to face the usual threat of the unknown. This is possible because all contingency is erased by the narrative's continuing reassurance that it reveals nothing that is not previously anticipated. Romance writers, in effect, supply a myth in the guise of the truly possible. It is precisely because the romance's surrounding universe is always portrayed so convincingly that romance readers might well be persuaded to believe that the romantic action itself is not only plausible but, like the already known ending, also inevitable. Reading in that case would be, as the women have said, a ritual of hope. Repetitive engagement in it would enable a reader to tell herself again and again that a love like the heroine's might indeed occur in a world such as hers. She thus teaches herself to believe that men *are able* to satisfy women's needs fully.

It should also be pointed out, however, that in participating in this "mixed" discourse with its contradictory suggestions about the contingency of human life on the one hand and its predetermined nature on the other, the Smithton women unconsciously perpetuate a familiar, ideological argument about female identity and freedom. Because romances are always novel-like narratives of the yet-to-be-determined destiny of *different* heroines, they suggest to the reader that all women, like the heroine about whom she reads, are unique individuals who live in ignorance of their own future and who are quite capable of living original existences. Simultaneously, however, the narrative's more surreptitious hints that this heroine's unforeseen destiny will prove to be just like that of her fictional sisters imply that such freedom is an illusion because, in fact, women live lives characterized by identical conclusions. Although they possess novel personalities and participate in some unprecedented events, women in romances, like mythical deities, are fated to live out a predetermined existence. That existence is circumscribed by a narrative structure that demonstrates that despite idiosyncratic histories, all women inevitably end up associating their female identity with the social roles of lover, wife, and mother. Even more successfully than the patriarchal society within which it was born, the romance denies women the possibility of refusing that purely relational destiny and thus rejects their right to a single, self-contained existence.

The conflicted discourse of the romance suggests, finally, that with respect to women at least, surface differences mask a more fundamental identity. By insisting so successfully on its superficial but nonetheless effective mimesis, the romance suggests to the reader that the heroine is as

individual as she and that, like events in her own life, those in the heroine's are merely chance occurrences that develop because she happens to
be in a certain place at a certain time. The heroine's happy union with the
hero is presented, consequently, not as a functional necessity dictated by
the needs of social and political institutions but as a combination of luck
and individual choice. The reader is invited to see her own fate in the same
light as a freely chosen course of her own making.

However, even as the narrative conveys its overt message that all
women are different and their destinies fundamentally open, the romance
also reveals that such differences are illusory and short-lived because they
are submerged or sacrificed inevitably to the demands of that necessary
and always identical romantic ending. Paradoxically, the inexorability of
the romance's *mythic* conclusion might be said to reproduce the "real," not
because all women actually find perfect fulfillment in romantic love but
because the conclusion's repeated overpowering of the heroine's individual difference by her enthusiastic assumption of an abstract, unvarying
role parallels a situation that women find difficult to avoid in actuality. Its
vociferous defense of human individuality and freedom notwithstanding,
American society is still remarkably successful at exacting the necessary
compliance from its female members. Through the use of rigid socializ-
ing procedures, instructional habits, and formal and informal sanctions
against deviance, the culture persuades women to view femininity solely in
terms of a social and institutional role that is essential to the maintenance
of the current organization of life. Therefore, while the act of romance
reading is used by women as a means of partial protest against the role
prescribed for them by the culture, the discourse itself actively insists on
the desirability, naturalness, and benefits of that role by portraying it not
as the imposed necessity that it is but as a freely designed, personally
controlled, individual choice. When the mythic ending of the romance
undercuts the realism of its novelistic rendering of an individual woman's
story, this literary form reaffirms its founding culture's belief that women
are valuable not for their unique personal qualities but for their biological
sameness and their ability to perform that essential role of maintaining
and reconstituting others.

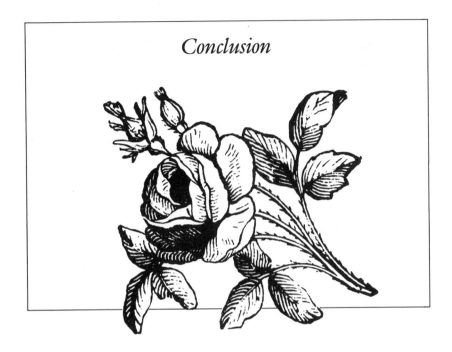

Conclusion

If in concluding these chapters, the reader remains unsure as to whether the romance should be considered fundamentally conservative on the one hand or incipiently oppositional on the other, that is not surprising. Until now, I have deliberately refrained from the formulation of a definitive conclusion. Indeed, the picture that emerges from this study of the romance-reading phenomenon is less distinct, though not less complete, than previous investigations of other mass-produced literary forms. Although the indistinctness is perhaps frustrating because it hinders the elaboration of a single conclusive statement about the meaning and effect of the romance, it is also an indistinctness born of ambiguity resulting from the planned superimposition or double exposure of multiple images. Those images are themselves produced by the several perspectives brought to bear upon the complicated, polysemic event known as romance reading. The indistinctness is not, then, simply the result of a faulty focus in a singular, comprehensive portrait of a fixed and unified object, the romantic text.

Had I looked solely at the act of reading as it is understood by the women themselves or, alternately, at the covert significance of the romance's narrative structure, I might have been able to provide one clear-cut, sharp-focus image. In the first case, the image would suggest that the act of romance reading is oppositional because it allows the women to refuse momentarily their self-abnegating social role. In the second, the image would imply that the romance's narrative structure embodies a simple recapitulation and recommendation of patriarchy and its constituent social practices and ideologies. However, by looking at the romance-reading behavior of real women through several lenses, each trained on a different component or moment of a process that achieves its meaning and effect over time, each also positioned differently in the sense that one attempts to see the women's experience from within while the other strives to view it from without, this study has consciously chosen to juxtapose multiple views of the complex social interaction between people and texts known as reading. Although I think each view accurately captures one aspect of the phenomenon of romance reading, none can account fully for the actual occurrence or significance of the event as such. In part, this is a function of the complexity inherent in any human action, but it is also the consequence of the fact that culture is both perceptible and hidden, both articulate and covert. Dot and the Smithton women know well both how and why they read romances. Yet at the same time, they also act on cultural assumptions and corollaries not consciously available to them precisely because those givens constitute the very foundation of their social selves, the very possibility of their social action. The multiple perspectives employed here have been adopted, therefore, in the hope that they might help us to comprehend what the women understand themselves to be gaining from the reading of romances while simultaneously revealing how that practice and self-understanding have tacit, unintended effects and implications.

Although it will be impossible, then, to use this conclusion to bring a single, large picture into focus simply because there is no context-free, unmarked position from which to view the activity of romance reading in its entirety, I can perhaps use it to remind the reader of each of the snapshots provided herein, to juxtapose them rapidly in condensed space and time. Such a review will help to underscore the semantic richness and ideological density of the actual process known as romance reading and thus highlight once and for all the complicated nature of the connection between the romance and the culture that has given rise to it.

If, as I have pointed out in the Introduction, we remember that texts are read and that reading itself is an activity carried on by real people in a preconstituted social context, it becomes possible to distinguish *analytically* between the meaning of the act and the meaning of the text as read. This analytic distinction then empowers us to question whether the significance of the act of reading itself might, under some conditions, contradict, undercut, or qualify the significance of producing a particular kind of story. When this methodological distinction is further complicated by an effort to render real readers' comprehension of each of the aspects of the activity as well as the covert significance and consequences underlying both, the possibilities for perceiving conflict and contradiction are increased even more. This is exactly what has resulted from this account of the reading preferences and behavior of Dorothy Evans and the Smithton women.

Ethnographic investigation, for instance, has led to the discovery that Dot and her customers see the act of reading as combative and compensatory. It is combative in the sense that it enables them to refuse the other-directed social role prescribed for them by their position within the institution of marriage. In picking up a book, as they have so eloquently told us, they refuse temporarily their family's otherwise constant demand that they attend to the wants of others even as they act deliberately to do something for their own private pleasure. Their activity is compensatory, then, in that it permits them to focus on themselves and to carve out a solitary space within an arena where their self-interest is usually identified with the interests of others and where they are defined as a public resource to be mined at will by the family. For them, romance reading addresses needs created in them but not met by patriarchal institutions and engendering practices.

It is striking to observe that this partial account of romance reading, which stresses its status as an oppositional or contestative act because the women use it to thwart common cultural expectations and to supply gratification ordinarily ruled out by the way the culture structures their lives, is not far removed from the account of folkloric practices elaborated recently by Luigi Lombardi-Satriani and José Limon.[1] Although both are concerned only with folkloric behavior and the way indigenous folk performances contest the hegemonic imposition of bourgeois culture on such subordinate groups as "workers, . . . peasants, racial and cultural minorities, and women,"[2] their definitions of contestation do not rule out entirely the sort of behavioral activity involving mass culture that I have discovered among the Smithton readers.

Lombardi-Satriani, for instance, argues that the folkloric cultures of subordinate groups may contest or oppose the dominant culture in two distinct ways. On the one hand, folklore may express overtly or metaphorically values that are different from or question those held by the dominant classes. On the other hand, opposition also can occur *because* a folkloric performance exists. Limon adds, however, that it is not the simple fact of a folkloric practice's existence that produces opposition: rather, opposition is effected when that performance "counter-valuates." What he means by counter-valuation is a process of inversion whereby the original socioeconomic limitations and devaluations of a subordinate group are first addressed by the folkloric performance and then transformed within or by it into something of value to the group. If the process is successful, Limon maintains, the performance contests by supplementation. In effect, it simultaneously acknowledges and meets the needs of the subordinate group, which, as the consequence of its subordination, are systematically ignored by the culture's practices and institutions.

When romance reading is examined, then, as an activity that takes place within a specific social context, it becomes evident that this form of behavior both supplements and counter-valuates in Limon's sense. Romance reading supplements the avenues traditionally open to women for emotional gratification by supplying them vicariously with the attention and nurturance they do not get enough of in the round of day-to-day existence. It counter-valuates because the story opposes the female values of love and personal interaction to the male values of competition and public achievement and, at least in ideal romances, demonstrates the triumph of the former over the latter. Romance reading and writing might be seen therefore as a collectively elaborated female ritual through which women explore the consequences of their common social condition as the appendages of men and attempt to imagine a more perfect state where all the needs they so intensely feel and accept as given would be adequately addressed.

I must stress here, as I have throughout the book, that this is *not* the only view of romance reading that might be taken. Women's domestic role in patriarchal culture, which is simultaneously addressed and counter-valuated in the imagination through a woman's encounter with romantic fiction, is left virtually intact by her leisure-time withdrawal. Although in restoring a woman's depleted sense of self romance reading may constitute tacit recognition that the current arrangement of the sexes is not ideal for her emotional well-being, it does nothing to alter a woman's social situation, itself very likely characterized by those dissatisfying patterns. In fact, this activity may very well obviate the need or desire to demand satisfaction in the real world because it can be so successfully met in fantasy.

By the same token, it should also be pointed out that although romance writing and reading help to create a kind of female community, that community is nonetheless mediated by the distances that characterize mass production and the capitalist organization of storytelling. Because the oppositional act is carried out through the auspices of a book and thus involves the fundamentally private, isolating experience of reading, these women never get together to share either the experience of imaginative opposition, or, perhaps more important, the discontent that gave rise to their need for the romance in the first place. The women join forces only symbolically and in a mediated way in the privacy of their individual homes and in the culturally devalued sphere of leisure activity. They do nothing to challenge their separation from one another brought about by the patriarchal culture's insistence that they never work in the public world to maintain themselves but rather live symbiotically as the property and responsibility of men.

In summary, when the act of romance reading is viewed as it is by the readers themselves, from within a belief system that accepts as given the institutions of heterosexuality and monogamous marriage, it can be conceived as an activity of mild protest and longing for reform necessitated by those institutions' failure to satisfy the emotional needs of women. Reading therefore functions for them as an act of recognition and contestation whereby that failure is first admitted and then partially reversed. Hence, the Smithton readers' claim that romance reading is a "declaration of independence" and a way to say to others, "This is my time, my space. Now leave me alone."

At the same time, however, when viewed from the vantage point of a feminism that would like to see the women's oppositional impulse lead to real social change, romance reading can also be seen as an activity that could potentially disarm that impulse. It might do so because it supplies vicariously those very needs and requirements that might otherwise be formulated as demands in the real world and lead to the potential restructuring of sexual relations. The question of whether the activity of romance reading does, in reality, deflect such change by successfully defusing or recontaining this protest must remain unanswered for the moment. Although it may appear on the surface that the leisure-time activity of reading an admittedly fantastic story could never provoke the women who recognize that they need such a "crutch" to act to change their situation, the women themselves indicate otherwise. In fact, they claim to be transformed by their hobby. Because recent developments in the social practices of romance writing and reading and variations in the romantic plot structure suggest that some change *is* being generated as a consequence of the phenomenon, I will return to this question of the cumulative effect of romance reading shortly after reviewing the significance of the traditional narrative itself, both as it is consciously constructed by the Smithton women and as I think they experience it unconsciously.

If one begins, as I have here, with the premise that the construction of a narrative is an activity that takes place over time, it becomes clear that the significance of the whole process of assembling and understanding the romantic story itself is as ambiguous and conflicted as the simple act of reading the book that contains the tale. As with the act of reading, the women construct and understand the story in a positive manner that both underscores their capabilities as readers and interprets the heroine's actions in the most favorable of ways. Nonetheless, it can also be shown that those conscious processes have tacit and sometimes contradictory consequences. They do so because the activities of constructing the narrative world and of interpreting the heroine's role within it leave intact the very cultural categories, assumptions, and institutions that prompt the readers' desire to demonstrate repeatedly that they are capable and to be told again and again of the worth and power of a romantic heroine.

As I have pointed out in Chapter 6, for instance, the narrative discourse of the romantic novel is structured in such a way that it yields easily to the reader's most familiar reading strategies. Thus the act of constructing the narrative line is reassuring because the romantic writer's typical discourse leads the reader to make abductions and inferences that are always immediately confirmed. As she assembles the plot, therefore, the reader learns, in addition to what happens next, that *she* knows how to make sense of texts and human action. Although this understanding of the process must be taken into account and attributed to a positive desire to assert the power and capability of the female self, it cannot be overlooked that the fictional world created as its consequence also reinforces traditional female limitations because it validates the dominance of domestic concerns and personal interaction in women's lives. The reader thus engages in an activity that shores up her own sense of her abilities, but she also creates a simulacrum of her limited social world within a more glamorous fiction. She therefore inadvertently justifies as natural the very conditions and their emotional consequences to which her reading activity is a response.

Similarly, in looking at the Smithton readers' conscious engagement with the manifest content of the ideal romance, it becomes evident that these women believe themselves to be participating in a story that is as much *about* the transformation of an inadequate suitor into the perfect lover-protector as it is about the concomitant triumph of a woman. Her triumph consists of her achievement of sexual and emotional maturity while simultaneously securing the complete attention and devotion of this man who, at least on the surface, admits her preeminent claim to his time and interest. The act of constructing the romantic tale thus provides the reader first with an opportunity to protest vicariously a man's initial inability to understand a woman and to treat her with sensitivity. Secondarily, the process enables a woman to achieve a kind of mastery over her fear of rape because the fantasy evokes her fear and subsequently convinces her that rape is either an illusion or something that she can control easily. Finally, by witnessing and approving of the ideal romantic conclusion, the reader expresses her opposition to the domination of commodity values in her society because she so heartily applauds the heroine's ability to draw the hero's attention away from the public world of money and status and to convince him of the primacy of her values and concerns.

It seems apparent, then, that an oppositional moment can be said to characterize even the production of the romantic story if that process is understood as the women themselves conceive it. I have elsewhere called this stage or aspect of the reading process a "utopian" moment,[3] drawing on Fredric Jameson's important argument that every form of mass culture has a dimension "which remains implicitly, and no matter how faintly, negative and critical of the social order from which, as a product and a commodity, it springs."[4] In effect, the vision called into being at the end of the process of romance reading projects for the reader a utopian state where men are neither cruel nor indifferent, neither preoccupied with the external world nor wary of an intense emotional attachment to a woman. This fantasy also suggests that the safety and protection of traditional marriage will not compromise a woman's autonomy or self-confidence. In sum, the vision reforms those very conditions characterizing the real world that leave so many women and, most probably, the reader herself, longing for affective care, ongoing tenderness, and a strong sense of self-worth. This interpretation of the romance's meaning suggests, then, that the women who seek out ideal novels in order to construct such a vision again and again are reading not out of contentment but out of dissatisfaction, longing, and protest.

Of course, in standing back from this construction of the romance's meaning, once again to assess the implications of its symbolic negation and criticism of the social order, it becomes possible to see that despite the utopian force of the romance's projection, that projection actually leaves unchallenged the very system of social relations whose faults and imperfections gave rise to the romance and which the romance is trying to perfect. The romance manages to do so because its narrative organization prompts the reader to construct covert counter-messages that either undercut or negate the changes projected on an overt level. To begin with, although the narrative story provides the reader with an opportunity to indulge in anger at the initial, offensive behavior of the hero, we must not forget that that anger is later shown to be unwarranted because the hero's indifference or cruelty actually originated in feelings of love. Thus while the experience of reading the tale may be cathartic in the sense that it allows the reader to express in the imagination anger at men that she would otherwise censor or deny, it also suggests to her that such anger as the heroine's is, in reality, unjustified because the offensiveness of the behavior prompting it was simply a function of the heroine's inability to read a man properly. Because the reading process always confirms for the reader that she knows how to read male behavior correctly, it suggests that her anger is unnecessary because her spouse, like the hero, actually loves her deeply, though he may not express it as she might wish. In the end, the romance-reading process gives the reader a strategy for making her present situation more comfortable without substantive reordering of its structure rather than a comprehensive program for reorganizing her life in such a way that all needs might be met.

In this context, I should also call attention once again to the hole in the romance's explanatory logic with respect to the hero's transformation from the heroine's distant, insensitive, and cold superior into her tender, expressive intimate. Although this crucial transformation in the romance clearly derives from writers' and readers' desires to believe in the possibility of such an ideal partner, the manner in which it is effected implies once again that the transfiguration is accomplished largely by a shift in the heroine's perceptual gestalt. Of course, the ideal hero does become more expressive in the course of the story, but because the early descriptions of him emphasized that this tender side was always part of his true character even though it was suppressed, the narrative structure places ultimate responsibility for its nurturance and flowering on the heroine herself. In reassuring him about the purity of her motives, it is *she* who frees him to respond warmly to her. This structure covertly suggests, then, that male reticence and distance cannot be transmuted into something else entirely. All that is possible, really, is the cultivation and encouragement of tendencies already there in the personalities of particular men. If a woman wants to be treated tenderly and attentively, the story ultimately suggests, she must find a man who is already capable of such expression though perhaps fearful of indulging in it. By having it both ways to begin with, that is, by beginning with a hero who is traditionally masculine and somewhat expressive in a feminine way, the romance manages to sidestep the crucial issue of whether the traditional social construction of masculinity does not rule out the possibility of nurturant behavior in men.

Little need be said here about the way in which the romance's treatment of rape probably harms romance readers even as it provides them with a sense of power and control over their fear of it. Although their distaste for "out-and-out" violation indicates that these women do not want to be punished or hurt as so many have assumed, their willingness to be convinced that the forced "taking" of a woman by a man who "really" loves her is testimony to her desirability and worth rather than to his power suggests once again that the romance is effectively dealing with some of the consequences of patriarchy without also challenging the hierarchy of control upon which it is based. By examining the whole issue of rape and its effect on the heroine, the romance may provide the reader with the opportunity to explore the consequences of related behavior in her own life. Nonetheless, by suggesting that rape is either a mistake or an expression of uncontrollable desire, it may also give her a false sense of security by showing her how to rationalize violent behavior and thus reconcile her to a set of events and relations that she would be better off changing.

Finally, it must also be noted here that even though the romance underlines the opposition between the values of love and those associated with the competitive pursuit of status and wealth, by perpetuating the exclusive division of the world into the familiar categories of the public and the private, the romance continues to justify the social placement of women that has led to the very discontent that is the source of their desire to read romances. It is true, certainly, that the romance accepts this dichotomy in order to assert subsequently that the commonly devalued personal sphere and the women who dominate it have higher status and the evangelical power to draw the keepers of the public realm away from their worldly interests. Yet despite this proclamation of female superiority, in continuing to relegate women to the arena of domestic, purely personal relations, the romance fails to pose other, more radical questions. In short, it refuses to ask whether female values might be used to "feminize" the public realm or if control over that realm could be shared by women and by men. Because the romance finally leaves unchallenged the male right to the public spheres of work, politics, and power, because it refurbishes the institution of marriage by suggesting how it might be viewed continuously as a courtship, because it represents real female needs within the story and then depicts their satisfaction by traditional heterosexual relations, the romance avoids questioning the institutionalized basis of patriarchal control over women even as it serves as a locus of protest against some of its emotional consequences.

Given the apparent power of the romance's conservative counter-messages, then, it is tempting to suggest that romantic fiction must be an active agent in the maintenance of the ideological status quo because it ultimately reconciles women to patriarchal society and reintegrates them with its institutions. It appears that it might do so by deflecting and recontaining real protest and by supplying vicariously certain needs that, if presented as demands in the real world, might otherwise lead to the reordering of heterosexual relationships. If true, romances would do all of this within the already fenced-off realm of leisure and the imaginary and thereby protect the more important arenas of the culture from women's collective elaboration of their dissatisfaction with patriarchy's effects on their lives.

I feel compelled to point out, however, that neither this study nor any other to date provides enough evidence to corroborate this argument fully. We simply do not know what practical effects the repetitive reading of romances has on the way women behave after they have closed their books and returned to their normal, ordinary round of daily activities. That kind of information can only be derived from a multidimensional cohort study carried out over time that would test the various hypotheses worked out here by attempting to trace real changes in women's behavior solely to leisure reading of romances and not to other factors. This could only be successful if both husbands and wives were interviewed in depth and a good deal more information about their marriages and sexual relationships than I have compiled here could be examined with care. This sort of study would be worth carrying out, however, because there is some evidence that indicates that the cumulative effect of giving rein to the utopian desire or impulse here identified as a crucial component of the romance may well be to change women in unforeseen and unintended ways, although perhaps always within certain limits.

As I have mentioned previously, Dot Evans and the Smithton readers believe very strongly that romance reading changes at least some women. They seem to feel that bad romances especially prompt them to compare their own behavior with that of passive, "namby-pamby" heroines who permit their men to abuse them and push them around. This comparison, they believe, then often leads to greater resolve on the part of the reader who vows never to let her spouse injure her in a similar fashion. Dot and her customers also believe that they learn to assert themselves more effectively as a consequence of their reading because they so often have to defend their choices of material to others and justify their right to pleasure.

Although I have no way of knowing whether this perceived assertiveness is carried over to their interactions with their husbands and families over issues beyond that of how to spend leisure time, the women's self-perceptions should not be ignored if we really do want to understand what women derive from reading romances. Of course, it could be the case that these readers develop assertive techniques in a few restricted areas of their lives and thus do not use their newfound confidence and perceived power to challenge the fundamental hierarchy of control in their marriages. However, it is only fair *not* to assume this from the beginning in order to guard against the danger of automatically assigning greater weight to the *way* a real desire for change is channeled by a culture into nonthreatening form than to the desire itself. To do so would be to ignore the limited but nonetheless unmistakable and creative ways in which people resist the deleterious effects of their social situations.

Other developments on the national romance scene suggest that the utopian current running through the experience of reading may move women in ways that conflict significantly with the more conservative push effected by the story's reaffirmation of marriage's ability to satisfy female needs completely. I am thinking here of the recent decision to organize among romance writers themselves. Founded by several Texas women in the spring of 1981, the Romance Writers of America has developed rapidly as a national organization that draws together writers and editors of romances and even some readers. Communicating through a monthly newsletter and at both regional and national conferences, these women are now sharing tips, techniques, and information about romance writing and reading. Indeed, the writers are, for the first time, disclosing facts and figures about their contracts with the express purpose of forcing better deals from publishers who the women now know are making enormous profits from the sales of their books.

Although the movement is still small given the apparent size of the romance audience, not to mention that of the female population as a whole, it is nonetheless significant because it counteracts women's traditional isolation from one another by bringing them together over an issue that concerns them alone. Of course, the purposes of the organization are very different from those of feminist groups that aim consciously to bring about radical change in the patriarchal balance of power. Yet once again it is unsafe to assume that the romance women share nothing with their avowedly feminist sisters. Indeed, in the December 1981 issue of *Romance Report*, the newsletter of the Romance Writers of America, the editors included a short article on a scholarly study that claims that romances "are moving 'feminist' messages to women who never read a Friedan, Steinem or Greer treatise on the role of women."[5] Marked by the headline, "Romance Survey—Finally! A Survey in Our Favor," this article describes with approval Carol Thurston's belief that paperback historical romances portray androgynous heroes and heroines, challenge the value of the macho male, and make new suggestions about female possibilities. Although I do not agree with Thurston's implicit definition of feminism and thus cannot concur with her claim that the message of the romance is *identical* to that of the women's movement, I do think it important that these romance writers approve of her findings and cite them to themselves as evidence of their progressivism and willingness to challenge traditional sex stereotyping. Their approval suggests strongly that changes in the perception of women and of their abilities *are* being generated in romance writers and readers who, until now, have been criticized as wholly traditional, if not reactionary.

While again it is impossible to say for sure whether these changes have been caused by external developments in the culture and merely reflected in romances or whether they are a logical development of the subterranean protest that has apparently been hidden within them all along, it is absolutely essential that we recognize that, for whatever reason, romance writers now find it possible to explore the acceptability of different ideal personalities for men and women. As a consequence, they seem to be incorporating a few of the least dangerous challenges to patriarchy into a literary form once thought to be a purely conservative reaffirmation or legitimation of it.

I do not want to pick up the threads of a wholly new argument here in order to show how romances have begun to develop a slightly different, perhaps more "feminist" orientation. Suffice it to say, then, that this process of absorbing new ideas is usually most evident in the coding of characters who have become of late even more independent and intelligent in the case of heroines, gentler and more expressive in the case of heroes. Although few of the books written in recent months advance the truly radical suggestions that women do not need men to define themselves or to be happy, that they might be able to operate in the public world on their own just as men do, still some have appeared that come remarkably close to making one or the other of these observations. Think of Victoria Kelrich's *High Fashion*, described in Chapter 5, which ends not with a projection of a blissful future for the newly wedded pair but with a note of uncertainty about the permanence of the romantic attachment while the heroine turns enthusiastically to her work! Although this ending was seen as ambiguous by Dot and her customers, the fact remains that *High Fashion* was written, published, and ranked by the Smithton readers only just below their favorite romances.

Whether such developments will be widespread and general in the future is impossible to say since we have no way of knowing how many women will give up their safe, limited, and barely conscious contestation of patriarchy for the uncertainty of feminism's conscious assault on both its categorization of the world and its institutional structure. The developments bear watching, however, for they may indicate that the romance's long-present but covert challenge to the notion that traditional marriages satisfy all women's needs is about to take on a more combative, questioning tone. This could occur if romance writers and readers ever discover through the collective sharing of experiences that together they have strength, a voice, and important objections to make about current gender arrangements. However, because I suspect a demand for real change in power relations will occur only if women also come to understand that their need for romances is a function of their dependent status *as women* and of their acceptance of marriage as the only route to female fulfillment, I think we as feminists might help this change along by first learning to recognize that romance reading originates in very real dissatisfaction and embodies a valid, if limited, protest. Then by developing strategies for making that dissatisfaction and its causes consciously available to romance readers and by learning how to encourage that protest in such a way that it will be delivered in the arena of actual social relations rather than acted out in the imagination, we might join hands with women who are, after all, our sisters and together imagine a world whose subsequent creation would lead to the need for a new fantasy altogether.

Perhaps one final observation about the implications of this study for future investigation of mass-cultural forms is necessary before bringing the work to its conclusion. I do not think it would be claiming too much to suggest that the very fruitfulness of the methodology employed here indicates that we may not yet understand the complexity of mass culture's implication in social life as well as we might. Certainly, my study does not challenge absolutely the notion that mass-produced art forms like the romance are ideologically conservative in the sense that they restore at least temporarily the claims of presently existing institutions and practices to the loyalty of those who participate vicariously in these forms. After all, the romance does assert on one level that the perfect heterosexual lover is a possibility as is an ideal marriage in which a woman achieves independence, dependence, excitement, and nurturance all at the same time. Nonetheless, the study's investigation of reading as act suggests that real people can use the romance to address their unmet needs experienced precisely because that ideal relationship is made highly improbable by the institutional structure and engendering practices of contemporary society. Furthermore, the focus on reading as a process of construction reveals that the early stages of a reader's interpretation and response to the romantic form can be characterized by the expression of repressed emotions deriving from dissatisfaction with the status quo and a utopian longing for a better life. The methodology highlights, then, the complicated and contradictory ways in which the romance recognizes and thereby protests the weaknesses of patriarchy and the failure of traditional marriage even as it apparently acts to assert the perfection of each and to teach women how to *re*-view their own imperfect relationships in such a way that they seem unassailable.

All of this suggests that we must be careful not to reproduce the reifying tendencies of late capitalism and its supportive perceptual and analytical strategies in our methodologies and interpretive work. We must not, in short, look only at mass-produced objects themselves on the assumption that they bear all of their significances on their surface, as it were, and reveal them automatically to us. To do so would be to assume either that perceptible, tangible things alone are worth analyzing or that those commodified objects exert such pressure and influence on their consumers that they have no power as individuals to resist or alter the ways in which those objects mean or can be used.

Commodities like mass-produced literary texts are selected, purchased, constructed, and used by real people with previously existing needs, desires, intentions, and interpretive strategies. By reinstating those active individuals and their creative, constructive activities at the heart of our interpretive enterprise, we avoid blinding ourselves to the fact that the essentially human practice of making meaning goes on even in a world increasingly dominated by things and by consumption. In thus recalling the interactive character of operations like reading, we restore time, process, and action to our account of human endeavor and therefore increase the possibility of doing justice to its essential complexity and ambiguity as practice. We also increase our chances of sorting out or articulating the difference between the repressive imposition of ideology and oppositional practices that, though limited in their scope and effect, at least dispute or contest the control of ideological forms.

If we can learn, then, to look at the ways in which various groups appropriate and use the mass-produced art of our culture, I suspect we may well begin to understand that although the ideological power of contemporary cultural forms is enormous, indeed sometimes even frightening, that power is not yet all-pervasive, totally vigilant, or complete. Interstices still exist within the social fabric where opposition is carried on by people who are not satisfied by their place within it or by the restricted material and emotional rewards that accompany it. They therefore attempt to imagine a more perfect social state as a way of countering despair. I think it absolutely essential that we who are committed to social change learn not to overlook this minimal but nonetheless legitimate form of protest. We should seek it out not only to understand its origins and its utopian longing but also to learn how best to encourage it and bring it to fruition. If we do not, we have already conceded the fight and, in the case of the romance at least, admitted the impossibility of creating a world where the vicarious pleasure supplied by its reading would be unnecessary.

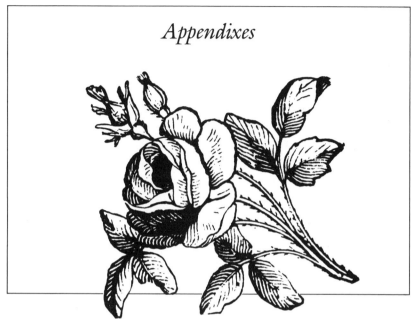

Appendixes

Appendix 1. Oral Interview Response Record

Reading History

I.   1. Age when began to read for pleasure.
    2. Favorite books (child).
    3. Favorite books (teenager).
    4. Age when first began reading romances.
    5. Reason for first reading a romance.
    6. Do you recall the title, author, or story of your first romance?
    7. Number of books read per month.
    8. Number of romances read per month.
    9. Kinds of books read other than romances.
    10. Read every day?
    11. Hours per week devoted to reading?
    12. When do most reading?
    13. Certain times a week devoted to more reading?
    14. Where do most reading?
    15. Discuss reading with others?
       a. With whom?
       b. Kinds of things talked about?
    16. Frequency of obtaining books from:
       a. Bookstore
       b. Library

c. From a friend
d. From a relative
17. Frequency of purchasing hardback and paperback:
a. Hardback
b. Paperback

Knowledge and Evaluation of Romances

II. 1. Definition of romantic novel.
2. Different kinds of romances.
a. Description of a typical ____ (heroine, hero, etc.).
3. Read certain kinds of romances more than others?
a. Most often read:
b. Never read:
4. Method of finding new romances.
5. Method of deciding which romances to read.
a. Favorite authors.
b. Ranking of favorite authors.
c. Features they have in common.
d. Reasons for liking better than others.
6. Kinds of characters which appear again and again.
a. Nature of their similarity from book to book.
b. Ways in which these characters differ.
7. Events which appear again and again.
a. Events which never happen.
8. Are people in romances like real people?
a. How?
b. Principal differences.
9. Are events like those in real life?
a. Which ones are similar?
b. Which ones are different?
10. Do characters change in the story?
a. Which ones?
b. How?
11. If we met at a party and began discussing romances, how would you describe your romance reading to me?
12. What makes romances different from other books?
13. Can you explain to me why you recently failed to complete a particular romance?
14. What do you do with your romances after you have finished reading them?

Personal Information

III. 1. Sex
2. Age
3. Marital status

4. Children ___ How many?
5. Ages of children
6. How do you spend your day?
7. What is your occupation?
   a. How long have you been employed outside the home?
   b. Have there been periods when you did not work outside the home?
   c. When?
8. What is your spouse's occupation?
9. What is your approximate family income?
10. Do you own or rent?
11. How many years of formal education do you have?

Leisure Patterns

IV. 1. a. Hours devoted to television viewing?
        b. Reading?
        c. Radio listening?
        d. Physical recreation?
     2. Other regular forms of leisure occupation?
     3. Number of times attend per week:
        a. Movies?
        b. Concerts?
        c. Theatre?
        d. Sports events?
        e. Church activities?
     4. Number of magazines read per week:
        a. Names
        b. Favorite?
        c. Why?
     5. Are there certain television shows you never miss?
        a. Names
        b. What is your favorite television show?
        c. Why?

Appendix 2. Pilot Questionnaire

ROMANCE READER SURVEY
Please Read the Following

I would appreciate it if you would take a brief amount of time to answer the questions on this form. The questionnaire is part of a project I am conducting about the reading habits and preferences of people who read romantic novels. I ask that you please do not identify yourself in any way and that you understand that your participation is completely voluntary. Feel free to skip any questions which you do not want to answer. Almost all the questions can be answered by placing an X in the appropriate space. I appreciate your cooperation very much.

Janice Radway
University of Pennsylvania

1. At what age did you first begin reading for pleasure?
   _____ a. 5–10 years
   _____ b. 11–20 years
   _____ c. 21–30 years
   _____ d. 31 or above

2. What were your favorite kinds of books to read *for pleasure* when you were a teenager?
   _____ a. biography
   _____ b. historical fiction
   _____ c. romances
   _____ d. westerns
   _____ e. mysteries
   _____ f. comic books
   _____ g. other (please specify)

3. At what age did you first begin reading romances regularly?
   _____ a. 5–10 years
   _____ b. 11–20 years
   _____ c. 21–30 years
   _____ d. 31 or older

4. About how many books of any sort (not including magazines) do you read *each* month?
   _____ a. 1–4
   _____ b. 5–9
   _____ c. 10–14
   _____ d. 15–20
   _____ e. 21 or more

5. About how many romances do you read *each* month?
   _____ a. 1–4
   _____ b. 5–9
   _____ c. 10–14

_____ d. 15–20
_____ e. 21 or more

6. Do you read every day?
_____ a. yes
_____ b. no

7. What kinds of books do you read for pleasure besides romances? Please check as many as you like.
_____ a. none
_____ b. biography
_____ c. historical fiction
_____ d. westerns
_____ e. mysteries
_____ f. horror-stories
_____ g. other (please specify)

8. About how many hours per week do you read?
_____ a. 1–5 hours
_____ b. 6–10 hours
_____ c. 11–15 hours
_____ d. 16 hours or more

9. When do you do *most* of your reading?
_____ a. in the morning, before going to work
_____ b. during the day while working around the house
_____ c. at lunchtime
_____ d. in the afternoon
_____ e. while traveling to and from work
_____ f. in the evening
_____ g. just before going to sleep
_____ h. other (please specify)

10. How often do you discuss romances with others?
_____ a. never
_____ b. rarely
_____ c. sometimes
_____ d. often

11. Where do you get *most* of the romances you read?
_____ a. bookstore
_____ b. library
_____ c. borrow from a friend
_____ d. borrow from a relative
_____ e. other (please specify)

12. If you buy romances, how often do you purchase hardcover romances?
_____ a. never
_____ b. rarely
_____ c. sometimes

_____ d. often
_____ e. almost always

13. Which of the following kinds of romances do you read *often*? Please check as many as you like.
_____ a. gothics
_____ b. historicals
_____ c. Harlequins
_____ d. Silhouettes
_____ e. Regencies
_____ f. other (please specify)

14. Which of the following kinds of romances do you *never* read? Please check as many as you like.
_____ a. gothics
_____ b. historicals
_____ c. Harlequins
_____ d. Silhouettes
_____ e. Regencies
_____ f. other (please specify)

15. How do you find out about new romances *most often*?
_____ a. I see them at the bookstore
_____ b. I see them at the supermarket or at a drugstore
_____ c. someone at the bookstore tells me about them
_____ d. I learn about them from friends
_____ e. I learn about them from relatives
_____ f. other (please specify)

16. How do you decide most often whether to read a romance or not?
_____ a. I like its cover
_____ b. I have already read something else by the author and liked it
_____ c. I like the title
_____ d. the publisher's descriptions on the cover and on the facing page make it sound interesting
_____ e. on the basis of someone else's recommendation
_____ f. other (please specify)

17. How closely do you think the characters in romances resemble the people you meet in real life?
_____ a. they are not at all similar
_____ b. they are somewhat similar
_____ c. they are very similar
_____ d. they are almost identical

18. How closely do you think the events in romances resemble those which occur in real life?
_____ a. they are not at all similar
_____ b. they are somewhat similar

_____ c. they are very similar
_____ d. they are almost identical

19. How closely do you think the romantic heroine's reactions and feelings towards people and events resemble your own?
_____ a. they are not like mine at all
_____ b. they are somewhat like mine
_____ c. they are very much like mine
_____ d. they are almost identical to mine

20. After you have finished with a romance, what do you most often do with it?
_____ a. put it on a bookshelf
_____ b. throw it away
_____ c. give it to a friend
_____ d. donate it to charity or a library
_____ e. other (please specify)

21. How often do you re-read romances you have read before?
_____ a. never
_____ b. rarely
_____ c. sometimes
_____ d. often

22. What is your sex?
_____ a. female
_____ b. male

23. What is your age?
_____ please fill in your age

24. What is your current marital status?
_____ a. single
_____ b. married
_____ c. widowed
_____ d. separated
_____ e. divorced

25. Last week were you working full-time, part-time, going to school, keeping the house, or what?
_____ a. working full-time (or more, including self-employment)
_____ b. working part-time
_____ c. working part-time and taking care of house and children
_____ d. have a job, but not at work because of illness, strike, or vacation
_____ e. unemployed, laid off, looking for work
_____ f. in school
_____ g. keeping house
_____ h. retired
_____ i. other (please specify)

26. If you have a job, what is your occupation or job description? _____

27. What is your *total* household income? (that is, not just yours if there are others)
    ____ a. less than $3,000
    ____ b. $3,000–5,999
    ____ c. $6,000–7,999
    ____ d. $8,000–9,999
    ____ e. $10,000–14,999
    ____ f. $15,000–24,999
    ____ g. $25,000–49,999
    ____ h. $50,000 or more

28. Do you own ____ or rent ____ your home?

29. How many years of education have you completed?
    ____ a. less than 8
    ____ b. K–8
    ____ c. 9–12
    ____ d. some college
    ____ e. completed college
    ____ f. some postgraduate work
    ____ g. Master's degree
    ____ h. Ph.D.

30. What is your religious preference?
    ____ a. none
    ____ b. Jewish
    ____ c. Catholic
    ____ d. Baptist
    ____ e. Lutheran
    ____ f. Methodist
    ____ g. Presbyterian
    ____ h. Episcopalian
    ____ i. other (please specify)

31. How often do you usually attend church services?
    ____ a. once per week or more
    ____ b. once or a few times a month
    ____ c. a few times a year or less often
    ____ d. not in the last two years

32. About how many hours per week do you watch television?
    ____ a. 7 hours or less
    ____ b. 8–14 hours
    ____ c. 15–20 hours
    ____ d. 21–30 hours
    ____ e. 31 hours or more

33. About how many magazines do you read per month?

34. Can you briefly describe what makes romances more enjoyable than other kinds of books available today?

Appendix 3. Final Questionnaire

ROMANCE READER SURVEY
Please Read the Following

I would appreciate it if you would take a brief amount of time to answer the questions on this form. I am conducting a survey to determine the reading habits of people who read romances. The questionnaire is designed to discover your own personal attitudes and opinion about the books you read. I ask that you do not identify yourself in any way and that you understand your participation is completely voluntary. Almost all the questions can be answered by placing a check in the appropriate space.
FOR EACH QUESTION, PLEASE SELECT ONLY ONE ANSWER
UNLESS THE QUESTION SPECIFIES OTHERWISE.

Thank you very much for your cooperation.   Janice Radway
University of Pennsylvania

1. At what age did you first begin reading for pleasure?
_____ a. 5–10 years
_____ b. 11–20 years
_____ c. 21–30 years
_____ d. 31 or above

2. What was your *most* favorite kind of book as a teenager?
_____ a. biography
_____ b. historical fiction other than romances
_____ c. westerns
_____ d. historical romances
_____ e. contemporary romances
_____ f. mysteries
_____ g. science fiction
_____ h. comic books
_____ i. fantasy
_____ j. none. I didn't read for pleasure.
_____ k. other (please specify)

3. At what age did you first begin reading romances regularly?
_____ a. 5–9 years
_____ b. 10–14 years
_____ c. 15–19 years
_____ d. 20–24 years
_____ e. 25–29 years
_____ f. 30–39 years
_____ g. 40 or older

4. When you were a child, did your mother or female guardian read romances?
_____ a. yes, very often
_____ b. yes, but only sometimes
_____ c. no
_____ d. I don't remember.

5. How many romances do you read *each* week?
      _____ a. 1–4
      _____ b. 5–9
      _____ c. 10–14
      _____ d. 15–19
      _____ e. 20–24
      _____ f. 25 or more

6. About how many books other than romances do you read each week?
      _____ a. none (If you select letter a, go on to question 8.)
      _____ b. 1–2
      _____ c. 3–4
      _____ d. 5–6
      _____ e. 7 or more

7. If you read other kinds of books besides romances, which of the following kinds of books are you *most* likely to read? (Remember, select only one.)
      _____ a. biography
      _____ b. historical novels other than romances
      _____ c. westerns
      _____ d. mysteries
      _____ e. horror stories or occult
      _____ f. fantasy
      _____ g. science fiction
      _____ h. non-fiction
      _____ i. other (please specify)

8. Do you read every day?
      _____ a. yes
      _____ b. no

9. About how many hours per week do you read?
      _____ a. 1–5 hours
      _____ b. 6–10 hours
      _____ c. 11–15 hours
      _____ d. 16–20 hours
      _____ e. 21 hours or more

10. Which of the following best describes your reading pattern?
      _____ a. I read mostly in the morning.
      _____ b. I read mostly during the day while working around the house.
      _____ c. I read mostly during lunchtime.
      _____ d. I read mostly in the afternoon.
      _____ e. I read mostly while traveling to and from work.
      _____ f. I read mostly in the evening.
      _____ g. It's hard to say when I do most of my reading since I read every chance I get.

11. Which of the following best describes what you usually do once you've begun a romance?

_____ a. I only continue reading it when I'm in the mood.

_____ b. I read a few pages each day until I'm done.

_____ c. I read as much of it as I can until I'm interrupted or have something else to do.

_____ d. I won't put it down until I've finished it unless it's absolutely necessary.

12. How often do you discuss romances with others?

_____ a. never

_____ b. rarely

_____ c. sometimes

_____ d. often

13. Who do you discuss romances with *most* often?

_____ a. my mother

_____ b. my daughter

_____ c. my sister

_____ d. a female neighbor

_____ e. other (please specify)

14. How often do you re-read romances you've already read?

_____ a. never

_____ b. rarely

_____ c. sometimes

_____ d. often

15. Where do you get *most* of the romances you read?

_____ a. bookstore

_____ b. library

_____ c. supermarket

_____ d. borrow from a friend

_____ e. borrow from a relative

_____ f. other (please specify)

16. If you buy romances, how often do you purchase hardcover romances?

_____ a. never

_____ b. rarely

_____ c. sometimes

_____ d. often

17. Which of the following kinds of romances do you read? Here you may check as many as you like.

_____ a. gothics

_____ b. contemporary mystery romances

_____ c. historicals

_____ d. contemporary romances

_____ e. Harlequins

_____ f. Regencies

_____ g. family sagas

_____ h. plantation series

_____ i. spy thrillers
_____ j. transcendental romances
_____ k. other

18. Which of the following kinds of romances is your favorite?
    _____ a. gothics
    _____ b. contemporary mystery romances
    _____ c. historicals
    _____ d. contemporary romances
    _____ e. Harlequins
    _____ f. Regencies
    _____ g. family sagas
    _____ h. plantation series
    _____ i. spy thrillers
    _____ j. transcendental romances
    _____ k. other

19. Which of the following best describes what usually makes you decide to read a romance or not?
    _____ a. I like the cover.
    _____ b. I have already read something by the author and liked it.
    _____ c. I like the title.
    _____ d. The publishers's blurb on the front and back cover makes it sound interesting.
    _____ e. Someone else recommended it to me.
    _____ f. other (please specify)

20. How often do you read the endings of romances before you begin reading the whole book?
    _____ a. never
    _____ b. sometimes
    _____ c. often
    _____ d. always

21. Which of the following best describes what you do when you realize you don't like a book that you have already begun reading?
    _____ a. I put it down and never finish it.
    _____ b. I read the ending to see how it came out.
    _____ c. I always finish it even if I don't like it.

22. Which of the following do you feel should *never* be included in a romance? Please select three and rank them by placing a number 1 next to the most distasteful element, a number 2 next to the second most distasteful, and so on.
    _____ a. rape
    _____ b. explicit sex
    _____ c. sad ending
    _____ d. physical torture of the heroine or the hero
    _____ e. an ordinary heroine

_____ f.   bed-hopping
_____ g.   premarital sex
_____ h.   a cruel hero
_____ i.   a weak hero
_____ j.   a hero who is stronger than the heroine
_____ k.   a heroine who is stronger than the hero

23. What are the three most important ingredients in a romance? Please pick the three which you think are essential and rank them by placing a number 1 next to the most important ingredient, a number 2 next to the second most important, and so on.
_____ a.   a happy ending
_____ b.   lots of scenes of explicit sexual description
_____ c.   lots of detail about faraway places and historical periods
_____ d.   a long conflict between the hero and heroine
_____ e.   punishment of the villain
_____ f.   a slowly but consistently developing love between hero and heroine
_____ g.   a setting in a particular historical period (Choose this one if you require your romances to be Regencies, Edwardians, about the Civil War, etc.)
_____ h.   lots of love scenes with some explicit sexual description
_____ i.   lots of love scenes without explicit sexual description
_____ j.   some detail about the heroine and hero after they have finally gotten together
_____ k.   a very particular kind of hero and heroine (Pick this one if you like the hero and heroine to have certain characteristics all the time)

24. What qualities or characteristics do you like to see in a heroine? Please select three and rank them by placing a number 1 next to the most desirable quality, a number 2 next to the second most desirable quality, and so on.
_____ a.   intelligence
_____ b.   independence
_____ c.   beauty
_____ d.   a sense of humor
_____ e.   assertiveness
_____ f.   femininity
_____ g.   aggressiveness
_____ h.   virginity
_____ i.   other (please specify)

25. What qualities or characteristics do you like to see in a hero? Please select three and rank them by placing a number 1 next to the most desirable quality, a number 2 next to the second most desirable quality, and so on.
_____ a.   intelligence
_____ b.   tenderness
_____ c.   protectiveness
_____ d.   strength
_____ e.   bravery

_____ f. a sense of humor
_____ g. independence
_____ h. attractiveness
_____ i. a good body
_____ j. other (please specify)

26. Which of the following best describes your attitude to the way the stories are told?
    _____ a. I like stories to be told by the heroine, in first person. (For example, "I couldn't believe my eyes, there was the most arrogant man I had ever seen.")
    _____ b. I dislike stories which are told by the heroine, in first person, but I will read them sometimes. My favorites give the point of view of both the heroine and hero.
    _____ c. I won't read a story if it is told by the heroine, in first person. I only read those which give the point of view of both the heroine and hero.
    _____ d. I have no preference whether the story is told by the heroine or by a narrator who gives the point of view of both the heroine and the hero.

27. How closely do you think the characters in romances resemble the people you meet in real life?
    _____ a. They are not at all similar.
    _____ b. They are somewhat similar.
    _____ c. They are very similar.
    _____ d. They are almost identical.

28. How closely do you think the events in romances resemble those which occur in real life?
    _____ a. They are not at all similar.
    _____ b. They are somewhat similar.
    _____ c. They are very similar.
    _____ d. They are almost identical.

29. How closely do you think the romantic heroine's reactions and feelings towards people and events resemble your own?
    _____ a. They are not like mine at all.
    _____ b. They are somewhat like mine.
    _____ c. They are very much like mine.
    _____ d. They are almost identical to mine.

30. How closely do you feel that the romantic hero's emotional responses to the heroine resemble the way the man in your life responds to you?
    _____ a. They are not like his at all.
    _____ b. They are somewhat like his.
    _____ c. They are very much like his.
    _____ d. They are almost identical to his.
    _____ e. There is not a steady man in my life right now.

31. After you have finished a romance which you liked, what do you most often do with it? (Remember, check only one.)

   ____ a. I put it on a bookshelf to keep although I sometimes lend my romances.

   ____ b. I throw it away.

   ____ c. I give it to a friend or relative. (Do not check this one if you only lend your books.)

   ____ d. I donate it to the library or to charity.

   ____ e. other (please specify)

32. Which of the following reasons best describe why you read romances? Please pick the three reasons which are closest to your reasons and rank them from the most important reason (number 1) to the third most important one.

   ____ a. to escape my daily problems

   ____ b. to learn about faraway places and times

   ____ c. for simple relaxation

   ____ d. because I wish I had a romance like the heroine's

   ____ e. because reading is just for me. It is my time.

   ____ f. because I like to read about the strong, virile heroes

   ____ g. because reading is at least better than other kinds of escape

   ____ h. because romantic stories are never sad or depressing

33. What are your three favorite romances? Please give the titles in order.

   1. _____

   2. _____

   3. _____

34. What are your three favorite authors? Please list them in order.

   1. _____

   2. _____

   3. _____

35. What is your sex?

   ____ a. female

   ____ b. male

36. In what age group are you?

   ____ a. under 15

   ____ b. 15–18

   ____ c. 19–24

   ____ d. 25–34

   ____ e. 35–44

   ____ f. 45–54

   ____ g. 55–64

   ____ h. 65 or over

37. What is your current marital status?

   ____ a. single (never married)

   ____ b. married

   ____ c. widowed

_____ d. separated
_____ e. divorced but not remarried

38. At what age did you first get married? _____

39. Do you have any children?
    _____ a. yes
    _____ b. no

40. If you do have children, what are their ages and sex? (Please specify, female child, age 6; male child, age 4 and so on.)
    _____
    _____

41. Last week, were you working full-time, part-time, going to school, keeping house or what?
    _____ a. working full-time (either for employer or self-employed)
    _____ b. working part-time
    _____ c. have a job but not at work because of illness, strike, or vacation
    _____ d. unemployed, laid off, looking for work
    _____ e. in school (or on summer vacation)
    _____ f. keeping house and/or caring for children
    _____ g. retired

42. If you have a full- or part-time job outside the home, what is your occupation or job title?
    _____

43. If married, what is your spouse's occupation?
    _____

44. What is your total household income? (that is, not just yours if there are others contributing to the family income)
    _____ a. less than $5,999
    _____ b. $6,000–9,999
    _____ c. $10,000–14,999
    _____ d. $15,000–24,999
    _____ e. $25,000–49,999
    _____ f. $50,000 or more

45. How many years of education have you completed?
    _____ a. less than 8
    _____ b. through grade 8
    _____ c. some high school
    _____ d. through grade 12 (graduated high school)
    _____ e. some college work (less than 3 years)
    _____ f. graduated from college
    _____ g. some graduate work
    _____ h. Master's degree
    _____ i. Ph.D.

46. If married, how many years of education has your spouse completed?
    _____ a. less than 8
    _____ b. through grade 8
    _____ c. some high school
    _____ d. through grade 12 (graduated high school)
    _____ e. some college work (less than 3 years)
    _____ f. graduated from college
    _____ g. some graduate work
    _____ h. Master's degree
    _____ i. Ph.D.

47. What is your religious preference?
    _____ a. none
    _____ b. Christian but non-denominational
    _____ c. Jewish
    _____ d. Catholic
    _____ e. Baptist
    _____ f. Lutheran
    _____ g. Methodist
    _____ h. Presbyterian
    _____ i. Episcopalian
    _____ j. Reformed Latter Day Saints
    _____ k. other

48. How often do you usually attend church services?
    _____ a. once per week or more
    _____ b. once or a few times a month
    _____ c. a few times a year or slightly less often
    _____ d. not in the last two years

49. About how many hours per week do you watch television for entertainment?
    _____ a. 3 hours or less
    _____ b. 4–7 hours
    _____ c. 8–14 hours
    _____ d. 15–20 hours
    _____ e. 21 hours or more

50. How many magazines a month do you read?
    _____ a. none
    _____ b. 1–2
    _____ c. 3–4
    _____ d. 4 or more

51. How often do you watch soap operas on television?
    _____ a. never
    _____ b. rarely
    _____ c. sometimes
    _____ d. often
    _____ e. almost every day

52. When you do watch television, what do you watch *most* often? (Please select only one.)
   ____ a. Masterpiece Theatre (PBS)
   ____ b. movies (either regular films or made-for-TV movies)
   ____ c. situation comedies (like Three's Company, Barney Miller, M*A*S*H)
   ____ d. hour-long dramas
   ____ e. variety or specials
   ____ f. documentaries
   ____ g. game shows
   ____ h. other (please specify)

53. Could you briefly describe what makes romances better than other kinds of books available today?

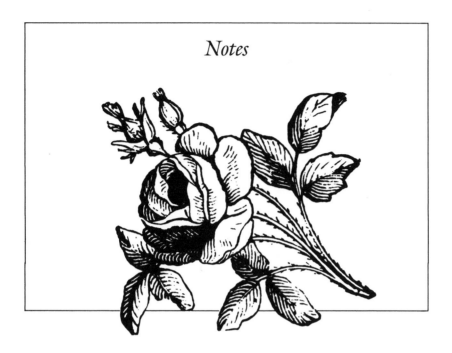

Notes

INTRODUCTION

1. Although I am still somewhat uncomfortable with the voice I have adopted here, in part because I fear this sort of discussion can be read as simple personal display, I have finally decided to use it because I agree with Angela McRobbie's argument in "The Politics of Feminist Research" (*Feminist Review* 12 [1982]: 54) that we must begin to acknowledge the ways in which our private, professional, and intellectual lives intersect. Thus what I have tried to do is to indicate the ways in which my personal situation and insertion into already existing social institutions and theoretical conversations both served as the conditions of possibility for *Reading the Romance* and structured its limitations.

2. See, for instance, Sandra Gilbert's review in the *New York Times Book Review*, 30 December 1984, p. 11; or that by Angus Calder in the *Times Literary Supplement*, 15 February 1985.

3. For a comprehensive history of these debates, see Gene Wise, "Paradigm Dramas," *American Quarterly* 31 (1979): 293–337.

4. See, for instance, Murray Murphey, "American Civilization at Pennsylvania," *American Quarterly* 22 (Summer 1970): 489–502.

5. See, for instance, Russel Nye, *The Unembarrassed Muse: The Popular Arts in America* (New York: The Dial Press, 1970).

6. Stuart Hall, "Cultural Studies and the Centre: Some Problematics and Problems," in *Culture, Media, Language: Working Papers in Cultural Studies, 1972–79* (London: Hutchinson, 1980), p. 19. See also his "Cultural Studies: Two Paradigms," *Media, Culture and Society* 2 (1980): 52–72.

7. Apparently, no one in my department knew at that time of the work carried out at the Birmingham Centre. I also remained unaware of this research until after I had completed *Reading the Romance*. I cannot now recall exactly how I learned of British ethnographic studies of media use, but I would like to express my great gratitude to Patrick Hagopian and Elaine Collins, who directed my attention to many references, photocopied chapters and articles in their possession not easily available in Philadelphia, and discussed all of it with me.

8. I am thinking here of Paul Willis's early work, including his "Notes on Method" in *Culture, Media, Language* and his *Profane Culture*, as well as of the work by the Women's Studies Group at Birmingham collected in *Women Take Issue: Aspects of Women's Subordination* (London: Hutchinson, 1978).

9. For a perceptive discussion of the dangers inherent in conceptualizing empirical work as objectively scientific and interpretive work as subjectively humanist and therefore as categorical opposites, see Lawrence Grossberg, "Critical Theory and the Politics of Research," *Mass Communication Yearbook* 6 (1987).

10. Willis, "Notes on Method," p. 90.

11. McRobbie, "The Politics of Feminist Research," p. 51.

12. See Jerry Palmer, *Thrillers: Genesis and Structure of a Popular Genre* (London: Edward Arnold, 1978); and Terry Eagleton, *Criticism and Ideology: A Study in Marxist Literary Theory* (London: New Left Books, 1976).

13. Janice Radway, "A Phenomenological Theory of Popular and Elite Literature," Ph.D. dissertation, Michigan State University, 1977.

14. I should not minimize the fact that significant differences in method and political perspective, particularly with respect to the audience for mass culture, continue to separate my approach from that taken by Modleski. See, for instance, her introduction to the recent *Studies in Entertainment: Critical Approaches to Mass Culture* (Bloomington: Indiana University Press, 1986), pp. ix–xix, where she specifically takes issue with the work of the Birmingham School and related approaches to the study of mass culture and charges that work with being celebratory rather than critical.

15. See Fish, *Is There a Text in This Class?*.

16. See the aforementioned titles by Willis; David Morley and Charlotte Brunsdon, *Everyday Television: Nationwide* (London: British Film Institute, 1978); David Morley, *The 'Nationwide' Audience* (London: British Film Institute, 1980); Angela McRobbie, "Working Class Girls and the Culture of Femininity," in *Women Take*

Issue, pp. 96–108; Angela McRobbie, "Settling Accounts with Subcultures: A Feminist Critique," *Screen* 34 (Spring 1980): 39–49; Angela McRobbie, "Jackie: An Ideology of Adolescent Femininity," in *Popular Culture: Past and Present*, ed. Bernard Waites et al. (London, 1982), pp. 263–83; Dorothy Hobson, "Housewives: Isolation as Oppression," in *Women Take Issue*, pp. 79–95; and Dorothy Hobson, *Crossroads: The Drama of a Soap Opera* (London: Methuen, 1982).

17. Morley, *The 'Nationwide' Audience*, p. 18.

18. Hobson, *Crossroads*, p. 170.

19. Ibid.

20. David Morley, *"The Nationwide Audience*—A Critical Postscript," *Screen Education* 39 (Summer 1981): 3–14.

21. I should perhaps note here that this boom was initiated in the United States by the Canadian firm Harlequin Enterprises, which began its rise to prominence in mass-market publishing by reprinting the romances of Mills & Boon in the 1950s and 1960s. The genre took off in the States when Harlequin began to issue romances written by American women and when other firms simultaneously introduced explicit sex into the genre. The Smithton women did not confine themselves to a single kind of romance but read widely in the genre and appreciated many different variations.

22. On this point, see Grossberg's discussion in his "Critical Theory and the Politics of Research," pp. 9–10 (typescript pages).

23. The tendency to deplore the "escapist" nature of popular fantasy seems much less pronounced in British work than in American. See, for instance, Valerie Walkerdine's sensitive discussion of the nature of fantasy escape for girls in "Some Day My Prince Will Come: Young Girls and the Preparation for Adolescent Sexuality," in *Gender and Generation*, ed. Angela McRobbie and Mica Nava (London: Macmillan, 1984), pp. 162–84.

24. The reader will no doubt note that this did not lead me to reconsider Chodorow's work and its relation to object-relations theory. Walkerdine's comments in "Some Day My Prince Will Come" (pp. 178–81) have since suggested to me that the revision romance reading caused me to propose in Chodorow's theory may be of more significance than I had thought. It may not be the case that mothering fails to work only for some (aberrant) women but in fact that the struggle over gender identity is never resolved as she suggests, following Freud, Lacan, and Rose.

25. For a somewhat different use of Chodorow that also connects romance reading to the search for preoedipal merging, see Angela Mile's fascinating unpublished article, "Confessions of a Harlequin Reader: Romance and the Fantasy of Male Mothering."

26. See my unpublished paper, "Romance and the Work of Fantasy—Feminine Sexuality and Subjectivity at Century's End."

27. Cora Kaplan has recently made an argument that suggests that readers do not identify only with the romantic heroine but in fact identify in multiple and wandering fashion with the seducer, the seduced, and the process of seduction itself. See "*The Thorn Birds*: Fiction, Fantasy, Femininity," in Kaplan, *Sea Changes: Feminism and Culture* (London: Verso, 1986), pp. 117–46. Although I found little evidence of this kind of multiple identification in the group I interviewed (at least at a conscious level), I have been told by many romance writers that the act of writing a romance is especially enjoyable because it gives them the opportunity to imagine themselves as the hero. It is also interesting to note that several American publishers of romances have recently permitted writers to experiment with the writing of a romance entirely from the hero's point of view. Thus it might be possible that this sort of multiple identification actually varies from reader to reader and therefore can be increased by cultural or personal changes.

28. Valerie Hey, "The Necessity of Romance," University of Kent at Canterbury, Women's Studies Occasional Papers, no. 3, 1983.

29. Alison Light, "'Returning to Manderley'—Romance Fiction, Female Sexuality and Class," *Feminist Review* 16 (April 1984): 7–25.

30. Ann Rosalind Jones, "Mills & Boon Meets Feminism," in *The Progress of Romance: The Politics of Popular Fiction*, ed. Jean Radford (London: Routledge and Kegan Paul, 1986), pp. 195–220.

31. Ibid., p. 210.

32. Catherine Kirkland, "For the Love of It: Women Writers and the Popular Romance," Ph.D. dissertation, University of Pennsylvania, 1984.

33. McRobbie, "The Politics of Feminist Research," p. 53.

34. Ibid., p. 57.

35. The phrases are Catherine Kirkland's and Angela McRobbie's respectively.

CHAPTER I

1. Douglas, "Soft-Porn Culture," pp. 25–29.

2. The distribution figure is that quoted by Harlequin itself in recent advertisements as well as in its 1979 annual report to its shareholders. A good example of Harlequin's advertising can be found in *Publishers Weekly*, 18 April 1980, pp. 26–27. The annual report is available from Harlequin Enterprises, Ltd., 225 Duncan Mill Road, Don Mills, Ontario, Canada M3B 3Z5. All facts and figures about Harlequin romances refer to the corporation's practices in 1982 unless otherwise noted.

3. Tebbel, *A History of Book Publishing in the United States*, 1:3. Tebbel's history of the American publishing industry is the single best source for details about the development of the business as a whole as well as about that of individual houses.

Although he keeps his interpretation to a minimum, Tebbel's treatment is so complete that it cannot be ignored by anyone interested in the industry. For an analysis of the "meaning" of the chronicle he presents in such detail, the reader should consult Escarpit, *The Book Revolution* and *The Sociology of Literature*, and Williams, *The Long Revolution*, especially pp. 125–292. For further information on American publishing, see Lehmann-Haupt et al., *The Book in America*, and Madison, *Book Publishing in America*.

4. Charvat, *Literary Publishing in America*, pp. 17–24. Charvat's extraordinary book remains one of the only attempts in American cultural studies to pursue the connections between form and literary activity as a social phenomenon. His book is an excellent example of a true sociology of American literature; as such, it deserves to be better known. Equally useful in both a methodological and substantive sense is his *The Profession of Authorship in America, 1800–1870*.

5. Charvat, *The Profession of Authorship*, pp. 29–43. I have used the male pronoun throughout this discussion because the early printer-publishers were men.

6. Tebbel, *A History of Book Publishing*, 1:240–41.

7. On Peterson and the Beadle brothers, see Tebbel, ibid., 1:245–51, and Schick, *The Paperbound Book in America*, pp. 50–53.

8. Tebbel, *A History of Book Publishing*, 1:242–43, and Schick, *The Paperbound Book in America*, pp. 48–50.

9. Charvat, *The Profession of Authorship*, p. 49.

10. The concept of fission is Fredric Jameson's. See his "Reification and Utopia in Mass Culture," pp. 130–48.

11. On the interim years between the nineteenth- and twentieth-century paperback revolutions, see Lehmann-Haupt et al., *The Book in America*, pp. 194–217, 241–54, 259–63, 317–22, 372–90; Madison, *Book Publishing in America*, pp. 49–60, 158–63, 395–98, 547–56; Schick, *The Paperbound Book in America*, pp. 55–63.

12. Schick, *The Paperbound Book in America*, p. 63.

13. Escarpit, *The Book Revolution*, p. 121.

14. Ibid.

15. Ibid.

16. Ibid.

17. Schick, *The Paperbound Book in America*, p. 79.

18. For full accounts of the creation of Pocket Books, see Schick, ibid., pp. 79–80, and Madison, *Book Publishing in America*, pp. 547–49.

19. De Graff's interest in the book's potential as a commodity is obvious in this comment taken from his announcement of the Pocket Books venture. De Graff queried his colleagues: "Has anyone ever considered publishing a special cheap edition . . . which people would *buy instead of lend*, that would not interfere with the sale of regular editions? It seems to me that might offer some solution, for then the author and the publisher through the sale of their cheap edition would get a revenue, however small, *from each person who reads the book*" (quoted in Schick, *The Paperbound Book in America*, p. 79, emphasis added). Although it would be unfair to say that de Graff is totally uninterested in securing *readers* for his authors, it is clear that his principal object is to get some pecuniary consideration every time knowledge of an author's book prompts the intention to read it

and therefore the simple need to *acquire* it. For him, the book is little more than a thing and the publisher an indispensable mediator who facilitates a material exchange between author and reader.

20. For an analysis of the various factors contributing to the rise of paperback publishing in the mid-twentieth century, see Schick, *The Paperbound Book in America*, pp. 96–98; Compaine, *The Book Industry in Transition*, p. 81; Roger H. Smith, *Paperback Parnassus*, pp. 65–76; Datus C. Smith, Jr., *A Guide to Book Publishing*, pp. 150–56.

21. For an analysis of the interaction between technology, economic factors, and production practices in paperback publishing, see Bodden, "An Economic Analysis of the Paper-Bound Book Industry," pp. 80–96.

22. Schick, *The Paperbound Book in America*, p. 97.

23. Roger Smith, *Paperback Parnassus*, pp. 68–70.

24. Returns to publishers generally run at or near 35 percent and sometimes as high as 60 percent. For a discussion of the returns problem, see Compaine, *The Book Industry in Transition*, pp. 90–94, and Roger Smith, *Paperback Parnassus*, pp. 25–31.

25. Escarpit, *The Book Revolution*, p. 122.

26. Escarpit, *The Sociology of Literature*, p. 68.

27. Compaine, *The Book Industry in Transition*, p. 145.

28. If the number of titles issued per year is used as a standard, mysteries have dominated paperback publishing since the twentieth-century revolution began. In the "Year in Review" issues of *Publishers Weekly* (usually the third week in January), this category has ranked number one since the first paperback listings were included. However, this ranking is based on titles rather than on sales. Although the mystery category continued to top the list in the 1940s and 1950s, sales of those titles varied considerably. Although *Publishers Weekly* rarely printed sales figures (because publishers did not—nor will they even now—release actual numbers of books sold), it instituted a mass-market section in the "review" series that included short interviews with individual houses. In those interviews, editors and publishers often commented about the difficulties with the sales of mysteries. See the issues of 22 January 1955, 21 January 1956, 20 January 1958, and 19 January 1959.

29. See Landrum, "Detective and Mystery Novels," p. 107, and Gruber, *The Pulp Jungle*.

30. It is extremely difficult to corroborate a publisher's observations about sales trends by using figures now generally available. As mentioned above, most statistics involve title production rather than actual sales or even distribution figures. Still, by noting the sometimes substantial variations in title production, one tends to conclude that some of those reductions probably resulted from deliberate decisions to curtail output in order to avoid returns rather than from a simple lack of publishable manuscripts.

31. I have relied here on Whitney's own account presented in "Writing the Gothic Novel," p. 11. I have not been able to discover corroborating evidence, nor have I been able to locate Gross himself. Still, several comments in Duffy, "On the Road to Manderley," pp. 95–96, suggest that Whitney's recollections are probably accurate.

32. Quoted in Proctor, "Phyllis Whitney," p. 20.

33. For a discussion of women's continuing interest in the family, see Degler, *At Odds*, especially pp. 418–35.

34. All of the preceding figures have been taken from "How to Identify, Display, and Sell the Gothic," an advisory bulletin for retailers issued by Speedy Shop Paperback Book Service.

35. Personal interview with Maureen Baron, executive editor, Gold Medal Books, 30 November 1979. Baron had been an editor at Dell during the gothic's peak years of popularity.

36. Quoted in Turner, "The Tempestuous World of Paperback Passion," p. 49.

37. For a discussion of Avon's introduction of the "original," see Davis, "The Cinderella Story of Paperback Originals," pp. 43–48.

38. Ibid., p. 44.

39. Rogers's manuscript had arrived at Avon in a brown paper envelope addressed "To the Editor of Kathleen Woodiwiss." See "Millions of Women Avid for Avon's Romances," p. 44.

40. McManus, "Editor's Report," p. 34.

41. Whiteside, "The Blockbuster Complex, I," p. 48. See also Doebler, "The Statistics of Concentration," pp. 26–30.

42. Whiteside, "The Blockbuster Complex, I," p. 52. See also Roger Smith, *Paperback Parnassus*, p. 75.

43. According to Benjamin Compaine, the total combined value of American publishers' receipts in 1976 amounted to $4.2 billion, which would place the industry only forty-first on *Fortune*'s list of individual industrial firms, immediately behind such corporations as Beatrice Foods, Xerox, and Firestone Tire (*The Book Industry in Transition*, p. 2). He also notes that the book publishing industry accounts for only 5.6 percent of personal consumption expenditures for recreation (p. 22). Leo Bogart has indicated that whereas the 1968 daily newspaper business was a $7 billion a year industry and the television industry was supported that same year by $3 billion, book publishing grossed only $2.4 billion. See his "How the Mass Media Work in America," pp. 165–85, especially pp. 169–70.

44. Whiteside, "The Blockbuster Complex, I," p. 56.

45. Ibid.

46. Ibid., pp. 56–58.

47. Ibid., p. 60.

48. Indeed, Roger Smith reports that, as of 1978, 75 percent of mass-market paperback sales "are not of best sellers." See "Paperback National Distributors— Part III," p. 79.

49. Davis, "The Cinderella Story of Paperback Originals," p. 44.

50. Ibid., p. 43.

51. Dayton, "B. Dalton, Bookseller, Foresees Growing Chain of Stores," p. 44. For reasons of space, throughout the following discussion of the impact of the bookstore chains on publishing, I will refer only to the practices employed by B. Dalton. Although Waldenbooks expanded more rapidly than did Dalton, it had less of an impact on the publishing houses, at least immediately, because it continued to rely on standard ordering procedures. Its returns rate was therefore consid-

erably higher than Dalton's and the company's orders were less reliable as indicators of public taste. While Walden concentrated on opening more stores, Dalton invested much of its capital in the computerized inventory and sales system for which it is now famous. Nonetheless, despite Walden's lower clout within the industry, its general approach to bookselling is similar to Dalton's and thus has acted to increase the impact of its practices on the publishers. Recently, Walden instituted computerized sales procedures similar to Dalton's, thus adding to the similarity between them. For information on Waldenbooks, see "Waldenbooks: Countering B. Dalton by Aping Its Computer Operations," pp. 116–21, and "Mass Merchandising Hits the Bookstores," pp. 80–86.

52. Whiteside, "The Blockbuster Complex, I," p. 94.

53. Quoted in Whiteside, "The Blockbuster Complex, II," pp. 136, 138.

54. Coser, Kadushin, and Powell, *Books*, p. 349.

55. For information on Dalton's computer, see Maryles, "B. Dalton," pp. 126–29; "Waldenbooks: Countering B. Dalton," pp. 116–21; Porter, "B. Dalton," pp. 53–57.

56. Thomas Whiteside attributes this claim to Morton Janklow, a lawyer-agent deeply involved in the publishing business. See his comments in "The Blockbuster Complex, II," pp. 65–70, and also his discussion of Dalton executive Kay Sexton, "The Blockbuster Complex, I," pp. 95–96.

57. Yankelovich, Skelly and White, *The 1978 Consumer Research Study on Reading*, pp. 137, 141, 143–48. For a discussion of the Yankelovich findings, see Chapter 2.

58. "Waldenbooks: Countering B. Dalton," p. 116.

59. The single best account of Harlequin Books' growing domination of the romance field can be found in Berman, "They Call Us Illegitimate," pp. 37–38.

60. "What Women Want," p. 94. See also Posner, "Show Business," pp. 72, 74, 76. Jensen has reported that among Harlequin's early titles were *Lady, That's My Skull*, *The Lady Was a Tramp*, and *Twelve Chinks and a Woman*; see "Women and Romantic Fiction," p. 71.

61. Berman, "They Call Us Illegitimate," p. 37.

62. Ibid., pp. 37–38.

63. Ibid.; Posner, "Show Business," p. 72.

64. All of the figures in this sentence are from a 1980 Harlequin publicity release entitled "Facts about Harlequin."

65. "The Romance of Harlequin Enterprises," p. 31.

66. Ibid., p. 31.

67. Posner, "Show Business," p. 72.

68. "The Romance of Harlequin Enterprises," p. 31.

69. Walters, "Paperback Talk," 12 October 1980, p. 47.

70. Berman, "They Call Us Illegitimate," p. 38.

71. "The Romance of Harlequin Enterprises," p. 31.

72. Berman, "They Call Us Illegitimate," p. 38.

73. Walters, "Paperback Talk," 24 February 1980, p. 47.

74. Davis, "The Cinderella Story of Paperback Originals," p. 45.

75. Personal interview with Vivien Stephens, series editor, Dell Publications, 12 April 1979.

76. Maryles, "Fawcett Launches Romance Imprint," pp. 69–70. All subsequent

details about the Fawcett venture have been drawn from this article.

77. Quoted by Maryles, ibid., p. 69.

78. Maryles, "S & S to Debut Silhouette with $3-Million TV Ad Campaign," p. 51.

79. Ibid., pp. 51–52.

80. Kakutani, "New Romance Novels," p. C13.

81. Yankelovich, Skelly and White, *The 1978 Consumer Research Study on Reading*, p. 48.

82. Compaine indicates that, as of 1978, $65 million worth of paperback book business was accomplished in food stores alone (*The Book Industry in Transition*, p. 89). A significant proportion of this sale must be attributed to the romance.

83. Davis, "The Cinderella Story," p. 43.

84. Harlequin advertisement, *Publishers Weekly*, 18 April 1980, pp. 26–27.

CHAPTER 2

1. In the course of completing this study of the Smithton readers, I have learned of at least five other such groups functioning throughout the country. Most seem to be informal networks of neighbors or co-workers who exchange romances and information about these books on a regular basis. I have also been told of a group similar to Dot's clustered about a Texas bookseller and have received information about the California-based "Friends of the English Regency," which also publishes a review newsletter and holds an annual Regency "Assemblee" at which it confers the "Georgette" award on favorite Regency romances. There is no way to tell how common this "reading club" phenomenon is, but it is worth investigation. If these clubs are widely relied upon to mediate the mass-production publishing process by individualizing selection, then a good deal of speculation about the meaning of mass-produced literature based on the "mass man" [*sic*] hypothesis will have to be reviewed and possibly rewritten.

2. These and all other figures about Smithton were taken from the *Census of the Population, 1970*. I have rounded off the numbers slightly to disguise the identity of Smithton.

3. Evans, "Dorothy's Diary," April 1980, pp. 1–2.

4. Ibid., p. 2

5. All spoken quotations have been taken directly from taped interviews. Nearly all of the comments were transcribed verbatim, although in a few cases repeated false starts were excised and marked with ellipses. Pauses in a speaker's commentary have been marked with dashes. I have paragraphed lengthy speeches only when the informant clearly seemed to conclude one topic or train of thought in order to open another deliberately. Lack of paragraphing, then, indicates that the speaker's comments continued apace without significant rest or pause.

6. Snitow, "Mass Market Romance," p. 150.

7. Brotman, "Ah, Romance!," p. B1.

8. Jensen, "Women and Romantic Fiction," p. 289.

9. Quoted in Brotman, "Ah, Romance!," p. B1.

10. See also Mann, *A New Survey*, passim.

11. Readers were instructed to identify the particular kind of romance they liked to "read the most" from a list of ten subgenres. The titles had been given to me by Dot during a lengthy discussion about the different kinds of romances. Although I expected the women to check only one subgenre, almost all of them checked several as their favorites. The categories and totals follow: gothics, 6; contemporary mystery romances, 5; historicals, 20; contemporary romances, 7; Harlequins, 10; Regencies, 4; family sagas, 1; plantation series, 3; spy thrillers, 0; transcendental romances, 0; other, 2.

12. It should be pointed out, however, that these findings could also indicate that romances were not heavily advertised or distributed when the majority of women in this sample were teenagers. Thus, the fact that so many have picked up the romance habit may be as much a function of the recent growth of the industry as of any particular need or predisposition on the part of women at a particular stage in their life cycle. Still, as I will make clear in this and subsequent chapters, romances do address needs associated with the role of mothering for *this* particular group of readers.

13. Jensen, "Women and Romantic Fiction," pp. 290–91.

14. Jensen also reports that all of the married women in her sample have children and that three-quarters have children still living at home (ibid., p. 291).

15. Cited in Yankelovich, Skelly and White, *The 1978 Consumer Research Study on Reading*, p. 325.

16. This compares with the eight-hour weekly average claimed by book readers who read fiction for leisure as reported in Yankelovich, Skelly and White, ibid., p. 126.

17. Although the Smithton women also commented, as did Jensen's informants, on the ease with which "light reading" like Harlequins and Silhouettes can be picked up and put down when other demands intervene, all of Dot's customers with whom I spoke expressed a preference for finishing a romance in one sitting. Jensen does not say whether her readers would have preferred to read in this way, although she does comment rather extensively on the fact that it is the material circumstances of their jobs as housewives and mothers that most often necessitate what she calls "snatch" reading. She refers to an alternate pattern of reading several books, one after the other, as the "binge." This is not exactly equivalent to the Smithton readers' practice with fat books, but some of them did mention engaging in such behavior as a special treat to themselves. See Jensen, "Women and Romantic Fiction," pp. 300–301 and 312–14.

18. Yankelovich, Skelly and White, *The 1978 Consumer Research Study on Reading*, pp. 141, 144.

19. The Smithton readers' patterns of explanation and justification will be explored in greater detail in Chapter 3.

20. Mann, *A New Survey*, p. 17.

21. For further discussion of this curious failure to trust that a new romance will end happily despite extensive prior acquaintance with the genre, see Chapter 6.

22. Evans, "Dorothy's Diary," April 1980, p. 1.

23. I included this choice on the final questionnaire because in many of the

interviews the women had expressed a distaste for romances that end abruptly with the declaration of love between the principal characters.

24. Faust, *Women, Sex, and Pornography*, p. 67.

25. Richard Hoggart is one of the few who disagrees with this argument. See his comments in *The Uses of Literacy*, pp. 171–75. Jensen has also acknowledged that many Harlequin authors "apparently share the backgrounds, attitudes, and fantasies of their women readers" ("Women and Romantic Fiction," pp. 118–19).

26. Quoted in Evans, "Dorothy's Diary," May 1980, p. 2.

27. Quoted in Evans, "Dorothy's Diary," Newsletter #4, 1980, p. 2. (This issue is not dated by month.)

28. Berman, "They Call Us Illegitimate," p. 38.

29. Whitney, "Writing the Gothic Novel," p. 10.

30. Ibid.

31. Ibid., p. 11.

32. Faust, *Women, Sex, and Pornography*, p. 63.

33. Whitney, "Writing the Gothic Novel," p. 43.

34. Quoted by Glass, "Editor's Report," p. 33.

35. Douglas, "Soft-Porn Culture," p. 28 (italics added).

36. Geertz, "Deep Play," p. 443.

37. Douglas, "Soft-Porn Culture," p. 25.

38. On the connection between patriarchy and marriage, see Hartmann, "The Family as Locus of Gender, Class, and Political Struggle," especially pp. 366–76.

39. None of the Smithton women commented on whether they had ever been hit, pushed around, or forced to have sexual relations against their will, although several did tell me that they know this goes on because it happens to their friends. In summarizing current studies on wife abuse, Rohrbaugh has commented in *Women: Psychology's Puzzle* that "many researchers in this field agree with Judge Stewart Oneglia's estimate that '50 percent of all marriages involve some degree of physical abuse of the woman'" (p. 350). Rohrbaugh also points out that "studies that define wife abuse as anything from an occasional hard slap to repeated, severe beatings suggest that there are 26 million to 30 million abused wives in the United States today" (p. 350). If these figures are accurate, it seems clear that a good many romance readers may very well need to be given a model "explanation" for this sort of behavior.

40. I would like to thank Star Helmer for giving me a copy of Gallen Books' "tipsheet" for contemporary romances.

41. The italics have been added here to indicate where Ann placed special emphasis and changed her intonation during her remarks. In each case, the emphasis conveyed both sarcasm and utter disbelief. Two of the most difficult tasks in using ethnographic material are those of interpreting meanings clearly implied by a speaker but not actually said and adequately conveying them in written prose.

42. See, especially, Modleski, "The Disappearing Act," pp. 444–48.

43. Again, the italics have been added here to indicate where special emphasis was conveyed through intonation. In each case, the emphasis was meant to underscore the distance between this heroine's behavior and that usually expected of women.

CHAPTER 3

1. See chap. 2, n. 5, for the method of citing spoken quotations in this chapter and elsewhere in the text.

2. These coupon ads appeared sporadically in national newspapers throughout the spring and summer of 1980.

3. Neels, *Cruise to a Wedding*, p. 190.

4. Maryles, "Fawcett Launches Romance Imprint," p. 70.

5. Hoggart, *The Uses of Literacy*, p. 196.

6. Harding, "The Notion of 'Escape,'" p. 24.

7. Ibid., p. 25.

8. For discussions of the growth of the reading public and the popular press, see Williams, *The Long Revolution*, pp. 156–213, and Altick, *The English Common Reader*, passim.

9. As Escarpit has observed in *The Sociology of Literature*, p. 91, "there are a thousand ways to escape and it is essential to know from what and towards what we are escaping."

10. Escarpit, ibid., p. 88. Although Dot's observations are not couched in academic language, they are really no different from Escarpit's similar observation that "reading is the supreme solitary occupation." He continues that "the man [*sic*] who reads does not speak, does not act, cuts himself away from society, isolates himself from the world which surrounds him. . . . reading allows the senses no margin of liberty. It absorbs the entire conscious mind, making the reader powerless to act" (p. 88). The significance of this last effect of the act of reading to the Smithton women will be discussed later in this chapter. For a detailed discussion of the different demands made upon an individual by reading and radio listening, see Lazarsfeld, *Radio and the Printed Page*, pp. 170–79.

11. Chodorow, *The Reproduction of Mothering*, p. 36.

12. Oakley, *The Sociology of Housework*, p. 179. See also Oakley, *Woman's Work*, pp. 60–155; McDonough and Harrison, "Patriarchy and Relations of Production," pp. 11–41; Kuhn, "Structures of Patriarchy and Capitalism," pp. 42–67; Sacks, "Engels Revisited," pp. 207–22; and Lopata, *Occupation Housewife*, passim.

13. In addition to Lopata, see Komarovsky, *Blue-Collar Marriage*; Myrdal and Klein, *Women's Two Roles*; Friedan, *The Feminine Mystique*; Mitchell, *Woman's Estate*; Steinmann, "A Study of the Concept of the Feminine Role."

14. With respect to this view of woman as a *natural* wife and mother, Dorothy Dinnerstein has observed in *The Mermaid and the Minotaur* that women are treated as "natural resources to be mined, reaped, used up without concern for their future fate" (p. 101).

15. Chodorow, *The Reproduction of Mothering*, p. 36.

16. Ibid.

17. It is worth remarking here that the feeling that housework ought to be done according to some abstract standard is apparently common to many women who work in the home. For a discussion of these standards, their origins in the generally unsupervised nature of housework, and the guilt they produce in the women who invariably feel they seldom "measure up," see Oakley, *The Sociology of Housework*, pp. 100–112.

18. Chodorow, *The Reproduction of Mothering*, p. 36. For studies of contemporary working-class versions of these networks, see Stack, *All Our Kin*; Young and Willmott, *Family and Kinship in East London*; Lamphere, "Strategies, Cooperation, and Conflict among Women in Domestic Groups," pp. 97–112.

19. Oakley, *The Sociology of Housework*, pp. 52–54, 75, 88–92; Oakley, *Woman's Work*, pp. 101–2; Lopata, *Occupation Housewife*, pp. 36, 244–45.

20. A few months before I arrived in Smithton, several of Dot's customers expressed an interest in getting together with other romance readers. Accordingly, Dot arranged an informal gathering in her home at which five to ten women socialized and discussed romances. Although the women claimed they enjoyed themselves, they have not yet met again. See also Chapter 2, note 1.

21. As I mentioned in Chapter 2, there is ample evidence to indicate that writers' and readers' perceptions of romances are remarkably similar. This holds true not only for the subject of the story itself but also for conceptions of the romance's function. For comments very similar to Dot's, see Van Slyke, "'Old-Fashioned' and 'Up-to-the-Minute,'" pp. 14–16.

22. It is important to point out here that certain behaviors of the Smithton readers indicate that they actually hold contradictory attitudes about the realism of the romance. Although they admit the stories are unreal, they also claim that they learn about history and geography from their reading. This contradiction and its significance will be explored later in this chapter and in Chapter 6.

23. Bettelheim, *The Uses of Enchantment*, pp. 121–23.

24. Ibid., p. 126.

25. The difficulty of eliciting honest answers from readers about their literary preferences and tastes is well known. As Escarpit has wryly observed, "The likelihood of lucid and sincere answers is extremely reduced as soon as someone's reading habits are examined. While the confession of one's sexual peculiarities may flatter a latent exhibitionist, the avowal of literary or anti-literary tastes . . . which lower one's position in society can only be painful" (*The Sociology of Literature*, p. 16). Indeed it was for this very reason that I decided to do some of my interviewing in groups. Because I knew beforehand that many women are afraid to admit their preference for romantic novels for fear of being scorned as illiterate or immoral, I suspected that the strength of numbers might make my informants less reluctant about discussing their obsession. The strategy seemed to work, for as the shyer women saw that I did not react negatively when others volunteered information, they too began to participate in the discussions. Group interviewing, of course, creates the possibility that one individual will influence the others, thus falsifying the results. I do not think this happened to any great extent because the answers to the questionnaires generally bear out what I discovered through the interviews.

26. Personal interview with Vivien Stephens, New York, 12 April 1979. Stephens is now an editor with Harlequin Books.

27. In fact, many romance authors do travel to the locales they intend to write about. This is especially true of the more successful writers. Most of the others manage to do at least rudimentary research in their local libraries. Indeed, it is not unusual to find expressions of gratitude to librarians included after the title page

of a romance. Phyllis Whitney, for example, included the following note in her novel, *Domino*: "My thanks to those who helped to make *Domino* possible. To Marlys Millhiser and Lucinda Baker, who know the West, and whose books I admire. To David Clemens of the Huntington Public Library, who found all that wonderful material about deringers for me. And especially to Sara Courant of the Patchogue Public Library who never fails me, no matter what peculiar roads of research I choose to follow" (unpaged).

28. On advertising, see Williamson, *Decoding Advertisements*, and Ewen, *Captains of Consciousness*.

CHAPTER 4

1. Propp, *Morphology of the Folktale*.

2. A function according to Propp is "the act of a character, defined from the point of view of its significance for the course of the action" (ibid., p. 21).

3. Wright, *Sixguns and Society*, pp. 124–29.

4. For a full discussion of semiotic coding, see Eco, *A Theory of Semiotics*, especially pp. 37–38, 48–150. For a more specific discussion of the coding or framing of literary characters, see the introduction to Eco's *The Role of the Reader*, pp. 3–43.

5. Jensen, "Women and Romantic Fiction," p. 141. For additional comments on the romantic heroine's sexual rival, see Douglas, "Soft-Porn Culture," pp. 26–27; Russ, "Somebody's Trying to Kill Me and I Think It's My Husband," pp. 668–70, 683, 691; Mussell, "Beautiful and Damned," pp. 84–89.

6. The seven with early marriages are *The Flame and the Flower*, *Shanna*, *Made for Each Other*, *The Proud Breed*, *The Black Lyon*, *The Fulfillment*, and *Moonlight Variations*.

7. Griffin, *Pornography and Silence*, passim.

8. I have come across no romance with a heroine described as ugly, homely, or simply plain. Harlequins do tend to have heroines who are not ravishing beauties, but, as Jensen notes, they are at least "plainly attractive" ("Women and Romantic Fiction," p. 142).

9. Ann Douglas emphasizes the violence in Harlequins, although she does not consider the implications of the fact that most of the stories conclude with the taming of the hero and with his transformation into a loving and attentive husband. She assumes, furthermore, that readers enjoy his early brutality rather than endure it precisely in order to be told later that such all-too-common behavior can be eradicated and transformed into something much more desirable. For further discussion of the role of male violence in the romance, see Chapter 5.

10. These heroines appear respectively in the following books: *The Flame and the Flower*, *Made for Each Other*, *Miss Hungerford's Handsome Hero*, *Ashes in the Wind*, and *Summer of the Dragon*.

11. Chodorow, *The Reproduction of Mothering*, pp. 169–70.

12. For an additional discussion of the continuing importance of her mother in a woman's relational life as an adult, see Flax, "The Conflict between Nurturance and Autonomy," especially pp. 179–84.

13. For a discussion of the widespread tendency to devalue all things associated with women and their duties, see Dinnerstein, *The Mermaid and the Minotaur*, pp. 124–56. See also Beauvoir, *The Second Sex*, pp. 129–85.

14. For extended discussions of the connection between patriarchy and the sexual division of labor that denies women access to arenas of production in the public sphere, see McDonough and Harrison, "Patriarchy and Relations of Production," pp. 11–41. See also Kuhn, "Structures of Patriarchy and Capital in the Family," pp. 42–67; in addition, see Hartmann, "The Family as the Locus of Gender, Class, and Political Struggle," pp. 366–94.

15. Molly Haskell, "The 2,000-Year-Old Misunderstanding—'Rape Fantasy,'" pp. 84–86, 92, 94, 96, 98.

16. Ibid., p. 94.

17. These terms were used by Dot herself in recounting the plot.

18. Both Ann Douglas and Tania Modleski have made this point; Douglas makes it in "Soft-Porn Culture," and Modleski argues this view in "The Disappearing Act."

19. Although Chodorow does not argue explicitly that real women are seeking the opportunity to regress to childhood when they marry, Flax suggests in "The Conflict between Nurturance and Autonomy" that the common "fantasy women . . . have about male therapists—the wish to have a baby with them—is on a deeper level a wish to *be* their baby" (p. 175). I think this same wish to be protected and cared for by an all-powerful parent is expressed through the romantic fantasy and its requisite infantilization of the heroine.

20. Geertz, "Deep Play," p. 449.

21. Ibid.

22. Ibid.

CHAPTER 5

1. For a similar argument about the functioning of gothic romances, see Radway, "The Utopian Impulse in Popular Literature," pp. 140–62.

2. For other similar passages, see Greer, *The Second Sunrise*, pp. 40–41, and Seymour, *Purity's Passion*, pp. 138–39.

3. Douglas, "Soft-Porn Culture," p. 28.

4. For an extended discussion of why a freely expressed female sexuality might be threatening to men, see Dinnerstein, *The Mermaid and the Minotaur*, pp. 59–66.

5. This passage is a bit more graphic in its representation of lovemaking than those in most ideal romances. Although the visual quality of the description may well have contributed to the book's lower rating, I did not pursue this line of reasoning with Dot or with the Smithton women. In reviewing the book in her September 1981 newsletter, Dot remarked only that "frankly, Rupert is a weak character and I don't see why she would return to him after he abandons her in China for a year."

6. Although I accept at face value the Smithton readers' assertion that they

know romances are not like real life, I also believe that their complex relationship to these texts, as revealed in their evaluative procedures and normative judgments, betokens an unconscious but nonetheless strong desire to believe that someday their lives might actually be like those lived by the romantic heroines. See the related discussion in Chapter 6.

7. Evans, "Dorothy's Diary," May 1981, p. 1.

CHAPTER 6

1. See, for instance, early issues of the *Journal of Popular Culture* where commentators characteristically admit that although popular art forms rarely provide unique insights about the human condition, they are nonetheless worthy of attention because, as fantasy, they can lead one to an understanding of the social situation necessitating that specific if temporary withdrawal into the imaginary.

2. Eagleton, "Ideology, Fiction, Narrative," p. 66.

3. Ibid.

4. For further discussions of literature as the imitation of ordinary discourse or speech, see Barbara Herrnstein Smith, *On the Margins of Discourse*, pp. 8–11, 15–40; Pratt, *Toward a Speech Act Theory of Literary Discourse*, passim; and Iser, *The Act of Reading*, pp. 62–68.

5. Mussell, "Romantic Fiction," p. 317.

6. Whitney, "Where It Happens," p. 29.

7. Evans, "Dorothy's Diary," November 1980, p. 1.

8. For a discussion of language's ability to function in this practical, utilitarian manner, see Mukařovský, "The Place of the Aesthetic Function," pp. 31–48.

9. In my discussion of the dual nature of the "realistic" discourse of romantic fiction I have been influenced by Roland Barthes's important observation that the task of writing in the novel is "to put the mask in place and at the same time to point it out." See his discussion of literary realism in *Writing Degree Zero*, pp. 29–40. See also Chaney, *Fictions and Ceremonies*, pp. 69–102.

10. Woodiwiss, *The Flame and the Flower*, p. 9.

11. Ibid.

12. For a discussion of the importance of the fairy-tale opening, see Bettelheim, *The Uses of Enchantment*, pp. 62–63.

13. Danton, *Star Sapphire*, p. 6.

14. Whitney, *Thunder Heights*, passim.

15. Dailey, *Ride the Thunder*, p. 1.

16. Eco, "Narrative Structures in Fleming," p. 166.

17. Ibid., p. 165.

18. Ibid., p. 167. See also Chaney's discussion of "realism of detail" in *Fictions and Ceremonies*, pp. 72–77.

19. I am adopting a phrase used by Peter Rabinowitz in his discussion of the relationship between fictional worlds and the world of a reader. Rabinowitz argues, in effect, that when a fictional world appears far different from the world of the reader, there is less of a possibility of infection from one to the other. See his

discussion, "Truth in Fiction," pp. 130–34, especially pp. 132–33.

20. Fredric Jameson has argued recently that *all* contemporary mass culture is characterized by the fact of its "sheer repetition." See his discussion in "Reification and Utopia," pp. 137–38.

21. For a discussion of mass culture as commodified aesthetic experience where value is not determined by the amount of labor required for its production but by the quantity and quality of the experience it promises, see MacCannell, *The Tourist*.

22. Whitney, *Thunder Heights*, p. 39.

23. James, *The Art of Fiction*, pp. 3–23. For a discussion of the difference between James's linguistic techniques and those employed in nineteenth-century popular fiction, see Veeder, *Henry James*, pp. 20–53.

24. For related comments on the realistic novel as a "paradigm of the structure of memory," see Iser, *The Act of Reading*, pp. 124–25.

25. Eco, "The Myth of Superman," p. 109.

26. Eco's introduction of a comparison between mythic ritual and mass culture is important because popular narratives are all too often dismissed in our post-modernist age as non-art simply because they do not explore new or unusual responses to human experience as do the prose and poetry of canonical modernism. But, as Raymond Williams has pointed out in an argument similar to Eco's, "[i]n many societies it has been the function of art to embody what we call the common meanings of the society." He asserts that "[t]he artist is not describing new experiences but embodying known experiences. There is great danger in the assumption that art serves only on the frontiers of knowledge" (*The Long Revolution*, p. 30).

27. Eco, "The Myth of Superman," p. 109.

28. On the novel as a contingent, personal narrative, see Watt, *The Rise of the Novel*, pp. 18–21. See also Jameson, *The Political Unconscious*, pp. 151–280, and Barthes, *Writing Degree Zero*, pp. 29–40.

29. Eco, "The Myth of Superman," p. 109.

30. Watt, *The Rise of the Novel*, pp. 14–15.

31. Evans, "Dorothy's Diary," January 1981, p. 1.

32. For a discussion of the novel's revolutionary method of representing time, see Kermode, *The Sense of an Ending*, pp. 35–64. See also Watt, *The Rise of the Novel*, pp. 21–25.

33. Watt, *The Rise of the Novel*, p. 22.

34. See Eco's discussion of this "sinusoidal" narrative structure in "Rhetoric and Ideology," p. 132.

35. Whitney, *Thunder Heights*, p. 217.

CONCLUSION

1. Lombardi-Satriani, "Folklore as Culture of Contestation," pp. 99–121, and Limon, "Folklore and the Mexican in the United States," pp. 1–21.

2. Limon, "Folklore and the Mexican in the United States," p. 3.

3. Radway, "The Utopian Impulse in Popular Literature," pp. 140–62.

4. Jameson, "Reification and Utopia," p. 144.

5. "Romance Survey," p. 19.

Bibliography

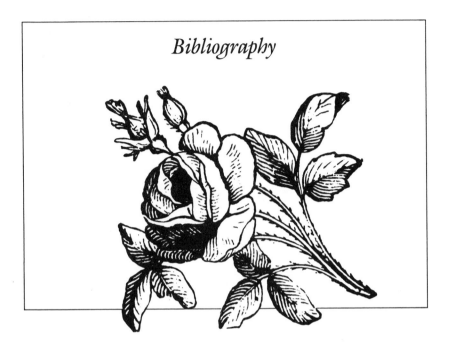

Altick, Richard. *The English Common Reader: A Social History of the Mass Reading Public, 1800–1900*. Chicago: University of Chicago Press, 1957.

Barr, Elisabeth (Irene Edwards). *The Sea Treasure*. New York: Playboy Paperbacks, 1979.

Barthes, Roland. *S/Z*. Translated by Richard Miller. New York: Hill and Wang, 1974.

———. *Writing Degree Zero*. Translated by Annette Lavers and Colin Smith. New York: Hill and Wang, 1968.

Beauvoir, Simone de. *The Second Sex*. Translated by H. M. Parshley. New York: Bantam Books, 1952.

Berman, Phyllis. "They Call Us Illegitimate." *Forbes* 6 (March 1978): 37–38.

Bettelheim, Bruno. *The Uses of Enchantment: The Meaning and Importance of Fairy Tales*. New York: Alfred A. Knopf, 1976.

Bodden, William Michael. "An Economic Analysis of the Paper-Bound Book Industry in the United States." M.B.A. thesis, The Wharton School, University of Pennsylvania, 1953.

Bode, Margot. *Jasmine Splendor*. New York: Richard Gallen Books, 1981.

Bogart, Leo. "How the Mass Media Work in America." In *Mass Media and Violence: A Report to the National Commission on the Causes and Prevention of Violence*, edited by Robert K. Baker and Sandra J. Ball, 9:165–85. Washington, D.C.: Library of Congress, 1969.

Bonds, Parris Afton. *Made for Each Other.* New York: Silhouette Books, 1981.

Bright, Elizabeth. *Desire's Legacy.* New York: Richard Gallen Books, 1981.

Brotman, Barbara. "Ah, Romance! Harlequin Has an Affair for Its Readers." *Chicago Tribune,* 2 June 1980, p. B1.

Burford, Lolah. *Alyx.* New York: Signet Books, 1977.

Burn, Helen Jean. *Savannah.* New York: Playboy Paperbacks, 1981.

Carter, Noël Vreeland. *Miss Hungerford's Handsome Hero.* New York: Dell Publishing Co., 1981.

Cawelti, John G. *Adventure, Mystery, and Romance: Formula Stories as Art and Popular Culture.* Chicago: University of Chicago Press, 1976.

———. *The Six-Gun Mystique.* Bowling Green, Ohio: Bowling Green Popular Press, 1970.

Chaney, David. *Fictions and Ceremonies: Representations of Popular Experience.* London: Edward Arnold, 1979.

Charvat, William. *Literary Publishing in America, 1790–1850.* Philadelphia: University of Pennsylvania Press, 1959.

———. *The Profession of Authorship in America, 1800–1870: The Papers of William Charvat.* Edited by Matthew J. Bruccoli. Columbus, Ohio: Ohio State University Press, 1968.

Chodorow, Nancy. *The Reproduction of Mothering: Psychoanalysis and the Sociology of Gender.* Berkeley: University of California Press, 1978.

Compaine, Benjamin. *The Book Industry in Transition: An Economic Study of Book Distribution and Marketing.* White Plains, N.Y.: Knowledge Industry Publications, 1978.

Coser, Lewis A.; Kadushin, Charles; and Powell, Walter W. *Books: The Culture and Commerce of Publishing.* New York: Basic Books, 1982.

Culler, Jonathan. *The Pursuit of Signs: Semiotics, Literature, Deconstruction.* Ithaca, N.Y.: Cornell University Press, 1981.

Dailey, Janet. *Night Way.* New York: Pocket Books, 1981.

———. *Ride the Thunder.* New York: Pocket Books, 1980.

Danton, Rebecca. *Star Sapphire.* New York: Fawcett Coventry, 1979.

Davis, Kenneth C. "The Cinderella Story of Paperback Originals." *Publishers Weekly,* 11 January 1980, pp. 43–50.

Dayton, E. N. "B. Dalton, Bookseller, Foresees Growing Chain of Stores." *Publishers Weekly,* 15 July 1968, pp. 44–45.

De Blasis, Celeste. *The Proud Breed.* New York: Fawcett Crest, 1978.

Degler, Carl N. *At Odds: Women and the Family in America from the Revolution to the Present.* New York: Oxford University Press, 1980.

Deveraux, Jude (Jude Gilliam White). *The Black Lyon.* New York: Avon Books, 1980.

Dinnerstein, Dorothy. *The Mermaid and the Minotaur: Sexual Arrangements and Human Malaise.* New York: Harper and Row, 1976.

Doebler, Paul D. "The Statistics of Concentration." *Publishers Weekly,* 31 July 1978, pp. 26–30.

Douglas, Ann. "Soft-Porn Culture." *New Republic,* 30 August 1980, pp. 25–29.

Duffy, Martha. "On the Road to Manderley." *Time,* 12 April 1971, pp. 95–96.

Eagleton, Terry. "Ideology, Fiction, Narrative." *Social Text* 2 (Summer 1979): 62–80.

Eco, Umberto. "The Myth of Superman." In *The Role of the Reader: Explorations in the Semiotics of Texts*, pp. 107–24. Bloomington: Indiana University Press, 1979.

———. "Narrative Structures in Fleming." In *The Role of the Reader: Explorations in the Semiotics of Texts*, pp. 144–72. Bloomington: Indiana University Press, 1979.

———. "Rhetoric and Ideology in Sue's *Les Mystères de Paris*." In *The Role of the Reader: Explorations in the Semiotics of Texts*, pp. 125–43. Bloomington: Indiana University Press, 1979.

———. *The Role of the Reader: Explorations in the Semiotics of Texts*. Bloomington: Indiana University Press, 1979.

———. *A Theory of Semiotics*. Bloomington: Indiana University Press, 1976.

Ellis, Leigh (Anne and Louisa Rudeen). *Green Lady*. New York: Avon Books, 1981.

Escarpit, Robert. *The Book Revolution*. London: George G. Harrap and Co., 1966.

———. *The Sociology of Literature*. Translated by Ernest Pick. Painesville, Ohio: Lake Erie College Press, 1965.

Evans, Dorothy. "Dorothy's Diary of Romance Reading." April 1980–September 1981. Mimeographed newsletters.

Ewen, Stuart. *Captains of Consciousness: Advertising and the Social Roots of the Consumer Culture*. New York: McGraw-Hill Book Co., 1976.

Faust, Beatrice. *Women, Sex, and Pornography: A Controversial and Unique Study*. New York: Macmillan Publishing Co., 1980.

Fish, Stanley. *Is There a Text in This Class?: The Authority of Interpretive Communities*. Cambridge, Mass.: Harvard University Press, 1980.

Flax, Jane. "The Conflict between Nurturance and Autonomy in Mother-Daughter Relationships and within Feminism." *Feminist Studies* 4 (June 1978): 171–89.

Fox-Genovese, Elizabeth. "Property and Patriarchy in Classical Bourgeois Political Theory." *Radical History Review* 4 (Spring/Summer 1977): 36–59.

Friedan, Betty. *The Feminine Mystique*. New York: W. W. Norton and Co., 1963.

Geertz, Clifford. "Deep Play: Notes on the Balinese Cockfight." In *The Interpretation of Cultures*, pp. 412–53. New York: Basic Books, 1973.

———. "Thick Description: Toward an Interpretive Theory of Culture." In *The Interpretation of Cultures*, pp. 3–30. New York: Basic Books, 1973.

Glass, Jeanne. "Editor's Report." *Writer* 90 (April 1977): 33.

Goodenough, Ward H. *Description and Comparison in Cultural Anthropology*. Chicago: Aldine Publishing Co., 1970.

Graff, Gerald. *Poetic Statement and Critical Dogma*. Evanston: Northwestern University Press, 1970.

Greer, Francesca (Frankie-Lee Janas). *The Second Sunrise*. New York: Warner Books, 1981.

Griffin, Susan. *Pornography and Silence: Culture's Revenge against Nature*. New York: Harper and Row, 1981.

Gruber, Frank. *The Pulp Jungle.* Los Angeles: Sherbourne Press, 1967.

Harding, D. W. "The Notion of 'Escape' in Fiction and Entertainment." *Oxford Review* 4 (Hilary 1967): 23–32.

Harlequin Enterprises Ltd. *Annual Report, 1979.* Ontario, Canada, 1979.

Hartmann, Heidi I. "The Family as the Locus of Gender, Class, and Political Struggle: The Example of Housework." *Signs* 6 (Spring 1981): 366–94.

――――. "The Unhappy Marriage of Marxism and Feminism: Towards a More Progressive Union." *Capital and Class* 8 (Summer 1979): 1–33.

Haskell, Molly. "The 2,000-Year-Old-Misunderstanding—'Rape Fantasy.'" *MS* 5 (November 1976): 84–86, 92, 94, 96, 98.

Hepburne, Melissa. *Passion's Blazing Triumph.* Los Angeles: Pinnacle Books, 1980.

Hoggart, Richard. *The Uses of Literacy: Changing Patterns in English Mass Culture.* Fair Lawn, N.J.: Essential Books, 1957.

Holland, Norman N. *The Dynamics of Literary Response.* New York: Oxford University Press, 1968.

――――. *5 Readers Reading.* New Haven: Yale University Press, 1975.

"How to Identify, Display, and Sell the Gothic." Speedy Shop Paperback Book Service, Lansing, Mich. Marketing bulletin distributed to booksellers, undated.

Hymes, Dell. *Foundations in Sociolinguistics: An Ethnographic Approach.* Philadelphia: University of Pennsylvania Press, 1974.

Iser, Wolfgang. *The Act of Reading: A Theory of Aesthetic Response.* Baltimore: Johns Hopkins University Press, 1978.

James, Henry. *The Art of Fiction.* New York: Oxford University Press, 1948.

Jameson, Fredric. "Marxism and Historicism." *New Literary History* 11 (Autumn 1979): 41–73.

――――. *The Political Unconscious: Narrative as a Socially Symbolic Act.* Ithaca, N.Y.: Cornell University Press, 1981.

――――. "Reification and Utopia in Mass Culture." *Social Text* 1 (Winter 1979): 130–48.

Jensen, Margaret. "Women and Romantic Fiction: A Case Study of Harlequin Enterprises, Romances, and Readers." Ph.D. dissertation, McMaster University, 1980.

Kakutani, Michiko. "New Romance Novels Are Just What Their Readers Ordered." *New York Times,* 11 August 1980, p. C13.

Kelly, R. Gordon. "Literature and the Historian." *American Quarterly* 26 (May 1974): 141–59.

Kelrich, Victoria. *High Fashion.* New York: Richard Gallen Books, 1981.

Kent, Katherine (Joan Dial). *Dreamtide.* New York: Pocket Books, 1981.

Kermode, Frank. *The Sense of an Ending: Studies in the Theory of Fiction.* London: Oxford University Press, 1977.

Komarovsky, Mirra. *Blue-Collar Marriage.* 1962. Reprint. New York: Random House, 1964.

Krieger, Murray. *The New Apologists for Poetry.* Westport, Conn.: Greenwood Press, 1977.

Kuhn, Annette. "Structures of Patriarchy and Capitalism in the Family." In *Femi-*

nism and Materialism: Women and Modes of Production, edited by Annette Kuhn and AnnMarie Wolpe, pp. 42–67. London: Routledge and Kegan Paul, 1978.

Kuklick, Bruce. "Myth and Symbol in American Studies." *American Quarterly* 24 (October 1972): 435–50.

Lamphere, Louise. "Strategies, Cooperation, and Conflict among Women in Domestic Groups." In *Woman, Culture, and Society*, edited by Michelle Zimbalist Rosaldo and Louise Lamphere, pp. 97–112. Stanford: Stanford University Press, 1974.

Landrum, Larry. "Detective and Mystery Novels." In *Handbook of American Popular Culture*, edited by M. Thomas Inge, 1:103–20. Westport, Conn.: Greenwood Press, 1978.

Lazarsfeld, Paul F. *Radio and the Printed Page: An Introduction to the Study of Radio and Its Role in the Communication of Ideas*. New York: Duell, Sloan and Pearce, 1940.

Lee, Elsie. *The Diplomatic Lover*. New York: Dell Publishing Co., 1971.

Lehmann-Haupt, Hellmut; Wroth, Lawrence C.; and Silver, Rollo G. *The Book in America: A History of the Making and Selling of Books in the United States*. New York: R. R. Bowker Co., 1951.

Lentricchia, Frank. *After the New Criticism*. Chicago: University of Chicago Press, 1980.

Limon, José. "Folklore and the Mexican in the United States: A Marxist Cultural Perspective." Unpublished paper.

Lindsey, Johanna. *Fires of Winter*. New York: Avon Books, 1980.

Lombardi-Satriani, Luigi. "Folklore as Culture of Contestation." *Journal of the Folklore Institute* 11 (June–Aug. 1974): 99–122.

Lopata, Helena Znaniecki. *Occupation: Housewife*. New York: Oxford University Press, 1971.

McBain, Laurie. *Moonstruck Madness*. New York: Avon Books, 1977.

MacCannell, Dean. *The Tourist*. New York: Schocken Books, 1976.

McDonough, Roisin, and Harrison, Rachel. "Patriarchy and Relations of Production." In *Feminism and Materialism: Women and Modes of Production*, edited by Annette Kuhn and AnnMarie Wolpe, pp. 11–41. London: Routledge and Kegan Paul, 1978.

McManus, Yvonne. "Editor's Report." *Writer* 90 (April 1977): 33–35.

Madison, Charles A. *Book Publishing in America*. New York: McGraw-Hill Book Co., 1966.

Mann, Peter H. *A New Survey: The Facts about Romantic Fiction*. London: Mills and Boon, 1974.

―――. *The Romantic Novel: A Survey of Reading Habits*. London: Mills and Boon, 1969.

Marten, Jacqueline. *Visions of the Damned*. New York: Playboy Paperbacks, 1979.

Maryles, Daisy. "B. Dalton, with 350 Outlets Due by 1979, Views Its Bookselling Future with Rosy Optimism." *Publishers Weekly*, 19 September 1977, pp. 126–29.

―――. "Fawcett Launches Romance Imprint with Brand Marketing Techniques."

Publishers Weekly, 3 September 1979, pp. 69–70.

————. "S & S to Debut Silhouette with $3-Million TV Ad Campaign." *Publishers Weekly*, 11 April 1980, pp. 51–52.

"Mass Merchandising Hits the Bookstores." *Business Week*, 9 February 1974, pp. 80–86.

Michaels, Fern (Roberta Anderson and Mary Kuczir). *Captive Splendors*. New York: Ballantine Books, 1980.

Millett, Kate. *Sexual Politics*. Garden City, N.Y.: Doubleday and Co., 1970.

"Millions of Women Avid for Avon's Erotic Historical Romances." *Publishers Weekly*, 6 October 1975, p. 44.

Mitchell, Juliet. *Woman's Estate*. New York: Pantheon Books, 1971.

Modleski, Tania. "The Disappearing Act: A Study of Harlequin Romances." *Signs* 5 (Spring 1980): 435–48.

Mukařovský, Jan. "The Place of the Aesthetic Function among the Other Functions." In *Structure, Sign, and Function*, translated and edited by John Burbank and Peter Steiner, pp. 31–48. New Haven: Yale University Press, 1978.

Murphey, Murray. *Our Knowledge of the Historical Past*. Indianapolis: Bobbs-Merrill, 1973.

Mussell, Kay J. "Beautiful and Damned: The Sexual Woman in Gothic Fiction." *Journal of Popular Culture* 9 (Summer 1975): 84–89.

————. "Romantic Fiction." In *The Handbook of American Popular Culture*, edited by M. Thomas Inge, pp. 317–44. Westport, Conn.: Greenwood Press, 1980.

Myrdal, Alva, and Klein, Viola. *Woman's Two Roles: Home and Work*. 2d ed. London: Routledge and Kegan Paul, 1968.

Neels, Betty. *Cruise to a Wedding*. Toronto: Harlequin Books, Harlequin Salutes Edition, 1980.

Oakley, Ann. *The Sociology of Housework*. New York: Pantheon Books, 1974.

————. *Woman's Work: The Housewife, Past and Present*. New York: Vintage Books, 1976.

Peters, Elizabeth. *Summer of the Dragon*. New York: Fawcett Crest, 1980.

Pike, Kenneth. *Language in Relation to a Unified Theory of the Structure of Human Behavior*. 2d ed. The Hague: Mouton, 1967.

Porter, B. "B. Dalton: The Leader of the Chain Gang." *Saturday Review*, 9 June 1979, pp. 53–57.

Posner, Michael. "Show Business: Give the People What They Want and They'll Turn Out for It." *MacCleans*, 20 February 1978, pp. 72, 74, 76.

Pratt, Mary Louise. *Toward a Speech Act Theory of Literary Discourse*. Bloomington: Indiana University Press, 1977.

Proctor, Pam. "Phyllis Whitney: She Writes Best Sellers the Old-Fashioned Way." *Parade*, 2 November 1975, p. 20.

Propp, Vladimir. *Morphology of the Folktale*. Translated by Laurence Scott. 2d ed. Austin: University of Texas Press, 1968.

Rabinowitz, Peter. "Truth in Fiction: A Reexamination of Audiences." *Critical Inquiry* 4 (Autumn 1977): 121–41.

Radcliffe, Janette (Janet Louise Roberts). *The Court of the Flowering Peach*. New York: Dell Publishing Co., 1981.

Radway, Janice. "The Utopian Impulse in Popular Literature: Gothic Romances and 'Feminist' Protest." *American Quarterly* 33 (Summer 1981): 140–62.

Ripy, Margaret. *A Second Chance at Love*. New York: Silhouette Books, 1981.

Rogers, Rosemary. *Dark Fires*. New York: Avon Books, 1975.

_____. *The Insiders*. New York: Avon Books, 1979.

_____. *Sweet Savage Love*. New York: Avon Books, 1974.

_____. *Wicked Loving Lies*. New York: Avon Books, 1976.

Rohrbaugh, Joanna Bunker. *Women: Psychology's Puzzle*. New York: Basic Books, 1979.

"The Romance of Harlequin Enterprises." *Publishers Weekly*, 3 September 1973, p. 31.

"Romance Survey." *Romance Report* 1 (December 1981): 19.

Russ, Joanna. "'Somebody's Trying to Kill Me and I Think It's My Husband': The Modern Gothic." *Journal of Popular Culture* 6 (Spring 1973): 666–91.

Sacks, Karen. "Engels Revisited: Women, the Organization of Production, and Private Property." In *Women, Culture and Society*, edited by Michelle Zimbalist Rosaldo and Louise Lamphere, pp. 207–22. Stanford: Stanford University Press, 1974.

Salvato, Sharon. *Bitter Eden*. New York: Dell Publishing Co., 1979.

Schick, Frank L. *The Paperbound Book in America: The History of Paperbacks and Their European Background*. New York: R. R. Bowker Co., 1958.

Scholes, Robert. *Semiotics and Interpretation*. New Haven: Yale University Press, 1982.

Sebeok, Thomas A., ed. *A Perfusion of Signs*. Bloomington: Indiana University Press, 1977.

_____. *Sight, Sound, and Sense*. Bloomington: Indiana University Press, 1978.

_____. *The Tell-Tale Sign: A Survey of Semiotics*. Atlantic Highlands, N.J.: Humanities Press, 1975.

Seymour, Janette. *Purity's Passion*. New York: Pocket Books, 1977.

Small, Bertrice. *Adora*. New York: Ballantine Books, 1980.

Smith, Barbara Herrnstein. *On the Margins of Discourse: The Relation of Literature to Language*. Chicago: University of Chicago Press, 1978.

Smith, Datus Clifford, Jr. *A Guide to Book Publishing*. New York: R. R. Bowker Co., 1966.

Smith, Roger H. "Paperback National Distributors—Part III: How Distributors Are Augmenting Their Role with Publishers." *Publishers Weekly*, 19 June 1978, pp. 78–80.

_____. *Paperback Parnassus: The Birth, the Development, the Pending Crisis . . . of the Modern American Paperbound Book*. Boulder, Colo.: Westview Press, 1976.

Snitow, Ann Barr. "Mass Market Romance: Pornography for Women Is Different." *Radical History Review* 20 (Spring/Summer 1979): 141–61.

Spradley, James P. *The Ethnographic Interview*. New York: Holt, Rinehart and Winston, 1979.

Stack, Carol. *All Our Kin: Strategies for Survival in a Black Community*. New York: Harper and Row, 1974.

Steinmann, Anne. "A Study of the Concept of the Feminine Role of 51 Middle-

Class American Families." *Genetic Psychology Monographs* 67 (1963): 275–352.

Stevenson, Florence. *Moonlight Variations.* New York: Jove Publications, 1981.

Suleiman, Susan B., and Crosman, Inge, eds. *The Reader in the Text: Essays on Audience and Interpretation.* Princeton: Princeton University Press, 1980.

Swezd, John. "The Ethnography of Literacy." In *Writing: The Nature, Development, and Teaching of Written Communication.* Vol 1. *Variation in Writing: Functional and Linguistic Cultural Differences,* edited by Marcia Farr Whiteman, pp. 13–23. Hillsdale, N.J.: Lawrence Erlbaum Associates, 1981.

Tebbel, John. *A History of Book Publishing in the United States.* 3 vols. Vol. 1, *The Creation of an Industry, 1630–1850.* Vol. 2, *The Expansion of an Industry, 1865–1919.* Vol. 3, *The Golden Age between Two Wars, 1920–1940.* New York: R. R. Bowker Co., 1972–78.

Tompkins, Jane P. "The Reader in History: The Changing Shape of Literary Response." In *Reader Response Criticism: From Formalism to Post-Structuralism,* edited by Jane P. Tompkins, pp. 201–32. Baltimore: Johns Hopkins University Press, 1980.

Trent, Brenda. *Winter Dreams.* New York: Silhouette Books, 1981.

Trevor, Meriol. *The Wanton Fires.* New York: Fawcett Coventry, 1979.

Turner, Alice K. "The Tempestuous, Tumultuous, Turbulent, Torrid, and Terribly Profitable World of Paperback Passion." *New York,* 13 February 1978, pp. 46–49.

U.S. Department of Commerce, Bureau of the Census. *Census of the Population, 1970.* Vol. 1. *Characteristics of the Population,* pt. 1, *United States Summary,* sec. 1. Washington, D.C.: Government Printing Office, 1973.

———. *A Statistical Portrait of Women in the United States.* Current Population Reports Special Studies, Series P-23, no. 58. Washington, D.C.: Government Printing Office, 1973.

Van Slyke, Helen. " 'Old-Fashioned' and 'Up-to-the-Minute.' " *Writer* 88 (November 1975): 14–16.

Veeder, William. *Henry James—the Lessons of the Master: Popular Fiction and Personal Style in the Nineteenth Century.* Chicago: University of Chicago Press, 1975.

"Waldenbooks: Countering B. Dalton by Aping Its Computer Operations." *Business Week,* 8 October 1979, pp. 116–21.

Walters, Ray. "Paperback Talk." *New York Times Book Review,* 24 February 1980, p. 47.

Watt, Ian. *The Rise of the Novel: Studies in Defoe, Richardson, and Fielding.* Berkeley: University of California Press, 1957.

"What Women Want, or, Kitsch Rewarded: Harlequin Enterprises." *Time,* 6 November 1972, pp. 94–95.

Whiteside, Thomas. "Onward and Upward with the Arts—the Blockbuster Complex, I." *New Yorker,* 29 September 1980, pp. 48–101.

———. "Onward and Upward with the Arts—the Blockbuster Complex, II." *New Yorker,* 6 October 1980, pp. 63–146.

Whitney, Phyllis. *Domino.* Garden City, N.Y.: Doubleday and Co., 1979.

———. *Thunder Heights.* New York: Fawcett Crest, 1960.

_____. "Where It Happens." *Writer* 85 (January 1972): 14–15, 28–30.

_____. "Writing the Gothic Novel." *Writer* 80 (February 1967): 9–13, 42–43.

Wilde, Jocelyn (John Toombs). *Bride of the Baja*. New York: Pocket Books, 1980.

Williams, Raymond. *The Long Revolution*. New York: Columbia University Press, 1961.

Williamson, Judith. *Decoding Advertisements: Ideology and Meaning in Advertising*. London: Marion Boyars, 1978.

Woodiwiss, Kathleen E. *Ashes in the Wind*. New York: Avon Books, 1979.

_____. *The Flame and the Flower*. New York: Avon Books, 1972.

_____. *Shanna*. New York: Avon Books, 1977.

_____. *The Wolf and the Dove*. New York: Avon Books, 1974.

Wright, Will. *Sixguns and Society: A Structural Study of the Western*. Berkeley: University of California Press, 1975.

Yankelovich, Skelly and White. *The 1978 Consumer Research Study on Reading and Book Purchasing*. Prepared for the Book Industry Study Group. Darien, Conn.: The Group, 1978.

Young, Michael, and Willmott, Peter. *Family and Kinship in East London*. London: Penguin Books, 1966.

Index